"A wonderful, thought-provoking book by Dick Couch and a quick study of human personalities; his conclusions are optimistic and uplifting."
—*Vice Admiral James Stockdale (USN, Ret.),
recipient of the Congressional Medal of Honor*

"*The Warrior Elite* offers superb insight into the making of a Navy SEAL."
—*Robert J. Natter, Admiral,
U.S. Navy, Commander in Chief, U.S. Atlantic Fleet*

"*The Warrior Elite* is a very accurate and authoritative look at basic SEAL training. A must-read for any young man who wants to become a Navy SEAL."
—*Rudy Boesch, MCPO (USN, Ret.),
BUD/S Class 6, and* Survivor *contestant*

"An authentic voice that spells out what it takes to become a SEAL—the sheer grit to overcome all obstacles. America is lucky that it continues to attract such men as these to serve."
—*Theodore Roosevelt IV, BUD/S Class 36*

"A story written of men's souls and the passion of deep personal challenge— an illuminating description of human endeavor. Dick Couch has delivered the best accounting yet of the extraordinary young men I was so privileged to lead."
—*Rear Admiral Ray Smith (USN, Ret.), BUD/S Class 54, and
former commander, Naval Special Warfare Command*

THE WARRIOR ELITE

THE
WARRIOR
ELITE

THE FORGING OF SEAL CLASS 228

DICK COUCH

PHOTOGRAPHS BY CLIFF HOLLENBECK

THREE RIVERS PRESS
NEW YORK

Published by Three Rivers Press, New York, New York.

Member of the Crown Publishing Group, a division of Random House, Inc.

www.randomhouse.com

THREE RIVERS PRESS and the Tugboat design are registered trademarks of Random House, Inc.

Originally published in slightly different form in hardcover by Crown Publishers, a division of Random House, Inc., in 2001.

Printed in the United States of America

Design by LEONARD W. HENDERSON

Library of Congress Cataloging-in-Publication Data

Couch, Dick, 1943–

  The warrior elite : the forging of SEAL class 228 / by Dick Couch.

    p. cm.

  1. United States. Navy. SEALs.   2. United States. Navy—Commando troops—Training of.   I. Title.

  VG87 .C68 2001

  359.9'84—dc21   2001028368

ISBN 1-4000-4695-5

10

First Paperback Edition

To
Mike "Doc" Thomas
1934–1999

Whiskey Platoon, SEAL Team One, 1970–1971
BUD/S Instructor, 1967–1969

Doc was our platoon corpsman; I was his platoon officer. We went to Vietnam together and we all came
home together. Doc has gone on ahead; he now walks
point for the old warriors in Whiskey Platoon. This
book is for Doc and for all those young men who enter
BUD/S training with the dream of becoming a SEAL
warrior.

ACKNOWLEDGMENTS

The focus of this book is the training of Navy SEALs, America's elite maritime warriors. This work is based on my interviews with Basic UDT/SEAL (BUD/S) trainees, BUD/S instructors, students and instructors in various advanced SEAL training programs, and SEALs preparing for operational deployment. With two exceptions, the names have not been changed; the men you will meet in *The Warrior Elite* are Navy SEALs, SEAL trainees, and SEAL training cadres. I was given full and unlimited access to the BUD/S and advanced training venues, and could speak freely with trainees and trainers alike. My only restriction was that I respect classified information and organizations. As a retired naval officer who held a top-secret clearance, I could not do otherwise. SEAL training and the forging of warriors is a dynamic business. Because SEALs continually try to find better ways to do things, SEAL training is a work in progress. *The Warrior Elite* represents SEAL training at BUD/S and in the teams during the fall of 1999 and early 2000.

I wish to thank all those in the Naval Special Warfare chain of command who gave their consent to, and cooperation in, the writing of this book. BUD/S training, the advanced training regimens, and the SEAL and SDV teams are a closed society. Reporters and TV journalists are occasionally allowed in, but they are politely shown only certain orchestrated events; the culture of the teams and their special brand of warrior training are kept well away from the public eye. I was allowed to see it all, even though I was technically an outsider—a guy in civilian clothes with a notebook. I may be an alumnus, but I am no longer an active warrior. SEAL training is dangerous, so I had to be supervised and accounted for. Therefore, I am particularly indebted to the BUD/S instructors and the advanced training cadres for graciously allowing me to roam so freely on their turf.

I want to thank Bob Mecoy, my editor at Crown, who came to me with the idea for this book. To Pete Fornatale at Crown, who picked up the load when Bob left, you did a great job. I also want to thank my wife, Julia, who patiently proofread my work and helped me through my second Hell Week. And thanks to my collaborator and photographer, Cliff Hollenbeck, who taught me that good pictures are as hard to produce as good words. For those officers and men in the Naval Special Warfare community who trusted me with your story, I can never thank you enough.

Contents

THE WARRIOR ELITE

INTRODUCTION

E ach year, U.S. military boot camps turn out tens of thousands of soldiers, sailors, and airmen. The Marine Corps builds about 20,000 new marines each year for their 174,000-man Force, and they do this remarkably well in only eleven weeks. In the U.S. Army special operations community, the ultimate gut check is Ranger School. This eight-week ordeal teaches young soldiers that they can fight and lead, even when they haven't eaten or slept for several days. The Army awards about 1,500 Ranger Tabs each year to these graduates. Ranger School is tough; a few graduates of Basic Underwater Demolition/SEAL training, or BUD/S, attend Ranger School each year to learn what the Army teaches. BUD/S, however, remains at the core of making a Navy SEAL—a "sea-air-land" commando.

The twenty-seven-week SEAL basic school graduates fewer than 250 men each year. Not all of them will become SEALs. BUD/S graduates must complete at least another six months of intensive training to qualify as SEALs. Only then are they awarded their SEAL pin, or Trident.

SEAL training is unique. It is designed to build warriors. The traditional military services train men and women together. The idea is that they will serve together during their military careers and should therefore train together, beginning with boot camp. There are women attached to the SEAL teams, but they serve only in support roles. Female Navy SEALs are only found in the movies.

SEAL training is unique in other ways. All services train their officers and enlisted personnel separately during their basic warfare instruction. In BUD/S training, officers and enlisted men train and suffer together, side by

side. BUD/S training is the glue that binds all SEALs together, from seaman
to admiral. Any Annapolis graduate is quick to claim that he is Class of
Whenever. And any carrier pilot can tell you the exact number of night carrier landings he has. A Navy SEAL can always tell you his class. In my case,
I was Class 45.

The first SEAL teams were commissioned just in time for the Vietnam
War, and the early character of the SEALs was formed in that conflict.
Forty-two SEALs were killed in action there. The spring of 1971 was not
a good time for Navy SEALs in Vietnam. At that time there were only six
operational platoons and some assorted advisers, all working in the
Mekong Delta—less than a hundred SEALs in all. In a five-month period,
more than 15 percent of them were killed or wounded. At that late stage
of the war, most new SEALs came directly from BUD/S to the SEAL teams.
After Army Airborne School and six weeks of training within the team,
they were eligible for assignment to an operational platoon and duty in
Vietnam. The corporate knowledge of SEAL operations in Vietnam rested
with the shrinking handful of veteran enlisted men, some of whom went
back for as many as seven tours.

In that spring of 1971, I was a navy lieutenant and the platoon commander of Whiskey Platoon, SEAL Team One—one of those six platoons
in the Mekong Delta. Whiskey Platoon had been lucky. My platoon chief
petty officer had picked up some shrapnel from a booby trap, but the
wound had not kept him out of action. Zulu Platoon, another Team One
platoon working in our area, had just gone home. Five of Zulu's fourteen
SEALs, including both platoon officers, were in the hospital with combat
wounds. There was also a squad of Vietnamese SEALs at our base, but a
Viet Cong ambush killed three of them and wounded most of the others.
In that same action, one American SEAL adviser was killed and another
wounded. The four American crewmen of our SEAL support craft were all
badly wounded.

We also had a five-man detachment of frogmen from Underwater
Demolition Team Twelve working with us. Not technically SEALs, they
had the same training and often operated with the SEAL platoons. A few

weeks earlier, three of the UDT men had been wounded while working with the South Vietnamese gunboats. It was decided not to send a SEAL platoon to replace Zulu and to withdraw the Vietnamese SEALs, but we did get a new UDT detachment. One of these UDT replacements I remember particularly well. His name was Kim Erskine, and his story is important, for it illustrates why SEAL training has to be so long and so difficult. When least expected, a SEAL may need all his training and then some.

In 1971, Kim Erskine was a young petty officer two months out of BUD/S training. He had just turned eighteen and didn't look old enough to drive. Kim was just over six feet tall and skinny. He still had acne and a fresh innocence that said he knew nothing of combat and jungle fighting. The thing I remember most about Erskine, other than his youth and inexperience, was his ability to spike a volleyball. We operated at night most of the time, but in the afternoons we played jungle-rules volleyball and drank beer. Kim dominated those volleyball games.

When Kim arrived, Whiskey Platoon had only about six weeks left in our tour. We were focused on running our operations and trying to take everyone home in one piece. I remember little of those last few weeks in Vietnam except for that slow-growing, delicious feeling that comes with the prospect of ending a combat tour. We were just starting to tease ourselves with visions of McDonald's burgers, clean sheets, and flush toilets. It was a tightly managed euphoria felt by everyone in the platoon, but we were careful not to give ourselves over to it. Even after we had ceased operations and only a few of us went into the field to break in our relief platoon, we never let ourselves believe it was over—not completely. We'd heard too many stories about SEALs finding trouble on that one last operation. Only when we were on the flight back did I know it was truly over. A platoon officer who took all his men home after a combat tour was uncommon in those days. I was immensely proud that all my men were on this flight with me.

After Vietnam, Kim Erskine attended college and earned his degree. Then he returned to the teams as an officer. I saw him briefly in the late '70s, a fresh ensign with gold bars and a gold SEAL pin on his khakis. He

was more mature, but he still had the boyish grin I remembered. It always made me feel good to see a former enlisted man back in uniform as an officer. I ran into Erskine again in 1987. I was on two-week reserve duty at the Naval Special Warfare Command in Coronado, California. After reporting in, I made my way down a laminated corridor to a small, sparse office with two desks. One was empty, but the other was occupied by a large, solid-looking man with a tanned, ruddy complexion. When he grinned, I realized that it was Kim Erskine.

"Hello, Commander," he said as he rose and offered his hand. "I heard you would be here this week. Welcome to staff officers' purgatory."

It was great to see him. Except for the grin and a glint in his eyes when he smiled, Kim had lost all his boyishness. He was a full lieutenant now. He also had a nasty series of scars on his right arm and the ribbons for a Silver Star and a Purple Heart just under his SEAL pin.

"What happened to you?" I asked. "You didn't get those when we were in the Delta way back when."

"Well, sir, it's kind of a long story."

"Grenada?" I ventured.

He nodded. "Commander, you know all that training we went through at BUD/S and in the teams? Well, it finally paid off. I got hung out there pretty far. If I hadn't been with a bunch of guys who went through BUD/S, I wouldn't be here."

I put my curiosity on hold while I got a cup of coffee. Then I pulled a metal folding chair alongside his desk and listened to Kim Erskine's story.

Operation Urgent Fury was the invasion and occupation of the island of Grenada in late 1983. This hastily mounted military operation against that Caribbean island was to curb growing Cuban influence and to restore the authority of the Grenadian governor-general. The opposing forces were a well-armed but poorly trained Grenadian army and a very seasoned cadre of Cuban advisers. The outcome was never in doubt, but there were pockets of fierce opposition. A squad of Navy SEALs was assigned to secure the governor-general, who was under house arrest. A second element was to capture a key radio station and transmitting facil-

ity, an installation located on the hilly, coastal region north of the capital. Kim was in command of the team of twelve SEALs assigned to take the radio station.

SEALs operate best in small units, and a key to their success has always been teamwork. In the years prior to Grenada, a great deal of additional training and qualification standards had been instituted for BUD/S graduates once they arrived in the teams. Predeployment training for SEALs was extended and made more rigorous. BUD/S was now just one step in the complex and comprehensive training of a Navy SEAL. This training is intense, continuous, realistic, and dangerous. Better training makes for better teamwork. Each man comes to know his role in the team and what to expect from his teammates. They react as one. At the time of Operation Urgent Fury, Kim led a special team of six Navy SEALs trained for mission tasking in Central and South America. When the order came to move against Grenada, they had only time to gather their gear and race for the airlift that would take them south. Once aboard the plane, Kim learned that his mission was the radio station at a place called Cape St. George Beausejour.

At the last moment, Kim and his five teammates were assigned six SEALs from another SEAL squad. He had never worked with the new SEALs. Since he hadn't trained with these new men, he tried to resist making them a part of his element. His commanding officer overruled him. Kim would take along the second group; he would lead a twelve-man squad. In spite of the additional men, he was assured the operation would be a "cakewalk." The initial airlift took them from Fort Bragg, North Carolina, to the island of Barbados, where they boarded an MH-60 Pavehawk helicopter for the final flight to the target area.

The helo took small-arms fire on the way in, but once on the ground, the SEALs quickly overran the station complex. By the time they seized the facility, the guards and station personnel had fled. Kim's orders were to hold the station until a broadcast team could be brought in. This would never happen. The operation had been staged quickly and the radio frequencies shifted without Kim's knowledge. Their state-of-the-art, crypto-capable, satellite radio was worthless, and their backup sets didn't have enough range. The SEALs had taken their objective, but they could tell no one about it.

Kim's squad and the SEALs of the newly assigned squad melded well. From basic small-unit tactics to urban-warfare procedures, their training was the same; they were SEALs. Having cleared the radio station, they set up defensive positions. Kim again briefed his team on the rules of engagement, or ROEs, and emergency procedures in the event they had to make a hasty withdrawal. This seemed unlikely, but standard special operations doctrine calls for it—hope for the best, but plan for the worst. While he was working with the backup radio to establish comms, they had their first visitors. A military truck pulled up to the station. Twenty armed Grenadian soldiers in their blue field uniforms piled off. They looked like service station attendants with automatic weapons.

The SEALs were on alert, concealed and well positioned to receive them. Kim stepped from behind cover and, in accordance with his ROEs, identified himself as an American military officer. He asked them to lay down their weapons and leave the area. They responded by opening fire, and paid a terrible price for it. The SEALs raked them with their automatic weapons and devastated the Grenadian unit. Half were killed immediately and the rest seriously wounded, many fatally. Kim's SEALs hastily converted one of the rooms in the station to a makeshift morgue for the dead and another to an infirmary for the wounded and dying Grenadians. No Americans had been hurt. The SEALs had expended a third of their ammunition and almost all of their medical kit on the Grenadian unit. Still, Kim had no communication. The SEALs redistributed ammunition, went to their defensive positions, and waited.

Kim scaled the radio tower with his backup transceiver, desperately trying to make contact with the American forces coming onto the island. No luck. Then one of his men called from the ground, "Hey, sir, looks like we got more company." From the tower, Kim could see an armored personnel carrier (APC) and three trucks making their way slowly up the hill to the radio station. The APC paused to disgorge a dozen Grenadian soldiers, then continued toward them. The three trucks stopped and each deployed a dozen or more armed men. It was clear that they had come to retake the radio station.

Kim quickly pulled his men back from the perimeter, intending to carry out a defensive action from the main station building. The Grenadians flanked the building and opened fire, while the APC drove right up to the front entrance. Then, with its 20mm gun, it began to tear into the wood-and-stucco building. Up close and personal, a 20mm cannon is a devastating weapon. The APC's turret swung back and forth, punching holes in the radio station. The SEALs could hold their own with the Grenadian infantry, but the armored vehicle with its cannon was another matter. With the building about to come down on their heads, one of the SEALs got a clear shot at the APC with a bullet-trap grenade and managed to jam the turret. The APC could still shoot, but the gunner was now unable to traverse the turret. This gave Kim and his SEALs a breather, but their situation was precarious.

The Grenadians were well armed with good reserves of ammunition. They were now pouring heavy automatic-weapons fire into the building. Inside, the walls were exploding, bullets splashing everywhere. Bullets, when they pass close by, carry a sonic wave and produce a distinctive *snap*. Kim Erskine was now hearing the *snap-snap* as the rounds broke close over his head. The SEALs were critically low on ammunition. If the 20mm came back on line, they had no chance.

Behind the radio station was a broad meadow leading to a path that cut between the cliffs to the beach. This was their preplanned escape route. When SEALs plan their first training missions in BUD/S, they include alternative escape routes and emergency procedures. Clearly, if Kim and his men remained to defend the radio station, they would all be killed. The APC surely had a radio and more soldiers could arrive at any moment. Kim gave the order to pull out. He told his SEALs to redistribute their remaining ammunition and prepare to leapfrog across the meadow for the beach. The SEALs needed no direction; they had done this many times, beginning at BUD/S, where they learned basic squad tactics. The open area behind the station was the size of a football field. They would be terribly exposed, but escape was their only hope.

As the SEALs fell back to the rear entrance of the radio station, incoming rounds continued to rip through the walls around them. The Grenadians were now ranging on both sides and would have them in a cross fire on the open ground. Kim had no option but to lead his men across the field and down a steep slope that led to the beach. When SEALs get into trouble, they always try to get back to the water.

In the movies, this scene would be played with scrappy, grim-faced men slapping their last magazine into their weapons—ready for the worst, but gamely determined to make a show of it. But this wasn't the movies. These were twelve real-live, scared Americans. Each thought he was going to die in that open field. Even Navy SEALs know fear, and here, we're talking about paralyzing, oh-please-God-no, pee-in-your-pants fear. They were scared, but they were also very well trained. In life-and-death situations, mortal fear can cause men to freeze—totally immobilize them. Often, only the confidence instilled by repetition and drill can get them moving. Often, there is a fine line between preparation and bravery.

"Go, go, go," Kim yelled as he and his squad bolted from the radio station to the base of the transmitter antenna. They laid down covering fire while his second squad sprinted into the field. Grenadian troops were moving along the chain-link fence on both sides. The radio station had become a death trap, and the field behind it could easily become a killing zone. Kim and his men had no choice but to cross it. To do this, the SEALs had to play the deadly game of leapfrog. Thirty yards into the field, using the antenna's cement anchors for cover, the second squad went down and began to return fire—single shots to conserve ammunition. It was now Kim's turn. He and his five SEALs sprinted across the field, past the other men who were now covering their dash.

The signal to halt and take up a firing position happens when the squad leader drops and begins to shoot. This decision was made when an enemy round clipped Kim's belt, shearing off his canteen and knocking him to the ground. Kim's squad went down with him and began to return fire, while the other squad ran past them to a new position. This leapfrog drill is rehearsed many times in SEAL platoon training; for most of the SEALs at the radio tower, this was the first time they had done it under fire.

Kim Erskine was knocked down three more times running across the field—once when the heel of his boot was shot off, and another time when a round glanced off a magazine strapped to his torso. The third time, a bullet destroyed his right elbow. At the end of the field, the SEALs were able to cut through a section of the chain-link fence and slip through. Kim, now seriously wounded, paused to get a quick count. A SEAL team leader, just like a boat-crew leader in BUD/S training, must always account for his men. Kim was a man short. Back in the field, his wounded radioman was making his way across the field, dragging the useless radio.

While the SEALs laid down a base of fire, Kim screamed for his wounded man to abandon the radio. The young man pulled his 9mm pistol and destroyed the satcom radio with its classified encryption components. As the SEALs expended the last of their ammunition, the final member of their team scrambled through the fence. Once in the dense brush behind the field, they had a brief respite from their pursuers. Yet their prospects were anything but good; they were outnumbered and they had no communications. No one knew where they were or whether they were still alive.

Quickly, they descended the path to the beach and waded out into the water. The shoreline arced in a shallow crescent that formed a scenic bay surrounded by rocky cliffs. The SEALs began swimming, but they knew it was a temporary sanctuary. It was evident that if they kept swimming, they would be sitting ducks for the Grenadians on the cliffs. Kim told them to ditch all their equipment except side arms and signal flares, and to swim parallel to the beach. A short way along the shoreline, they came back into a rocky portion of the beach and made their way up into the cliffs where they were protected from above by overhanging ledges and vegetation. The Grenadians were still following, but very carefully now. The running firefight across the field had left a number of them dead and wounded. They understood now that these Americans could shoot as well as run.

Once down on the beach, the pursuing Grenadians found the tracks leading into the water and assumed the invaders had probably escaped out to sea. Still yet more Grenadians arrived and searched along the shore and high on the cliffs until nightfall. Kim and his men could hear them talking as they searched above and around them, but they remained undetected. At dusk, the Grenadians finally pulled back to the radio station.

Soon after dark, two U.S. Hughes 500D observation helos, or "Little Birds," made a pass over the radio station. The SEALs heard the choppers roar in over the beach and assumed they were looking for them, but the men huddled in the side of the cliff could do nothing. Kim, in consultation with his senior petty officers, decided to wait until after midnight before trying to swim out to sea. Kim's wounded arm was throbbing and he had lost all feeling below the elbow. The radioman was also in a great deal of pain, but holding on. Another SEAL suffered from a wound in his upper leg. They settled in to wait, but just before ten o'clock the SEALs again came under fire.

Unknown to Kim, the Little Birds had taken fire from the Grenadians at the radio station and a nearby antiaircraft battery. Since nothing had been heard from the SEALs and the Grenadians held the radio station, the U.S. force commander assumed they had been killed. He sent an air strike against the radio station. While the SEALs burrowed into the rocks and vegetation, a section of Navy A-7 attack jets made several strafing runs on the radio station and surrounding area. Again the SEALs were on the wrong end of 20mm fire, this time from the A-7s' Vulcan gun pods— 20mm fire at seven thousand rounds per minute. Stray rounds splashed around them, chipping at rocks and bringing down tree limbs. After the A-7s left, Kim's chief petty officer turned to him and said, "Sir, maybe it's time we got the hell out of here."

Kim agreed. The Grenadians at the radio station were now probably more concerned with A-7s than SEALs. And the SEALs had had enough friendly fire. Descending the rocky cliff would have been dangerous in the dark, but there was an outcropping from which they could jump. With a strong leap, they could clear the rockface and make the water. Kim's right arm was useless and he was in a great deal of pain. The SEALs had pain drugs in their medical kit, but Kim feared the side effects; he was still in command. Unsure if he had the strength to make the leap from the cliff, he had two of his SEALs throw him off. All twelve of them made the water and began to swim seaward. Kim had to drag his useless arm through the water; the other wounded had to swim as best they could. But SEALs prepare for this. In BUD/S training, the trainees are bound, hands and feet, and made to swim this way. They call it drown proofing.

Kim knew that a SAR Bird (search-and-rescue C-130 aircraft) would be circling the island on a regular schedule. They had been in the water for close to six hours when the SAR Bird flew near them. The men in the water fired off several pencil flares and the aircraft turned toward them. The C-130 found the SEALs in the water with its powerful searchlight, and vectored a Navy ship to their position. Just before dawn, the SEALs were picked up by the USS *Caron* (DD-970).

By this time, Kim had been awake for over forty-eight hours. The last time he had been this beat up and sleep-deprived was during his Hell Week with Class 52. Once on the deck of the *Caron,* he again counted his men. During every BUD/S Hell Week, exhausted, half-dead officers and petty officers again and again count their men. BUD/S instructors do unspeakable things to leaders who lose track of their men. So Kim counted his men. Once the count was right and he knew his men were safely aboard, he passed out. When he awoke a day later in the hospital at the Bethesda Naval Hospital, his first question was "Where are my men?"

· · ·

The account of Kim Erskine and the SEALs at the radio tower on Grenada is extreme, but perhaps not unusual. Intelligence about enemy troop strength and opposition forces is usually accurate. The radios usually work. But what if they don't? Then, it's all about the men in the fight. Are they true warriors? In the face of overwhelming odds, do they have the training and the will to fight and win?

SEAL training, beginning from day one at BUD/S, is designed to create warriors. This is a book about Navy SEALs and their training. It is also about their warrior culture. It is a sorting process that finds young men who would rather die than quit, then instills them with a relentless desire to fight and win as a team. Once a prospective SEAL trainee reports for BUD/S training, he is immediately immersed in the culture of the teams. Most SEALs never have their courage and training put to the test as severely as the SEALs on Grenada. But many have.

Modern SEALs are much like policemen. Their operational deployments often take them into dangerous and volatile situations, but they may well spend their entire careers without firing a shot in anger. Yet, at any time, they may have to fight—to risk death in combat. From the days of the World War II frogmen, through the establishment of the first SEAL teams in 1962, to the present, SEAL training has evolved to meet new mission requirements and changing threat scenarios. In World War II and Korea and Vietnam, a young frogman or SEAL could find himself in a firefight after three or four months of training. Today, it takes more than *thirty months* to train a Navy SEAL. At that point, he is certified and ready for deployment—an apprentice warrior in the SEAL trade and still a "new guy." When he comes back from his first deployment, he is called a "one-tour wonder"—no more than a journeyman in the trade.

As SEAL training has become longer and more comprehensive in recent years, one aspect of this training has remained the same; in order to get one good man, it's necessary to begin with five good men. Since the birth of the Navy frogmen at Fort Pierce, Florida, during World War II, this forging of warriors through adversity and attrition has always been unlike any military training in the world. It is a ruthless process; for every man who succeeds, four men will fail. It's a rendering for men of character, spirit, and a burning desire to win at all costs. It is a unique and often brutal rite of passage that forms the basis of this distinctive warrior culture.

So who are these guys, really? Taking examples from the public sector, are they like Bob Kerrey—the quiet, charismatic former senator and governor from Nebraska, who as Ensign Kerrey was awarded the Medal of Honor in Vietnam? Or are they like Jesse Ventura, A.K.A. Petty Officer Jim Janos—a veteran of UDT Twelve and the World Wrestling Federation, and the governor of Minnesota? The senator was Class 42 and the governor, like Kim Erskine, was Class 58. Or are they like Rudy Boesch, Class 6? Rudy was a "survivor" for forty-five years as a SEAL on active duty; the television series was a piece of cake.

To examine SEAL training today, I was allowed to follow BUD/S Class 228. It was an opportunity for me to journey back in time, and to revisit an important and meaningful time in my life. This time, as an observer, I thought it would be without the pain or the emotion. I was wrong. At times, watching young men battle cold water, mud, swollen joints, and days without sleep was almost more than I could bear. Sometimes when the instructors sent them back out into the surf at night, I would begin to shake uncontrollably and have to walk up the beach to regain my composure. Even after thirty years, there's still scar tissue. Here, you're going to meet the young men who want to be SEALs, to see where they come from and exactly what they must do to join this elite band of warriors. And you're going to see why they do it and what motivates them to willingly suffer so much.

If the Marines are "the Few—the Proud," then the survivors of Class 228 are "the Courageous—the Driven." I was privileged to have been allowed to share a small part of their journey. And I'm both proud and grateful that such fine young men are still willing to pay the price to become modern warriors and to serve in the Navy SEAL teams.

CHAPTER ONE

THE BEGINNING

Monday, 4 October 1999. A fine mist hangs over the Naval Amphibious Base on Coronado as a cool marine air layer steals in from the Pacific, extinguishing the stars. The lights along Guadalcanal Road are a harsh, haloed yellow. The base is quiet. Behind a chain-link fence with diagonal privacy slats, Class 228 waits anxiously, seated on the concrete pool deck. The new BUD/S trainees wear only canvas UDT swim trunks. They are compressed into tight rows, chests to backs, in bobsled fashion to conserve body heat. The large clock on the cinder-block wall reads 5:00 A.M.—0500, or zero five hundred, in military jargon. They are wet from a recent shower. Neat rows of duffel bags that contain the students' uniforms, boots, and training gear separate each human file. The pool—officially called the combat training tank, or CTT—has already been prepared for the first evolution. The students had arrived thirty minutes earlier to roll and stow the pool covers and string the lane markers.

"Feet!" yells the class leader.

"FEET!" The voices of nearly a hundred young men answer in unison as they scramble into ranks.

"In-struct-tor Ree-no!" intones the class leader.

"HOOYAH, INSTRUCTOR REE-NO!" the class responds in full roar.

The first day of training has begun for Class 228. It's pitch black except for the building lights that cut into the mist and the underwater pool lights that illuminate a blue mirror surface. The members of Basic Underwater Demolition/SEAL Class 228 stand at attention in fourteen files, each file forming a boat crew of seven BUD/S trainees. Instructor Reno Alberto, Class 228's proctor for the two-week BUD/S Indoctrination Course, surveys the pool. Apparently satisfied the CTT is ready, he turns and regards Class 228 for a long moment.

"Drop," he says quietly.

"DROP!" 228 echoes as the class melts to the deck, each student scrambling to claim a vacant piece of concrete. They wait, arms extended, holding their bodies in a rigid, leaning-rest position.

"Push 'em out."

"Push-ups!" yells the class leader.

"PUSH-UPS!" responds 228.

"Down!"

"ONE!"

"Down!"

"TWO!"

Class 228 loudly counts out twenty push-ups, then returns to the leaning rest. "In-struct-tor Ree-no," calls the class leader.

"HOOYAH, INSTRUCTOR REE-NO!" the students yell in unison.

Reno stands off to one side, arms folded, apparently uninterested in the mass of students leaning on their outstretched arms.

"Push 'em out," he commands softly.

"Push-ups!"

"PUSH-UPS!"

After two more rounds of this, Reno leaves them in the leaning rest for close to five minutes. By now the students are twisting and thrusting their buttocks into the air in an effort to relieve the burning in their arms.

"Recover," he says in the same measured voice.

"FEET!" the class responds, this time with less zeal.

"Give me a report, Mister Gallagher."

Lieutenant (junior grade) William Gallagher takes the class muster board from Machinist Mate First Class Robert Carreola, 228's leading petty officer, or LPO. Gallagher and Carreola are the class leader and class leading petty officer, respectively, as they are the senior officer and senior enlisted trainee in Class 228. Carreola is five-ten, but he appears shorter—partly because he has a broad, highly developed upper body and partly because his lieutenant is six-two.

Bill Gallagher is a slim, serious young man with a shy smile. He came to the Naval Academy from northern Virginia, recruited to play lacrosse for Navy. Gallagher has wanted to be a Navy SEAL since 1982, when his father gave him an article from *Parade* magazine with pictures of SEALs and BUD/S training. He was seven years old. Bill Gallagher was unable to come to BUD/S from Annapolis, so he went directly from the Academy to the fleet. Now, as a qualified surface warfare officer with two years at sea, he stands at the head of Class 228. His goal is still to become a Navy SEAL. Bob Carreola has been in the Navy for eleven years; this is his second try at BUD/S. He is thirty-one years old with more than a decade of service in naval aviation squadrons. His goal is also to be a Navy SEAL.

"Instructor, Class Two-two-eight is formed; ninety-eight men assigned, ninety-five men present. I have one man on watch and two men at medical for sick call."

"Ninety-five men present, Lieutenant?"

"Hooyah, Instructor Reno."

"That's wrong, sir. Drop and push 'em out. You too, Carreola."

While Gallagher and Carreola begin pushing concrete, Reno turns to the class. "The rest of you, seats."

"SEATS!" bellows Class 228 as the young men hit the concrete. They return to their compressed boat-crew files. They will sit like this often in the days and weeks ahead, hugging the man in front of them to stay warm. Gallagher and Carreola finish their push-ups and chant, "Hooyah, Instructor Reno!"

"Push 'em out," Reno replies.

This is not the last time that Lieutenant Gallagher and Petty Officer Carreola will personally pay for the sins of the class. One of the boat-crew leaders failed to report to Gallagher that one of his men was UA, or an unauthorized absence. This oversight caused Gallagher to give a bad muster; the actual number of men on the pool deck this morning is ninety-four. When one man in the class screws up, sometimes the whole class pays the tab. Sometimes a single boat crew pays or just the class leaders. But someone always pays.

"Now listen up," Reno says, turning to the class, finally raising his voice. He glances at his watch; it's 0510. "This is bullshit. You guys better get it together . . . now! Things are going to start to get difficult around here. We know most of you won't be here in another two months, but if you don't start pulling as a team, none of you will be here! It's a simple muster, gentlemen. If you can't get that done, what are you going to do when you get into First Phase and things really become difficult?" The class listens silently. Gallagher and Carreola continue to push concrete.

Reno regards the files of young men seated on the pool deck, then turns to the two sweating trainees. "Recover." They scramble up and take their places at the head of their boat crews. "This morning, gentlemen, we're going to take the basic screening test. You all passed this test at your last command or you wouldn't be here. If you can't pass it again this morning, you'll be back in the fleet just as soon as we can get you there. Understood?"

"HOOYAH, INSTRUCTOR RENO!"

. . .

BUD/S training is conducted in three distinct phases. First Phase is the conditioning phase, followed by Second Phase—diving—and Third Phase—weapons and tactics. In order to prepare them for the rigors of First Phase, the trainees must first complete the two-week Indoctrination Course. Here they will learn the rules and conventions of BUD/S training. They will learn how to conduct themselves at the pool, how to run the obstacle course, and how to maneuver small boats through the surf. They will also learn the complex set of procedures and protocols needed in First Phase and the rest of BUD/S training—customs they must observe if they hope to survive this rite of passage. During this indoctrination period, they also begin to learn about SEAL culture and begin to absorb the ethos of this warrior class. In these first few minutes of the Indoctrination Course, Class 228 has already learned something about accountability and leadership. An officer or petty officer must always account for his men. SEALs have died in combat, but never has one been left behind.

The Indoctrination Course, or Indoc, also helps the trainees to physically prepare for First Phase. Some members of Class 228 have been at BUD/S for a few days, a few for as long as two months. Eight are rollbacks from a previous class—men recently injured in training who are beginning again with Class 228. These two weeks of pretraining are designed to physically and mentally bring the class together. This is a very important time. Most of the students have prepared for this individually. Now they will live and train as a class—as a team.

One hundred fourteen souls were originally assigned, or had orders, to BUD/S Class 228. Most are relatively new to the Phil E. Bucklew Naval Special Warfare Center, Coronado, California, where BUD/S is conducted. Twelve members of 228, like Bob Carreola, are here for a second time. If a student quits, he must return to fleet duty for at least eighteen months before he can return for another try—if he demonstrated potential on his first attempt and was recommended for a second try.

Class 228 had 114 men who thought they wanted to become Navy SEALs. But only 98 are on the roster on the first day of indoctrination. A few of the no-shows were sailors who were unhappy with their ship or duty station. They were fit enough to pass the BUD/S screening exam and accepted the orders to BUD/S as a way to make a change. Others found the relatively modest conditioning swims and runs before Indoc more than they bargained for. And there are always a few who, upon their arrival at BUD/S, are simply intimidated. When they see what SEAL trainees are asked to do, they quit before they begin. So the attrition began even before Class 228 started its first official day of training. Any student at BUD/S, at any time, can DOR—drop on request. All he has to do is say, "I quit."

Those assigned to Class 228 who quit prior to the beginning of Indoc will be reassigned back to the fleet.

Today, Class 228 has to earn the privilege of continuing with the Indoctrination Course. Each trainee must again pass the BUD/S screening test:

1. A five-hundred-yard swim using the breast- or sidestroke in twelve minutes, thirty seconds
2. A minimum of forty-two push-ups in two minutes
3. A minimum of fifty sit-ups in two minutes
4. A minimum of six dead-hang pull-ups
5. A mile-and-a-half run in eleven minutes, thirty seconds wearing boots and long pants

All but one in Class 228 passes the screening test. This buys the trainees a ticket to proceed with their training for two more weeks. A few of the men are close to the minimums, but most handle the run and the swim with at least a minute to spare. Eighty push-ups, a hundred sit-ups, and fifteen pull-ups are not uncommon. There are those in the teams and among the instructor staff who think the screening minimums are too low—that the bar should be higher for those entering BUD/S.

This test is not a perfect predictor for who will succeed and who will fail. In the demanding days ahead, a few of those who struggled to pass the screening test will make it to graduation. Those are the ones who arrived at BUD/S with a soft body and a strong spirit. Some of the more physically gifted will find that they have no stomach for the punishment that lies ahead, and they will quit as soon as they become tired and cold. They will be timed and tested during Indoc, but only two things can remove a student from the two-week Indoctrination Course: a DOR or failing a comprehensive psychological evaluation given to each new arrival. Only one member of Class 228 fails the psych exam.

After the screening test, the men of Class 228 gather their gear from the pool deck and hustle off to chow. Following their morning meal, they will run in formation across the Naval Amphibious Base to the Special Warfare Center located on the ocean side of Highway 75, which bisects the base. The Amphibious Base is the host facility for the West Coast SEAL teams and other Naval Special Warfare commands, as well as the Naval Special Warfare Center.

Coronado is a near-island that sits in the center of San Diego Bay, connected at its southernmost tip to the mainland by way of a narrow, eight-mile-long sand spit called the Silver Strand. The Naval Amphibious Base is located on the northern portion of this narrow strand, just south of the village of Coronado. The north end of Coronado proper is occupied by the massive North Island Naval Air Station. Known as NAS North Island, this facility is a major maintenance, training, and repair depot for the naval air arm of the Pacific Fleet. Aircraft Carrier Number One, the USS *Langley*, moored at North Island in 1924 and pioneered naval aviation in the Pacific. Today, North Island is home for two West Coast–based aircraft carriers. The Naval Amphibious Base, built on reclaimed land in 1943, is a relative newcomer.

Nestled between NAS North Island and the much smaller Naval Amphibious Base on the Silver Strand is the idyllic resort community of Coronado. "Idyllic" is an understatement; Coronado is a neat, manicured residential setting of expensive homes with broad, white-sand beaches on the Pacific side and the San Diego skyline on the bay side. Anchoring the western end of Orange Avenue, a palm-lined main boulevard of eateries, boutiques, and art galleries, is the famous Hotel del Coronado. This historic hotel has been a favorite of presidents, royalty, and movie stars for over a century. When it was built in 1887, it was the largest resort hotel in the world. Today it stands as an elegant architectural monument to the grace and splendor of a past era. Just south of the Hotel del (as it's sometimes called), between the hotel and the Amphibious Base, is a series of modern, high-rise beach condominiums. These stark, concrete towers, punctuated by pools, gardens, and verandas, couldn't be more dissimilar to the graceful wooden curves and red-pinnacled roofs of the historic and charming Hotel del Coronado. Further south, the contrast increases. Less than three hundred yards from the concrete condo towers on this gorgeous strip of white-sand beach, the U.S. Navy conducts the toughest military training in the free world.

. . .

"Feet!"

"FEET!"

There is a mass scraping of chairs as Class 228 comes to attention. Some are already standing along the back and side walls of the classroom because there are more students than seats. This student-chair ratio will change as the number of DORs increases. The room is ripe with the smell of sweat, chlorine, and wet clothing. Instructor Reno works his way to the front of the room and the raised podium. Once again he quietly surveys the class.

"Drop," he deadpans.

"DROP!" the class responds. Now there is a serious amount of commotion as the members of Class 228 compete with the school chairs for a piece of the classroom floor. While the class pushes linoleum, other BUD/S instructors assigned to Indoc quietly make their way to the front of the room. When the twenty push-ups are completed, the trainees "hooyah" Reno and are allowed to take their seats.

The origin of the term "hooyah" is unclear. It originated on the West Coast, as it was seldom heard on the East Coast during those years when the Navy conducted UDT/SEAL training on both coasts. One theory attributes the expression back to a popular mid-1950s UDT instructor named Bud Juric. An aggressive volleyball player, he used to yell "poo-yah" when he spiked the ball. It is said that the trainees of that era took the term and converted it to "hoo-yah." Other old SEALs claim that another BUD/S instructor in the mid-'50s named Paul McNalley coined the term. A third theory simply holds that earlier training classes simply adopted a syllable reversal of "yahoo." Whatever the origin, it has evolved into a universal trainee response during all phases of BUD/S training and a favored expression in the teams.

Petty Officer Reno Alberto, who insists the trainees use his first name, is one of the junior BUD/S instructors assigned to Indoc. At five-six he is also one of the shortest, but he is compact, muscular, and very fit. He speaks with the precise, measured accent of someone for whom English is a second language. Reno has a degree in business administration from USC; he left the corporate world to become a Navy SEAL. He opens a three-ring binder and sweeps his eyes over the class.

"All right, listen up. I will be your class proctor for the two-week Indoc course. I have some word to put out and it will behoove you all to pay attention. Better still, take notes." He watches while some of the trainees pull out Ziploc bags with dry paper and pencils. Other students don't move or look down to avoid Reno's stare. "How many of you do not have paper and pencil?" Several hands go up. "Drop—all of you!" Reno lets them push out a set of twenty and holds them in the leaning rest.

"Listen up, people. You were told to have a pencil and paper on you at all times. So why don't you?" Silence. "This is a school for warriors and it's serious business. If you don't want to do this, then get the hell out. Start thinking. Get your heads in the game. Anticipate. Now, push 'em out."

"HOOYAH, INSTRUCTOR RENO!"

When the students complete the round of push-ups, Reno orders them back to their chairs and the class quiets down. They're starting to sweat again, and the air in the classroom reeks. One by one, Reno introduces the other BUD/S instructors who will be putting Class 228 through the Indoctrination Course. Each instructor steps forward with a modest ten- or fifteen-second oral bio. Most have ten or more years in the teams and are veterans of multiple SEAL platoon deployments. They file out and Reno has the class to himself. He is taking the trainees through a litany of what they can expect for the next two weeks, when he sees a man start to nod off.

"Feet!"

"FEET!" The class members scramble to their feet.

"Seats." The class sits and Reno steps from behind the podium. "You've got to pay attention, gentlemen. If you start to fall asleep, stand up. What I have to say is important. It's for your benefit, so I want all eyes on me, understood?"

"HOOYAH!"

"This is high-risk training. We define high-risk training as any evolution where there is potential for serious injury or loss of life. Safety is our primary consideration. If you observe any unsafe condition or feel that your own safety is in jeopardy, you are to call it to the attention of an instructor, or the attention of your boat-crew leader or the class leader. Understood?"

"HOOYAH!"

"We've already talked about accountability. Use the chain of command. Let your boat-crew leaders and class leaders know if you're excused from an evolution. Stay with your swim buddy. I don't care if you're going to the head, you stay with your swim buddy, understood?"

"HOOYAH!"

"Respect. I expect you to show respect for the instructor staff, the class officers, and the senior petty officers. You're in the military; you will be courteous at all times. Understood?"

"HOOYAH!"

"Integrity. It's a simple thing, gents: you don't lie, cheat, or steal. If you lose a piece of gear, you put in a chit and report it. You do not take someone else's gear. That's happened here in the past and those guys are gone. You respect your classmate and his gear, and that means you don't take what is not yours. Got that?"

"HOOYAH!"

"I'm your class proctor for the next two weeks. I'm here to help you if you need help. If you have a pay problem, we'll get you over to the disbursing office and get it fixed. If you have a personal problem or a family problem, I'll see that you get to the chaplain. If you become injured, go to medical, get it fixed, and get back into training. I'm your proctor; I'm not your mother. I'm here to teach you. You stay in the box and I'll help you. You get outside the box and I'll hammer you. Understood?"

"HOOYAH!"

"One more thing. For those of you who make it through this training and go on to the teams, your reputation begins here. Your reputation as a class begins here. And your reputation as a class is a reflection of your proctor. I take that very personally. Reputation is everything. Pay attention. Keep your head in the game. Put out a hundred percent, because we'll know it if you're not. And never leave your swim buddy." He looks at the class and closes the notebook. "Any questions?"

"NEGATIVE!"

"Fair enough. Lieutenant Mahoney will be here in a few minutes. Stand by for him."

"Feet!" Carreola yells as Reno leaves the podium.

"FEET!"

Class 228 stirs about the classroom while it waits for Lieutenant Mahoney. One member of the class stands guard at the door to alert the others of the approach of the instructor. The others mill about near their seats or in the back of the room. The guard announces the arrival of Mahoney and Class 228 comes to attention.

"Take your seats, gentlemen, and welcome to your first day of Indoc." Lieutenant Bill Mahoney is a sturdy six-footer dressed like the rest of the enlisted BUD/S instructors: blue T-shirt, khaki shorts, and polished black military boots with white socks rolled over the top. Lieutenant Mahoney, a Villanova graduate, is the basic training officer. He is responsible for the three regular phases of BUD/S, as well as the Indoctrination Course. He looks up from his notes and surveys the class.

"This block of instruction is designed to give you an idea about life in the teams and the overseas deployment opportunities available to those of you who graduate from BUD/S and go on to earn your Trident pin." He squares his shoulders and looks directly at the class. "Now, I'm really only talking to the twenty percent or so of you men who will actually make it to graduation. The rest will be long gone by then. Most of you have already decided if you're going to make it. Whether you're at graduation or not is entirely up to you." Mahoney pauses and rubs the side of his face. "You see, it's like this; if you can get through training, life in the teams can be terrific. There's excitement, adventure, travel, and a chance to serve with a great bunch of guys—a chance to be one of the best. But you have to get through this first. Some of you can see the cost-benefit of what we do here. You'll take the pain and the cold water because you think it's worth it to get to the teams; you'll pay your dues because you want to be in the club. A few of you will stay no matter how hard we try to get rid of you—no matter how cold you get or how much you hurt. We'd have to kill you because you won't quit. And that's okay; that's what we're here to find out. Who wants to be in the teams and who's willing to pay the price of admission? Most of you here simply don't want it that bad. We'll see."

Mahoney drags a computer keyboard to the top of the podium and taps in a few commands. The presentation software kicks into gear and an overhead projector flashes the Naval Special Warfare emblem onto the screen— the gold SEAL Trident that all qualified SEALs proudly wear.

"So let's see what's in store for you if you manage to survive the next twenty-seven weeks." Mahoney presents a brief history of the teams, beginning with the frogmen in World War II through the formation of the first SEAL teams in 1962, and up to the current configuration of the SEAL and SDV (SEAL Delivery Vehicle) teams. Then he clicks through a slick presentation that highlights the ongoing training, deployment, and operational life of a Navy SEAL. For the most part, he has their attention, but a few of them succumb to the warm classroom and start to nod off.

· · ·

Each day of Indoc seems to be a little longer and a little more intense than the previous one. Each morning of Indoc begins at the pool at 0500. After a two-hour pool evolution that is half physical harassment and half water training, the students don their fatigues and boots. When they are fully dressed, the instructors usually order them into the pool along with their gear. They then run to the chow hall for a quick breakfast and back across the base to the Special Warfare Center to continue their training. Days— and sometimes nights—at BUD/S are a series of training evolutions. As the days become weeks, the evolutions seem endless. The students run six miles each day just to eat. BUD/S trainees live on the run and are always cold and wet. When they are at the Center, they make several trips a day to the Pacific and are made to roll on the beach after returning from the surf. Now they are cold, wet, and sandy.

The instructors appear insensitive and often cruel. A great deal of what they do is to test the spirit and character of their charges, individually and as a class. They are instructors, but they are also gatekeepers, and they take this job very seriously. Yet, along with the harassment and misery, there is the teaching. Even though the primary purpose of Indoc is to prepare the students for the physical ordeal that will begin in First Phase, they also begin to learn skills they will need as Navy SEALs here.

The teaching begins in the pool. "You have to be good in the water," Instructor Tim King tells Class 228. Like Reno, King is a short, powerful man. And like many enlisted SEALs, he has a college degree; Tim King's is in criminal justice. "This is what separates us from all other special operations forces. For them, water is an obstacle; for us, it's sanctuary." I noted many changes at BUD/S since Class 45 graduated, but the most dramatic are in the swimming curriculum. In the past, it was simply a matter of showing the trainees a basic stroke and making them swim laps; kick, stroke, and glide. Now it's all about technique. The instructors begin with teaching buoyancy control and body position in the water. The basic stroke is a modified sidestroke that the trainees will later adapt to the use of fins. Much of what is taught is taken from the work of Terry Laughlin and his "Total Immersion" training technique. Laughlin is a noted civilian instructor who developed innovative long-distance swimming techniques for competitive and recreational swimmers. A few in Class 228 were competition swimmers before coming to BUD/S, but most are not. All will learn the Laughlin method. According to Laughlin, it's all about swimming more like a fish and less like a human. The instructors say it's like swimming downhill. It has to do with making one's body physically longer in the water and reducing drag.

"Before Terry Laughlin," King says, "it was just a matter of getting in the water and getting it done. When I was in BUD/S training, my instructors taught us the way they learned it from their instructors. Now, that's all changed; technique is everything."

The trainees do lengths in the pool using just their legs. Then they add a new method of breathing, rolling in the water to get a breath rather than lifting their heads. Arms are used for balance and to make the swimmer longer in the water. As the trainees practice, the instructors are right there, coaching and teaching.

"There's not a lot we can do to make them run faster," explains Instructor King. BUD/S instructors are addressed as "Instructor" unless they are a chief petty officer, in which case they are addressed by their title. "But if they can master these techniques in the water, we can dramatically get their swim times down. The staff here at BUD/S can be a very skeptical bunch. We tend to resist anything from the outside. But when our personal swim times came down using Laughlin's methods, well, we knew this was good information. We try to do as much teaching as possible here in Indoc—help them improve their technique. The First Phase instructors can't do this; they don't have the time. They'll just put them in the water and expect them to perform. They'll have to make the minimum swim times or they'll be dropped from the class. For some of them, this training will make the difference between making it to graduation or washing out. We've been able to cut swim drops by twenty-five percent," he adds with a measure of pride. "This stuff really works."

During the first week of Indoc, the trainees practice surface-swimming skills without fins. The second week they put on standard-issue duck feet. The instruction and coaching continue—along with the physical harassment.

A number of other pool competency skills are taught during Indoc. There are basic knots the trainees need to know and must be able to tie underwater while holding their breath. These are knots that they will later use to rig underwater explosives in simulated combat conditions. The Indoc instructors explain each knot, some of its applications, and how it can be tied quickly underwater. Each student carries a section of line tied to the neck of his canteen with which to practice and to take into the water for knot-tying drills. Along with knot tying, the trainees are graded on underwater swimming. In Indoc, they have to swim underwater without fins for thirty-five meters. The secret to underwater swimming is going deep early. The trainees learn that if they swim along the bottom in deeper water, the increased partial pressure of oxygen in their lungs will allow them to hold their breath longer and swim farther.

The most intimidating of the pool competency skills is drown proofing. Trainees' ankles are bound together and their hands tied behind their back. Trussed in this manner, they are introduced to a number of underwater maneuvers and drills they will be required to perform during First Phase. The point of these exercises is to teach trainees to be comfortable in the water and to stay calm. The instructors constantly remind them to relax, but it's not easy for some. Tim King watches as members of 228 are bound hand and foot then rolled off into the deep water. Alert instructors with fins and masks swim among them like sharks.

"Now we find out which ones played in the swimming pool as kids and which ones played in the fire hydrant." He grimaces slightly as one student wriggles to the surface for a bite of air and disappears. "You guys have to be good in the water," he reminds other members of 228 waiting for their turn at drown proofing. "You'll never be a SEAL unless you first become a frogman."

Next to swimming, the obstacle course is the most technically demanding challenge for the Indoc trainees. There are fifteen major obstacles the trainees have to negotiate. This obstacle course is a tough one—a series of walls, vaults, rope bridges, and logs with a short sprint in the soft sand between obstacles. One of the most daunting is the cargo net—a rope latticework stretched on a tall wooden frame. They must climb this rope web and slither over a log at the top, some sixty feet in the air. Other obstacles require that they crawl under barbed wire and hand walk on parallel bars. On the first day at the "O-course," the instructors walk them through the course and explain the various ways to handle each barrier. Then Class 228 runs it for time. This is not a confidence course, as some are called; these are real obstacles, and the Indoc trainees struggle with their first attempt.

"Each one of these obstacles was designed to challenge you in some specific way and prepare you to function as a Navy SEAL," the trainees are told. "Whether it's parachuting, working in small boats, boarding a ship under way, or rappelling down the face of a cliff, this course will make you a more proficient operator. Guys in the teams come here and run this O-course to prepare for overseas deployment."

The O-course requires a blend of technique, stamina, confidence, agility, and upper-body strength. "You have to attack it; throw your body into it," an instructor shouts as one of the trainees scrambles up a vertical wall. "Don't hold back."

It's also a little man's game. The taller and stockier trainees tend to have more trouble with the O-course. Some of the best times are registered by the smaller men. The O-course is a venue in which some members of 228 will excel. It will weed a few of them out. In any case, it's high-risk training, as Class 228 quickly finds out. One obstacle, called the Slide for Life, features a long, three-inch diameter nylon line that loops down from a thirty-foot tower to a ten-foot vertical bar. The trainees have to pull themselves up the three-story tower a level at a time to get to the top, then slide or pull themselves down the line. One member of 228 loses his grip on the line and falls to the sand below. He breaks his arm and pelvis and the class shrinks by one.

Indoctrination also introduces Class 228 to group physical training, or PT. Physical training is a full range of highly regimented calisthenics led by an instructor. During First Phase, the class will do PT on the famous BUD/S grinder, the blacktop expanse in the middle of the main BUD/S compound. But Indoc trainees do not have that privilege. For now, they will do PT on the beach behind the BUD/S compound.

"A-one, two, three—"

"ONE!"

"A-one, two, three—"

"TWO!"

No single exercise, in itself, is too strenuous or difficult, and many are designed to balance and stretch certain muscle groups. But two areas are hammered again and again: abs and arms. Each third or fifth exercise is a set of push-ups, usually a count of twenty but often as many as fifty. For the abdomen, there are sit-ups and leg levers, but the ab exercise of choice at BUD/S is flutter kicks. Again and again the trainees will be on their backs, legs six inches off the deck. In this position they will count off flutter kicks with their legs straight, toes pointed. This builds stomach muscles and will help prepare Class 228 for the long ocean swims later in training. While one instructor calls the cadence and leads the class in exercises, the other instructors walk among the trainees offering encouragement and a liberal dose of verbal harassment. During PT the trainees, individually and as a class, must show spirit and motivation, and loudly maintain the exercise count. If they don't, the instructor leading PT will periodically send them into the surf—cold, wet, and sandy.

Following PT, Class 228 forms up for a four-mile conditioning run in the soft sand. The uniform for PT and the beach runs is white T-shirts, long pants, and boots. Several times during the run, 228 is sent up and over the large berm dunes, across the hard sand, and into the surf. Cold, wet, and sandy is a permanent condition for a BUD/S class, and it will take its toll. By the end of the first week there are seventy-four members in Class 228.

Indoc includes instruction as well as physical training. One lesson that is particularly helpful is a one-hour presentation on nutrition. This is the province of Hospital Corpsman Second Class Brandon Peterson, one of three hospital corpsmen assigned to the Indoc staff. HM2 Peterson is a full-time BUD/S instructor, a part-time triathlete, and a part-time college student. His wife is a nutritionist. Like Instructors King and Reno, he is not a big man, but very fit. His presentation on nutrition is a slick PowerPoint delivery, but he begins the class in the normal fashion.

"Drop."

"DROP!"

"Push 'em out."

After three sets of twenty, he commands, "Seats." Class 228 scrambles into the one-arm classroom chairs. There are now enough for everyone, and all of them have paper and pencil ready.

"I want you all to pay attention because what I have to say is important to you and your success here at BUD/S. Today we're going to cover what you should be eating and taking and what you shouldn't be eating and taking. You guys getting enough to eat at the chow hall?" There is a rumble of negative comments. "Well, that's bullshit. You should be getting all you want to eat over there. We'll look into that." He pauses to jot down a notation. "Let's talk about what you should be doing." He takes up a laser pointer and stabs at the screen as various food groups slide into view.

"It really comes down to this: there is no substitute for a well-balanced diet that is heavy in complex carbohydrates with lots of fruits and vegetables. Some of you guys think you need a high-protein diet or an all-protein diet. Not so. You need sixty percent carbohydrates with a blend of fats and protein. Don't forget the fat, especially you thin guys. When you get into the long ocean swims, you're going to need those calories to fight the cold. Eat whenever you can and eat all you can. If you can sneak a PowerBar between meals, do so, but stay away from the quick fixes like sugar or honey. You'll get a spike of energy and then you'll go flat. Otherwise, eat sensibly and eat often. No one burns calories like a BUD/S trainee. You can take in as much as six thousand calories a day and we'll see that you burn them off. Feet."

"FEET!"

"Seats."

"SEATS!"

"Don't be nodding off on me," Peterson warns them. "Supplements," he continues. "Stay away from them. The only thing you might need is a good multivitamin. If you take vitamin C, take no more than six hundred milligrams—otherwise it might give you diarrhea. Vitamin E, no more than four hundred milligrams. Nothing else. Aside from the illegal stimulants that you all know about, stay away from Creatine. I know it's an over-the-counter supplement and that it's legal, but it's strictly illegal here at BUD/S. Half the time when we find one of you musclemen face down in the sand on a beach run, we find Creatine in your locker. It causes leg cramps. It may help build bulk and upper-body mass, but it will not make you a stronger trainee. If we find Creatine in your locker, we'll kick you out of here, understand?"

"HOOYAH!"

"The best thing you can do to help yourself through BUD/S is to eat a balanced diet, heavy on carbohydrates, and—I can't stress this enough—eat a lot. And don't forget to hydrate. Keep those canteens full. You should all be drinking one and a half to two gallons of water each day. When the instructors give you a water break, take it. Mister Gallagher, I want you and your officers to see that your men get plenty to drink and that they begin each evolution with a full canteen."

"Hooyah, Instructor Peterson."

"There are no shortcuts here—no secret formulas and no magic potions. Give your body what it needs—a balanced diet and lots of fluids. Take care of your body just like you take care of your equipment, and your body will take care of you. Then you can give a hundred percent to this training, which you will have to do if you hope to make it through. Any questions?"

A hand goes up. In keeping with BUD/S classroom protocol, the student comes to attention and states his name and rate.

"Instructor Peterson, what about things like Motrin and aspirin?"

Peterson smiles. "You mean vitamin M. Most of you will need ibuprofen, especially during Hell Week. In fact, it's tough to get through Hell Week without it. The Medical Department will see that you get all the ibuprofen you need, but no more than you need. As for Excedrin, Tylenol, or Aleve, don't exceed the recommended doses. They're okay if you have a fever or for some of your aches. But don't overuse these drugs. You're going to hurt while you're here. Part of our job is to induce pain—not permanent injury, but we will make you hurt. You're all going to have to learn to play the game with pain. It's all part of becoming a SEAL. Your best defense against the pain and abuse is your personal motivation and your class spirit. Just how much do you really want to be here? You must decide that. Any more questions?" No hands. "Okay, then, that's it. Feet."

"FEET!"

The class scrambles to attention as Peterson steps from the podium and leaves the room. The men form up on the grinder and run to the next training evolution.

Class 228 will run the gauntlet of BUD/S training as a class. The trainees will acquire an identity as a strong class or a weak one; one that is motivated and pulls together or one that struggles. But between the training and the testing there is a good deal of leeway. The instructors can make the students' lives simply miserable or nearly impossible. They can cause a man to drop the course as surely as a failed swim or a broken leg. The class's only defense against this discretionary harassment is spirit and teamwork. This is the primary lesson of Indoc for 228. Teamwork makes life easier for the class as a whole, but for many in Class 228, it will also mean the difference between becoming a SEAL or a BUD/S dropout.

During the second week of Indoc, Class 228 begins IBS surf passage. IBS officially stands for inflatable boat, small; unofficially, itty-bitty ship. Up to this point, the trainees have functioned as individuals and as a class. Now they will learn to perform as boat crews. An IBS crew is made up of six to eight men. In the SEAL teams, the basic combat unit is the same size, only they will be called squads or fire teams. During First Phase training and especially during Hell Week, boat crews have to function as a team.

The IBS is an unwieldy, 170-pound, thirteen-foot rubber boat. It would be a miserable choice as a recreational boat for running a white-water river. They are poorly designed and too cumbersome for just about anything except teaching BUD/S trainees to work together in the surf zone—to pull together as a team. Initially, 228 learns the procedures and protocol for rigging the IBSs and aligning them on the beach for inspection. When the boats are rigged and the trainees are ready, the men stand at attention in life jackets by their boats. Their fatigue hats are attached to their blouses by a length of orange parachute cord. The paddles are wedged in a particular manner between the main tube and the two cross tubes; bow and stern lines are carefully coiled on the rubber floor. After each surf passage race, the crews must return to this same spot, prepare their craft for inspection, and wait at attention for the next race.

In front of the line of boats the coxswains, or boat-crew leaders, stand in a line abreast holding their paddles at the order-arms position, as if they were some kind of a long-barreled rifle. In turn, each coxswain salutes the instructor in charge and reports his boat rigged and his crew ready for sea.

Meanwhile, the other instructors roam the line of boats looking for discrepancies. If they find a paddle that is not tightly stowed, they fling it across the beach. If a student runs to retrieve it without his swim buddy, the whole boat crew drops for push-ups. During IBS drills, trainees do push-ups with their boots atop the main tube of their boat and their hands down on the sand. Instructor Steve Ryback is in charge of Class 228 for their first day of surf passage. He is a wiry man who grew up in Chicago. Ryback served with SDV Team Two on the East Coast before coming to BUD/S. He gives the coxswains the rules of each surf passage race. The coxswains then brief their boat crews and direct their crews as they paddle out through the surf zone, clear of the breakers, and back. After several races, Ryback drops the coxswains for several sets of push-ups.

"Recover, gentlemen," he says. They grab their paddles and come to attention. "I'm not seeing enough teamwork and spirit out there. We'll be here all day unless you guys start pulling together. Mister Gallagher."

"Hooyah, Instructor Ryback."

"You and your crew take seats."

"Hooyah, Instructor."

Gallagher's crew won the last race, so it is allowed a rest while the other crews must go back out. Class 228 is not only learning the value of teamwork, but that it also pays to be a winner.

"The rest of you guys listen close, because I will not repeat myself. Now, here's the drill." He motions the leaders into a close horseshoe formation and gives them their sailing orders. "Coxswains, you have one minute to brief your crews. Go!"

Ensign Jason Birch races back to his boat. He's not in the best mood; it's been a long day and this is now their fifth boat race in the 63-degree water. His boat has finished last or next to last in all the races. Birch is at a slight disadvantage because his is one of the smurf crews. The boat crews are organized by height since the trainees must often carry the boat on their heads. Seven bigger men are generally able to lift and carry more weight than seven smaller men—less IBS per inch of trainee. Many training evolutions at BUD/S favor the smaller men, but IBS surf passage is not one of them. Ensign Birch races back to his IBS, where his boat crew is completing a set of push-ups for doing so poorly in the last race.

"Okay, guys," he tells them, "here's the deal." Birch is a powerful twenty-three-year-old Annapolis graduate from Crofton, Maryland. While at the Naval Academy he boxed and ran cross-country, a good combination for a BUD/S trainee. "We gotta paddle out past the surf line, dump boat, then hang a left and paddle up the beach to that range marker." The crew follows his outstretched hand, which points to a wooden tower with a marking stripe on it. "We dump boat again and come straight in to the beach. Now here's where we gotta pull together; we take the boat at a head carry up the sand dune, around the ambulance, and sprint back down the beach to here. Got it? Okay, guys, get ready!"

While the crews prepare, instructors work the line of boats. Some of them use boat paddles to shovel sand onto the backs of trainees still doing push-ups and into their boats. Others remind the trainees that if they don't want to go back out into the cold water, all they need to do is quit; there's a warm shower in the barracks back in the BUD/S compound. As Ensign Birch finishes his brief, Jeff Rhodes approaches from behind. Rhodes is a chief petty officer with a great deal of experience in the teams and at BUD/S. During this tour at BUD/S, he is finishing his M.B.A. at San Diego State.

"Okay, Ensign, pull your head out this time," he says quietly. "You should already be watching those sets of breakers as they come in. Learn to anticipate. If you get a strong set, try to lay back and let them spill over before you take them on. If you can't wait for a slack set, don't take your boat out where they're plunging unless you can take the wave directly bow on. If you get sideways, have the guys on the seaward side backpaddle. As soon as you're bow on, give it hell. And try to stay out of traffic, understand?"

"Hooyah, Chief Rhodes."

"Hit the surf," Ryback calls over the bullhorn and nine boats charge the water. Gallagher and his crew watch. The trainees move their craft along at a low carry just off the sand, one hand grasping the lifting strap and the other clutching their paddle. With the boat crews dead even, they splash into the shallows. The surf waiting for them is a moderate line of breakers just under six feet. There's a slight offshore breeze blowing straight into the curl, making their plunge a little more vicious.

"One's in!" Birch calls and the first two men vault into the bow and start to paddle.

"Two's in!" The next two board the IBS amidships and pick up the stroke. When the water surges to his chest, Birch orders his last two men into the stern of the boat. They struggle aboard, and then reach back to drag their officer over the stern. Birch sees a few low breakers just in front of him and a big set following just beyond them. His boat is headed straight into them and he has a chance.

"Let's go for it! Stroke, stroke, dig, dig . . . !" While his fellow smurfs paddle hard, Birch fights to keep the bow heading straight into the breakers. They punch through one wave and ride dangerously high over the second, but they make it. "Keep digging!" he yells. Without taking his eyes from the line of oncoming waves, he catches a glimpse of an IBS to his left as it capsizes, scattering its trainees and paddles. "Stroke! Stroke!" the six paddlers cry in unison. They manage to clear the surf zone as another big set of swells begin to break. Once safely past the breakers, Birch orders them to dump boat.

The three starboard paddlers tumble over the side, taking their paddles with them. The three remaining men on the port side lean across the IBS and grab the inside carrying straps, canvas loops attached to the starboard main tube near the bottom of the IBS. Standing on the port main tube, they pull the boat over on top of them. As the boat goes over, the three men from the starboard side scramble atop the overturned boat, grab the starboard outside carrying handles, and pull the boat back upright. Ensign Birch and his six paddlers pull themselves quickly back into the boat as the swells nurse them dangerously back toward the surf zone. All the while Birch is watching the waves and the beach.

"Let's do it!" Birch yells. "Starboard ahead, port guys backpaddle." The IBS spins around. "Okay, give way together—stroke, stroke!" As they paddle in unison heading south just outside the surf zone, Birch notes they are fifth in the nine-boat regatta—an improvement, but still not good enough.

Ensign Jason Birch has already gained the attention of the instructor staff. At the end of one of the first-week pool sessions, the class was quickly dressing on the pool deck to get to the next evolution—breakfast. The pool session had dissolved from instruction to harassment, and the trainees were being given a steady diet of push-ups as they struggled into their fatigues. Two instructors worked the class over with water hoses, ensuring the men would run to chow in wet clothes. Instructor Troy Casper watched from the three-meter concrete tower as his tired, wet charges struggled with their gear.

"Okay, gents, let's see if you like to gamble," he called over the bullhorn from his perch. "If one of you can give me twenty dead-hang pull-ups from my tower, I'll let you go five minutes early for chow. But, if your champion fails, you owe me—all of you."

Birch came forward. "I'll take that bet, Instructor Casper." Casper motioned him up to the tower. Birch quickly climbed onto the platform and slipped over the side. He is in full fatigues and boots—and he is soaking wet. Hanging over the water with only his fingers grasping the concrete ledge, he does twenty dead-hang pull-ups. The last ones are not easy, but his class is with him, counting them off: ". . . EIGHTEEN . . . NINE-TEEN . . . TWENTY!"

"Okay," Casper conceded. He tried to sound gruff, but like all the BUD/S instructors, he's pleased to see leadership and spirit in the class. "You're secured early."

"Stroke . . . stroke . . . ," Birch exhorts his crew now as they continue to paddle south along the Strand just outside the surf zone. Ensign Birch keeps a close eye on the swells to his right, the breakers on his left, and the boat just ahead of him. Occasionally, he glances over his shoulder at the crew that's trying to gain on him. As the boat crews come abreast of the range marker on the beach, the crews begin to dump their boats. But Birch encourages his men to paddle past the other boats.

"Now, sir?"

"Keep paddling; I'll tell you when." His head's on a swivel, alternating between the breakers and the swells. "Now!" he yells when they are finally well past the other boats. "Dump boat!"

The crew repeats the drill, flipping the boat and righting it. The cold is starting to take its toll and their movements are clumsy. They appear to be in slow motion. They've been in the water or standing in wet fatigues on the beach for close to two hours.

Once back in the boat, Birch gets them pointed toward the shore. He watches as a large wave capsizes one of the boats just ahead and off to his left. The capsized boat falls onto another IBS, knocking one of the paddlers into the water. His swim buddy quickly tumbles into the water to join him.

"Now!" Birch calls to his crew. "Stroke! Dig! Dig hard!" With a quick glance back at the swells, he steadies the boat with his paddle, which he uses as a rudder, and studies the breakers ahead. He commits his crew into the surf zone. They catch a big roller and surge forward. As the wave breaks around them, the IBS slews precariously to the right.

"Port side back! Port side back!" he yells desperately and the three men on the left side of the boat backpaddle furiously. The IBS hesitates, then straightens and rides the next wave into the shallow foam off the beach. They're through.

"One's out!"

"Two's out!"

"Three's out!"

Birch and his men quickly dump the water from their IBS. They sling it between them at a low carry as they run up to the soft sand. There they heave it up over their heads as they shuffle heavily across the soft sand to the base of the dune. The crews who spilled in the surf zone are quickly sorting themselves out and crossing the beach. Birch and his crew have moved into third place as they climb the sand dune, but another two boats are closing on their heels.

While the six crewmen carry the IBS up the fifteen-foot berm dune on their heads, Birch pushes from the stern. They're bone-weary, but they struggle over the dune and around the parked ambulance. Instructor Tim

Cruickshank, the duty corpsman, shouts encouragement as they head for home. A hospital corpsman is present for every physical training evolution. Birch shifts his command to the bow of the IBS for the trek down the dune and across the soft sand to the finish. When in the head carry, the coxswain cannot carry his share of the weight from his position at the stern. Going downhill, most of the weight is carried by two men in the bow. One of his "ones" is struggling, so Birch trades places with him as they begin their shuffle-sprint to the finish. One of the tall guys' boats overtakes them, but they are able to hold off the other for a fourth-place finish.

"Good goin', guys," Birch tells his crew as they line up their IBS and prepare for inspection.

"Not bad, Ensign; you guys are learning."

"Hooyah, Chief Rhodes."

"Now get down there and start pushing them out with the rest of the losers."

"Hooyah, Chief Rhodes."

. . .

The last day of Indoc for Class 228 is graduation day for Class 225. The normally sterile BUD/S compound at the Naval Special Warfare Center has taken on a festive look. Known simply as the grinder, the blacktop where BUD/S trainees in First Phase endure grueling PT is now lined with metal folding chairs shrouded in blue cloth. Surrounding the chairs on three sides of the grinder, flags of the fifty states partly hide the BUD/S training offices and classrooms. A huge, two-story American flag hangs from the second-story balcony of the west end of the compound, serving as a backdrop for a raised platform with an elegant wooden podium. The raised dais is decorated with red-white-and-blue bunting. Three naval officers and a civilian in a coat and tie sit in a shallow arc around the podium. Their attention is focused on twenty-two men in crisp white uniforms seated in the first two rows of chairs. Behind these men in uniform are several hundred guests. Most are friends and family who have come to witness the graduation. Sprinkled among the gallery are SEALs, active and retired. Like old parishioners of an orthodox faith, they have come to renew their ties to the church.

Lieutenant (jg) Gallagher's voice echoes across the grinder, "Two . . . Two . . . Five!"

"HOOYAH, CLASS TWO-TWO-FIVE!" roars Class 228.

Class 228 is in tight formation dressed in starched fatigues, spit-shined boots, and starched covers. The trainees are standing tall off to the side of the seated guests, at attention and looking good. There are now seventy of them.

"Two . . . Two . . . Eight!"

"GOOD LUCK, CLASS TWO-TWO-EIGHT!" the twenty-two soon-to-be-graduates loudly reply.

This is all part of the ritual. The junior class hooyahs the graduating class and the graduating class wishes the junior class good luck. Classes 226 and 227 are absent, both away from the Center on training evolutions. In keeping with current tradition, the graduation speech is delivered by an older BUD/S graduate. In the case of Class 225, the graduates are honored by having Lieutenant Commander Scott Lyons, USN (Ret.), Class 25, as their speaker. Scott Lyons graduated from an early equivalent of BUD/S training in the mid-1950s and served as First Phase officer in the early 1970s. Lyons also saw his share of combat with multiple tours in Vietnam, where he collected a Silver Star, five Bronze Stars, and a Purple Heart. Class 225 began with 146 men reporting to BUD/S. Today it graduates 22 men— 3 officers and 19 enlisted personnel.

The remarkable thing about the members of Class 225 is their overall appearance; these BUD/S graduates look terribly average. They are all alike—white, boyish, clean, and healthy; most are five-foot nine or ten with a few just over six feet. This is not lost on Class 228, where the trainees range from six-foot seven on down to five-six.

Lieutenant John Dowd, 225's class leader, mounts the raised dais and salutes the Navy captain who has stepped up to the podium. "Sir, request permission to ring out Class Two twenty-five."

Captain Ed Bowen, the commanding officer of the Naval Special Warfare Center, returns his salute. His smile is almost as wide as Dowd's. "Permission granted, Lieutenant."

Lieutenant Dowd turns and bails from the platform in a single bound. Tossing his hat to a classmate, he sprints around the seated guests to where the famous BUD/S bell is lashed to a stanchion just outside the First Phase office. He rings it three times, almost tearing the lanyard from the clapper. A roar goes up from the men of Class 225; it's officially over. They are not yet SEALs, but they are now BUD/S graduates.

"I've never been so jealous of anyone in my life," Ensign Chad Steinbrecher will remark later that evening at 228's Indoc party. "I watched three classes graduate ahead of me at Annapolis and never felt the envy that I did for those guys in Two-two-five."

Class 225's graduation was just one evolution during Class 228's last day of Indoc. Like all Indoc mornings, 228's day began at the pool at 0500. This is the trainees' last morning at the pool with the "teachers" of the Indoctrination Course. First Phase, which begins on Monday, will be light on the teaching and heavy on the trauma. For many trainees in 228, it seems like they just arrived at BUD/S. As one student put it, the days are long but the weeks go by quickly. It's important that the class has a strong finish and builds momentum going into First Phase. After an intensive pool session, the men run to breakfast, then across the base to the Naval Special Warfare Center. After PT on the beach, a run in the soft sand, and a few trips into the surf, they double-time back to the barracks to change for the graduation ceremony. Indoc is essentially over for 228. While Class 225 celebrates at a reception for family and friends at the Naval Special Warfare Center, Class 228 runs across the base for noon chow. The trainees are back in the classroom at the Center at 1300.

"Feet!"

"FEET!"

"Push 'em out."

Bill Gallagher counts them down and 228 cranks off twenty and waits in the leaning rest.

"Recover."

"HOOYAH, INSTRUCTOR RENO!"

"Seats."

"SEATS!"

"Give me a muster, Mister Gallagher."

"Seventy men assigned, Instructor Reno. All present except for one man over at medical."

"That's close, sir, but not your fault. Since you mustered, another man quit out back, just a few minutes ago." With Reno's announcement, the heads of the boat-crew leaders snap around surveying their boat crews. It's starting to get personal and they want to know if it was one of their men who quit. "So this is it, gents. You'll class up in First Phase with sixty-nine men."

Class 228 gives out with a roar. Reno gives the men a rare smile and lets them go on for a moment, then calls for quiet.

"All right, listen up. This is your final Indoc briefing. You guys had a tough two weeks; I think you're ready for First Phase. And it's going to get a lot tougher. It will never be easy—not here; not in the teams. We're in a tough business. If you think the staff did a good job here in Indoc these past two weeks, you can show your appreciation by spending some time with these critique sheets. Now, we don't want a free pass. If you've got a bitch, we want to know about it. Each and every one of the instructors at Indoc will read these critiques, so give us your best shot, okay?"

"HOOYAH!"

"Now, I've got a few things to say. You're on your way to First Phase, so make me proud of you. After Hell Week, those of you who survive will still have to face the scuba pool comps in Second Phase and weapons practicals in Third Phase. I'll want to shake your hand at graduation. When you get there, I want to think of you as one of Reno's warriors."

There's another roar from the class. Reno is very popular with Class 228. While he has frequently made them suffer, the trainees know that Reno and the other Indoc instructors have tried to give them what they need to survive in First Phase.

"Be on time. Be alert. Be accountable for your actions in and out of uniform. You officers, look out for your men and your men will look out for you. Your reputation is everything in the teams. Remember this if you remember nothing else. For each of you, a chance to build on that reputation begins on Monday morning at zero five hundred in First Phase." He looks around the class; every eye is on him. "For those of you who do get to the teams, I want you to take this on board. The guys in the teams are a brotherhood. You'll be closer to them than you ever were to your friends in high school or college. You'll live with them on deployment and some of you may even die with them in combat. But never, ever forget your family. Family comes before teammates. Most of us will grow old and die in bed, and the only people who will be there to help us die will be our family. Put your family first. I want you to never forget that."

Reno's eyes sweep across the class. "Good luck, gentlemen," he says as he heads for the door.

"Feet!" Gallagher shouts.

"FEET!"

"In-struct-tor Ree-no!"

"HOOYAH, INSTRUCTOR REE-NO!"

After Reno leaves them, the trainees begin to mill about and talk quietly. They're excited, they're pumped—and they're very apprehensive. Most of them hurt and all are very tired. During Reno's epilogue, an instructor had quietly slipped into the back of the room. He is not one of the Indoc instructors. Class 228 has yet to notice him.

"Drop," he quietly commands.

"DROP!"

He threads his way to the front of the classroom through the sea of prone bodies frozen in the leaning rest.

"Recover and take your seats," he says, and the class scrambles for their chairs.

He's taller than Reno and has a rounded, softer look to him. Reno hardly ever smiled, but this instructor seems to have a permanent, affable grin.

"My name is Instructor Mruk [pronounced Mur-rock], and I'll be your First Phase proctor. Do we have any first class petty officers here?" Only Carreola raises his hand. "Okay, how many second class?" A number of hands go up. "And how many rollbacks?" This time he counts them.

"Seven rollbacks—good. You rollbacks know the deal. You can help the others with all the after-hours stuff—prepping the boats, the vehicles, the supply chits, that kind of thing. As you guys know by now, a lot of things have to get done outside of training hours. In First Phase, you'll have a lot less time and a lot more to do. It all has to get done or you'll pay for it as a class, believe me.

"I've been here for about two years and you're the second class I've proctored. I made some mistakes with my first class, but I'm going to try to do a better job with you." The class stares at Mruk dumbly; it's like God saying he's sorry. "But you have to pay attention and give me a hundred percent. That means that you put out during training and don't slack off on the after-hours stuff. Get all your gear ready to go before you secure for the night and keep your assigned spaces in order. The days are long, but you have to get it all done. Understand?"

"HOOYAH!"

Sean Mruk graduated with Class 162. Like a surprising number of SEALs, he is from the Midwest—in his case, Lakewood, Ohio. He came to BUD/S from SEAL Team Two, where he completed three deployments in Europe. The measure of an instructor—or of a Navy SEAL, as Class 228 is coming to understand—is the number of deployments he has made. The more deployments, the more experienced the SEAL. It's a measure of knowledge and respect. As Mruk moves through a litany of things 228 has to do to get ready for First Phase training, Class 228 scribbles in their tattered notebooks.

"Class leader?" Gallagher is on his feet. "Did you get your guys moved over to the other barracks?"

"Hooyah, Instructor."

During Indoc, Class 228 lived in the small barracks just behind the BUD/S grinder. Now the class will live on the third deck of the Naval Special Warfare barracks, about 150 yards north of the Center. These newer barracks are relatively spacious two-man rooms with a shared bath between rooms. The building is situated directly on the white-sand beach with an unobstructed view of the Pacific. If these were condominiums, they would be priced at close to a million dollars each. But the cost to Class 228 will be much higher. To remain at the Special Warfare barracks, a trainee has to stay in Class 228. If they DOR or get rolled back to another class, it's back to the cramped quarters at the Center.

"Good," Mruk continues. "I'll be over there on Sunday at ten hundred and show you how to prepare your rooms for inspection. You have to keep your rooms and the drying cages picked up and squared away. And the rooms have to be spotless, understand?"

"HOOYAH!"

"Now, as you know, First Phase starts with PT here on the grinder at zero five hundred Monday morning. Use your time well between now and then. There's a stack of helmets by the First Phase office. Get them repainted and your class numbers blocked on. You're officially a class now; First Phase owns you. Any questions?" There are none. Either 228 has no questions or they do not entirely trust an instructor who is this civil to them. "Uh-oh." Mruk frowns for just a moment as he looks past the class to the rear entrance. "Here comes Instructor Register. He was the proctor for Class Two-two-seven and I was kind of rough on his class. Looks like it might be payback time." Then the pleasant grin returns to Instructor Mruk's face.

"Drop!" calls a harsh voice from the back of the room.

"DROP!"

"Push 'em out," Instructor Bill Register tells the new First Phase trainees.

. . .

The class-up party on Gator Beach gets under way at 1800, just as the last of the commuters pour out of NAS North Island and down Highway 75 for Imperial Beach. It's 15 October—twelve days after they began Indoc. The Gator Beach picnic area is conveniently located a half block from the Special Warfare barracks. This is the first time 228 has been together out of uniform and in a nontraining, nonmilitary environment. Off duty, the trainees look like any other gathering of college students—baggy shorts, T-shirts, jeans, baseball caps. A few of them are in bib overalls, others are in sweats. The class-up party is a traditional celebration of sorts to mark the end of their two-week Indoc and the beginning of First Phase. They've come a long way in a short time. Their spirits are good. Yet the specter of First Phase and what's ahead of them hangs over the gathering. There are overtones of a wake as Class 228 celebrates the end of Indoc.

The Indoc instructors are invited and many of them show up. Sean Mruk is the only First Phase instructor present. I, too, was invited, as I have become an unofficial member of Class 228. My presence has added a very subtle element to the journey of this class, a guy in his mid-fifties following them around with a notebook. I can usually be found wandering about the O-course or behind a row of IBSs as they prepare for surf passage. I'm often in the back of the classroom or jogging along behind the class from one evolution to the next. Some trainees think it's neat that someone is going to write about their class, but most are too busy to give it much thought. Occasionally, I'm favored with a "Hooyah, Captain Couch." Once a week I do one PT with the class and go on a conditioning run with them. This goes a long way with Class 228 and the staff. It's like someone trying to speak the language in a foreign country.

My official permission to mingle with the inmates at BUD/S only goes so far. BUD/S training is administered by the enlisted instructors under the supervision of the phase officers. It's well-guarded turf. I carefully maintain a *Star Trek*–like prime directive; I do not interfere with training or talk with trainees during training evolutions. One by one, the instructors approach me and ask about what I'm doing, even though most of them already know. They are invariably polite. Many of them have read my novels because they were about SEALs and by an ex-SEAL. They usually ask, "Has training changed much since you went through?"

That's not an easy question. Only two members of Class 228 were alive when I came through training on the East Coast with Class 45. Structurally, training was very different then; there were no Indoc or pretraining courses in 1968. My training was less regimented and I don't recall my class being so pressed for time as is 228. We had fewer duties and responsibilities outside of training hours. On the other hand, much of it was the same. We ran to the pool and learned to swim with our hands and feet bound. We did the same basic exercises at PT, but without the stretching routines. There was no such thing as hydration; you drank water at meals to wash down food. My O-course was much the same as the one 228 must negotiate. We ran daily in the soft sand. Mine was also a winter class, but winter in southern Virginia is different than in southern California. The waves were smaller and the waters of the Chesapeake much colder when Class 45 did the same surf passage drills as Class 228.

"But was it harder?" they all ask.

I don't know yet. I think BUD/S training may be like childbirth; the pain is quickly pushed aside by the joy of having it behind you. Unlike BUD/S graduates, women don't sit around and brag about how hard it all was. If Indoc is any indication, the days are longer, but most of the trainees arrive in better condition than in my day. They are wet much more than I was during the first weeks of training. Like Class 228, I'll have to wait for First Phase to see just how hard the training really is.

"Ready for next week, Billy?" I ask Lieutenant Gallagher as he comes over to say hello.

"I don't know, sir; I guess so. I know I want to get started with First Phase. The sooner it begins, the sooner it'll be over." He grins and shrugs. "I guess I don't need a lot of time to sit around and think about it."

I was surprised to see Bill Gallagher at the head of Class 228. We first met, by chance, when he was a plebe at the Naval Academy. He was assigned as my escort for noon meal in King Hall; that was seven years ago, in the fall of 1992. He was almost as tall as he is now but much thinner. I recall asking my standard Academy midshipmen question:

"Mister, Gallagher, what do you want to do when you graduate from here? Aviation? Submarines?"

I remember that he didn't hesitate. "I want to be a Navy SEAL, sir."

Now Bill Gallagher will lead sixty-eight other young men into First Phase BUD/S training. It is a small world, and one of cycles—old guys, new guys. I retired with thirty years of active and reserve service the same day Bill Gallagher was commissioned an ensign in the U.S. Navy. We are

Academy men, thirty years apart: Class of 1967—Class of 1997. I, too, came to BUD/S from the fleet as a junior grade lieutenant; I was also my class leader. A little more than seventy trainees began with Class 45; only thirteen of us graduated. I wonder how many of Class 228 will make it through the next twenty-five weeks to graduation. Will Bill Gallagher graduate with his class? I think so. It seems to me he has the right stuff, but so do all of them. I envy Gallagher and the others. I envy their youth and their chance to come of age in the Navy SEAL teams. I don't envy them the price they'll have to pay to get there.

Each trainee I talk with is both optimistic and apprehensive. One man is at the grill flipping burgers. A short distance away, a trainee-turned-barber is shaving the heads of his fellow BUD/S trainees. This, too, is a class-up tradition. On Monday, the first day of First Phase, the entire class will pay if just one of them shows up with more than a stubble on his head. Suddenly, there is a slight commotion as a man in T-shirt and jeans walks from his car to the picnic area.

"In-struct-tor Ree-no!" shouts one of the class officers.

"HOOYAH, INSTRUCTOR REE-NO!" Class 228 crowds around its former proctor. This is a cultural shift from the days of Class 45. We never socialized with our instructors until after graduation. For me, it's fascinating to watch. Reno and the other instructors were pounding on these trainees only a few days ago; in some cases, a few hours ago. Now here they are sharing a beer and talking about how to get through First Phase.

CHAPTER TWO

FIRST PHASE

The morning of 18 October is clear and cold. The day holds the promise of sunshine and temperatures in the seventies, but at 0500 it is fifty-three degrees. The sun will not be over San Diego Bay for another two hours.

"Class Two-two-eight is formed, Chief," Lieutenant Gallagher reports. "Sixty-nine men present."

Chief Stephen Schultz quickly returns his salute. "Hit the surf, sir—all of you. Then get into the classroom."

Class 228 races out of the compound and across the beach to the Pacific. A few moments later the men slosh into the First Phase classroom. After dropping several times for push-ups, they are given "seats." The First Phase instructors file in and parade across the front of the room.

"Welcome to First Phase, gentlemen. Training begins today." Ensign Joe Burns is a hard, well-conditioned six-footer with short salt-and-pepper hair. There is nothing frivolous or forgiving about him. He left college to enlist in the Navy and to become a SEAL. After rising through the enlisted ranks, he earned his commission and is now the First Phase officer. His brother is a lieutenant in the teams. Burns has a reputation as a harsh man with a wry sense of humor. This morning he is all business.

"This is a small class, but I understand all of you want to be frogmen, is that right?"

"HOOYAH!"

"Well, we're going to see about that. We'll see just how bad you really want it. I'm Ensign Burns. This is my phase and this is my staff."

There are fourteen instructors including Burns. They go down the line and introduce themselves, names only—no background or bio. Instructor Mruk, the class proctor, introduces himself only as "Mother." Introductions made, Chief Schultz drops the trainees for more push-ups as the instructor staff files out.

"Okay, on the grinder, ready for PT," Schultz yells at them. "Move, move, move!"

At 0510 the class is back in PT formation. The men are arrayed in boots, long fatigue pants, and white T-shirts. This is their first PT inside the BUD/S compound, an honor reserved for First Phase trainees. They stand in places marked by miniature frog flippers painted on the blacktop. The paint and macadam are chipped and stained where generations of BUD/S trainees have toiled and suffered. They are armed only with canteens that stand in formation alongside each trainee.

"Okay, people, hit the surf; get wet and sandy!" Schultz orders, and the class races from the grinder. Moments later 228 tramples back onto the grinder. This time the men roll in the soft sand after diving into the breakers. They now have the texture of sugar cookies.

"Too slow, people, much too slow. Drop!"

There is a raised podium or platform on the north side of the BUD/S grinder. The three-foot platform fascia bears the tall gold numbers "226." Class 226, now in Third Phase, is the senior class at BUD/S. From here, Chief Schultz leads Class 228 in its initial First Phase PT. The rest of the instructors move among the class like prowling lions, tearing into individual trainees.

"You're doing push-ups like a girl. Is that what they taught you in Indoc? Go get wet."

Getting wet is different from hitting the surf. Before 228 formed up for PT, the men had to prepare two IBSs, one on each side of the PT platform. Both are filled with an ice-water slurry and have the two cross tubes deflated. A trainee ordered to get wet slides over the bow or stern and "swims" under the flat cross tubes to emerge from the other end. It only takes about five seconds to make the plunge. The trainee is no longer sandy, just wet and very cold. Two instructors roam among the lines of struggling trainees with water hoses, blasting their shaved heads with a stream of cold water. By a conservative count, Class 228 will do over five hundred push-ups and sixty pull-ups before First Phase training is an hour old. Chief Schultz takes the men from one exercise to the next with no break. For good measure, he mixes in an extra ration of flutter kicks and sit-ups.

Class 228 knew this was coming; the trauma of the first day of First Phase was passed on to them by Classes 226 and 227. But neither Indoc nor warnings from the senior classes prepared them for the intensity of this PT session. For the First Phase instructors, it is a calculated mayhem, designed to force each man in the class to reassess his personal commitment to the goal of becoming a Navy SEAL. Many in Class 228 are asking themselves, "Four weeks of this, then Hell Week? I don't know if I can I do it!" Across the grinder, a few members of Class 227 peek at the havoc being visited on the junior class. They are in Second Phase—dive phase. Many of them shudder as they remember their first day on the grinder. But they don't watch for long. It is too painful, and they are too busy with diving physics and air decompression tables.

"Hydrate!" Schultz calls from the platform. Stephen Schultz is a prototype BUD/S instructor: short, compact, and very muscular. He has a bachelor's degree in education. Before becoming a SEAL, he served with Special Boat Unit 24. Prior to coming to the Special Warfare Center as an instructor, Schultz completed an exchange tour with the British Royal Marines as an assault team leader with the famous Special Boat Squadron. Leading PT for Class 228, he does everything he asks the trainees to do, yet he seems to do it without effort.

"HYDRATE!" the exhausted trainees respond.

The men of Class 228 grab their canteens and chug. Thirst is the last thing on their minds, but they drink anyway. The order to hydrate is the only respite Chief Schultz gives them.

"Canteens down!"

"HOOYAH!"

"Push-ups!"

"READY!"

At 0615, they are sent into the surf one final time and released for breakfast.

"Form it up, running formation!" Gallagher calls to his classmates. "C'mon, guys, we don't have a lot of time."

They seem tentative and confused. Their biceps and stomach muscles are on fire. Many in 228 are confused and in shock. Others are feeling sorry for themselves. A few of the stronger trainees try to help their classmates, but most think only of themselves; they are not yet a class. For the run to chow, they don their fatigue blouses, canteen belts, and helmets. The Naval Amphibious Base is still asleep as Class 228 jogs across the base to the chow hall for the first time in their green helmets—helmets that have 228 stenciled on each side in white letters. They have an hour to eat and make the mile run back to the BUD/S compound for the next evolution, a four-mile timed run on the beach. Three men quit after breakfast—the first three DORs from 228 in First Phase.

Last Friday there was a line of green helmets along the grinder next to the First Phase office, helmets with 227 stenciled on the side. Each helmet represented a trainee from that class who DORed. This morning at 0500 there were none. When Class 227 moved on to Second Phase, the helmets were removed to make room for the new class. Now the first green 228 helmets appear on the grinder next to the bell.

Secured to a stanchion just outside the First Phase office is a famous BUD/S institution—the bell. Tradition calls for a student who quits in First Phase to ring the bell three times and place his helmet on the grinder. Indoc DORs don't count. There was a time at BUD/S when there was no bell. Pressure from a kinder and gentler Navy thought it too demeaning to ask that a trainee publicly declare his failure in this way. But the bell came back. Since it returned in 1995, the bell has been a part of BUD/S training.

Many think the bell is a tradition that dates back to the early days of training Navy frogmen. Not so. When the current BUD/S training compound was built in 1970, training moved from the World War II–vintage Quonset huts on the Amphibious Base to the new facility on the Pacific side of Highway 75, or the Strand Highway, as it is commonly called. Before 1970, trainees who wanted to DOR went to the instructor hut, banged three times on the doorjamb with their helmets, and yelled, "I quit!" Master Chief Terry Moy was a legendary instructor at BUD/S in the late 1960s and early '70s. "Mother" Moy, as he was called, moved across the Strand Highway with BUD/S when they occupied the new facility. Moy, Class 35, was an old-school frogman who was justly proud of his new office quarters. When the first trainee banged on his new door to quit, he had to put a stop to it—not the quitting, the abuse of his new door. The next day he brought in a tugboat bell and lashed it to the stanchion outside the First Phase office. Except for the three-year exile in the early '90s, Mother Moy's bell has been there ever since.

After the brutal PT session on the grinder and a two-mile round trip for breakfast, Class 228 faces its first timed evolution in First Phase. It's a terrible day for running on the beach. The tide is dead high, which means the runners will have to thread their way along the high-water mark between the soft dry sand and the not-so-soft wet sand. The cutoff for this first timed run is thirty-two minutes. Eight-minute miles don't sound too demanding, but in wet trousers and boots, at high tide, it's not an easy run. The trainees stretch for a few moments behind the BUD/S compound, then line up across the beach near the water's edge.

"Okay, fellows, listen up," says Chief Ken Taylor. "We're going south today. It's down and back in thirty-two minutes. This is your first timed evolution. Two miles down, two miles back, and you best be back here in thirty-two minutes—or else. Any questions?"

"NEGATIVE!"

"Get ready . . . Go!"

Class 228 charges down the beach toward Mexico. Soon the trainees begin to string out, each man trying to find that sweet, firm spot between the upsurge from the breakers and the soft dry sand. The first man, Petty Officer Lawrence Obst, arrives back in just over twenty-seven minutes. But twenty of them fail to cross the line under thirty-two minutes. Those that make it in the allotted time are allowed to turn right and join Obst in the soft sand. They form in ranks at a slow jog to cool down. Those who arrive later than thirty-two minutes turn left. First they do push-ups, then bear-crawl into the surf and join the growing line of slow runners in the Pacific. Here they link arms in a line, with the sixty-two-degree water up to their necks.

While the slow twenty endure the cold water, Lieutenant Gallagher leads the rest of the class in stretching exercises on the beach. Instructor Dan Maclean watches the trainees in the water carefully and checks his watch. Maclean is the corpsman on this evolution. He came to BUD/S from SEAL Team Five, where he made four platoon deployments. Maclean is responsible for the trainees' immersion times. Over the years, the BUD/S medical department has developed an immersion table based on water temperature and activity. Hypothermia is no stranger at BUD/S training, and Maclean scans the line of immersed men for any sign of it. At sixty-two degrees, trainees whose movements are restricted can stay in the water for only twenty minutes. Within the hour they can go back in, but not for as long. While the faster portion of the class continues to stretch, the slow runners are called out of the water one at a time. Chief Taylor logs their times and scolds them for failing the evolution. The trainees return to the edge of the surf zone and are made to lie on their backs, feet toward the sand. They now do flutter kicks while the expended waves surge up over their heads and shoulders. By doing flutter kicks, they go off the restricted-activity time limit and can stay in the water longer.

"All right, listen up," Taylor tells the men kicking in the surf. "See the rest of your classmates up there on the beach taking it easy?"

"HOOYAH!"

"Those guys are winners; you guys are losers. You better start taking this training seriously or you're not going to be around here much longer. They paid the price up front and now they get a little time off. You didn't. You failed. And now you're paying a bigger price. Is there anybody here who does not understand the difference between putting out and giving up?"

"NEGATIVE!"

"Anybody not understand the difference between a winner and a loser?"

"NEGATIVE!"

"Give me twenty, then get up there with your class."

The slow runners push them out while still in the surf, then join the class as they move on to the next evolution, log PT.

Log PT is older than the Navy frogmen of World War II. In 1943, the U.S. Marines landed at Tarawa. Because of faulty intelligence about the offshore reefs surrounding the Tarawa beaches, the Marines suffered terrible casualties. Something had to be done. A colorful officer by the name of Draper Kauffman was sent to Fort Pierce, Florida, to train men who would go onto the landing beaches ahead of the Marines. Fort Pierce became the incubator of the Navy frogmen and Kauffman the father of UDT. Prior to his service in the U.S. Navy and our entry into World War II, Kauffman served as an ambulance driver and bomb disposal expert in England. There he observed the newly formed British commandos exercising with sections of telephone poles to build strength and teamwork. He introduced those same techniques at Fort Pierce when he began to train the first Navy frogmen. Much like surf drills with the IBSs, log PT encourages teamwork and spirit. It also pays to be a winner.

When the instructors arrive at the log PT area, Class 228 is standing by its logs, one log for each boat crew. The trainees now wear their long-sleeved fatigue blouses buttoned to the collar and soft hats. Each log is eight feet long and a foot in diameter—about 150 pounds each. A single log sits at the head of the two files of logs and their crews. This log is engraved with the title "Old Misery." It is slightly shorter than the other logs, but bigger in diameter and much heavier.

"Get wet and sandy, people," Instructor Michael Getka tells them over the electronic bullhorn. "I don't want to see any piece of green fabric or flesh that does not have sand on it."

The log PT area is directly behind the BUD/S training compound. Between the log PT area and the Pacific is a fifteen-foot, dunelike sand berm built by the Seabees to protect the compound from the winter storm surf. Class 228 charges up the berm and down to the surf some fifty yards away. Once again the men are cold and wet. On the way back they roll down the berm to the log PT area—cold, wet, and sandy.

"The logs, people. I want the logs wet and sandy." The boat crews retrieve their logs and head back for the surf. They carry the logs in front of them at a waist carry to go over the berm, then up to a shoulder carry to the water. On the return trip, the boat crews carefully roll their logs down the berm. One crew's sandy log slips from their grasp and they drop it.

"Don't pick it up; drop down and push 'em out. The rest of you get those logs in the extended-carry position." Instructor Getka turns his attention back to the crew doing push-ups. Michael Getka is a lanky six-footer from upstate New York, with thick blond hair and mustache. He served with the East Coast SEAL platoons before coming to BUD/S and is a Gulf War veteran. "If you ever drop one of my logs again, your pain will be legendary."

"HOOYAH!"

Soon all the crews are standing under their logs. While they hold them over their heads at arms' length in the extended-carry position, instructors roam among them with IBS paddles, shoveling sand on them. Whenever they see or sense that a trainee is not supporting his share of the log, the instructors drop him. The individual pays with push-ups and his boat crew pays with one less man to bear the weight of the log. As the boat crews twist and strain under the weight of their logs, more individual trainees are dropped for push-ups.

"This slacker was holding back on you; he wasn't holding up his end of the log. You want him back?"

"HOOYAH, INSTRUCTOR!"

"He was cheating you—and himself." The trainee pushes sand and the rest of the crew fights to keep the log aloft. "You sure you want him back?"

"HOOYAH, INSTRUCTOR!"

"Get back under there, slipknot, and quit making your crewmates pull your weight."

After more extended-arm harassment, the trainees circle up and learn the mechanics of log PT. Log PT is the only evolution Class 228 did not learn in Indoc. Using the class rollbacks as demonstrators, the rest of 228 learns the basic exercises for log PT: squats, jumping jacks, sit-ups, overhead tosses. Most of these are four-count exercises.

"Now pay attention," Instructor Maclean tells them. "If I hear a loud head-to-log crack, or one of you sees a man go down, put up your hand and call out, 'Man down!' We'll be right there. The safest way to do this is to work as a team. If you work as team, nobody'll get hurt."

"Fall in on your logs," yells Getka over the bullhorn. Class 228 breaks from the circle and races for their logs. "Too slow, too slow. Get wet and sandy."

The class finally settles on their logs and Getka begins to drill them. Log PT puts a premium on teamwork and spirit. Strength is important, but secondary. The midsize crews of uniform height have a slight advantage. Ensign Birch's smurf crew is the first to lose momentum and teamwork in handling their log. After fifty push-ups as a crew, they take up Old Misery for punishment drills. The big log is heavy and hard to handle, straining arms and backs that are already tired and cold. The smurfs struggle as best they can and are spared only when Ensign Clint Burke and the big crew are singled out for extra instruction.

Ensign Burke and Ensign Birch. The instructors confuse the names but not the trainees. The two boat-crew leaders couldn't be more physically dissimilar. Birch is short, burly, and black. Burke is tall—about six-five—rangy, and blond. They were classmates at the Naval Academy and both want to be Navy SEALs. Ensign Burke's crew is very tall. They begin at six-foot one and go up to a lanky seaman who is six-seven. This six-inch height differential is not helping them with log PT, and Old Misery emphasizes their problems. The tall men are butt to belly button as they crouch under the big log.

The boat crews gradually begin to get the hang of working together; they talk it up, motivate each other, and pull as a team. The First Phase staff is on them relentlessly—shouting, dropping individuals and whole crews for push-ups. In the midst of this, one crew begins to excel; it is the other smurf crew. They have a lot of spirit and are able to loft their log well above their extended hands on the overhead toss. They're beginning to move as one. Instructor Getka, who has been in a mock rage since the evolution began, stalks over to them.

"Right-hand starting position," Getka orders. Ensign Chad Steinbrecher and his crew bring their log down to the sand on their right side and crouch next to it, expecting the worst. "Seats."

"SEATS!"

"Good job, guys. You're showing some teamwork. Take a break." Getka moves on to the other crews.

"Nice goin', guys," Steinbrecher tells his men as he sits warily at the head of the crew, watching the instructors continue hammering the other crews, "but let's stay alert."

They sit quietly like grade school kids who have survived the first round of a spelling bee. They have earned a brief respite, but they know they'll be back in the fray soon enough.

This crew is led from the front by Steinbrecher, another ensign from the Naval Academy, and from the rear by Airman Harry Pell. Junior enlisted men in the Navy are designated seamen, airmen, or firemen. Airmen are normally assigned to naval aviation squadrons. The airmen at BUD/S are usually parachute riggers, and will be in great demand if they can make it through training to the teams. Pell is just one of the interesting personal stories of Class 228. Airman Harry Pell used to be First Lieutenant Harry Pell, U.S. Marine Corps. He is a short, powerful man who left the Corps to become a Navy SEAL. Pell is about five-six and very fit. He is average in the water, a solid runner, and very strong at PT. But he has spirit, and spirit in a BUD/S boat crew is contagious. He either genuinely loves BUD/S training or he should be up for an Oscar. Whenever an instructor sends an individual trainee out to the surf, that trainee has to take along a swim buddy—an innocent classmate who must also suffer. No SEAL or aspiring SEAL goes in the water without his swim buddy. When the call goes out, "Need a swim buddy," Pell is the first to his feet. This is not lost on the instructors. He brought a reputation as a team player with him from Indoc, and he's keeping it up in First Phase. All the First Phase instructors are curious about this little guy with the bulldog and USMC tattoos—the one who gave up his commission in the Marines to become an enlisted BUD/S trainee.

After log PT, the class quickly gets into running formation and slogs off to chow. Three of them don't; they go to the First Phase office. An instructor leaving the office sees them lined up on the grinder just outside the office, next to the three helmets that were deposited by the bell after breakfast.

"What are you doing here? Drop." The trainees drop and start doing push-ups. "So, why are you here? How come you're not on your way to chow?"

While two of them continue to push away, the third looks up from the leaning rest. "We want to DOR, Instructor."

"You want to quit?"

"Yes, Instructor."

The instructor is at a loss for words. "Uh, recover. Wait right here." He returns to the office. "Hey, Mruk, get over here. I got some of your guys outside."

Mruk steps from the office and looks at the three wet trainees. "You're quitting?"

"Yes, Instructor."

"All three of you?"

"Yes, Instructor."

"I hate you," he grumbles. "Go sit on the bench." The three trainees shuffle over to the green bench between the First Phase office and the First Phase classroom. They quietly take a seat.

Instructor Sean Mruk doesn't really hate them. Few instructors have much empathy for trainees who quit so early in the program, and most have learned not to take it personally. They prefer that those trainees who want to leave do so; it's better for the class and better for the men who don't want to be there. But Mruk does hate the process. If a trainee DORs during a training evolution, he first goes to the senior instructor in charge of the evolution and tells him that he wants to quit. The instructor may or may not try to talk him back into the evolution and back into training. Then he sends the DOR requestee to the class proctor. If a trainee quits between evolutions—as these three did—he goes straight to the proctor. The proctor will either counsel him, if he feels there may be something to salvage, or process him for disenrollment. For these three trainees, at this stage of the game, there is little to be saved.

Mruk retrieves the three men's training records and attaches DOR chits to them. All trainees who quit must do so by the chain of command.

"Okay, guys," Mruk says as he again emerges from the First Phase office, "let's get this done." He sets off across the grinder with the three trainees in tow to find Ensign Burns.

. . .

Following lunch, Class 228 is standing by for its first barracks and personnel inspection of First Phase. Inspection is a weekly event. Over the weekend, the class buffed out their rooms and carefully stowed all their personal gear. When the instructors arrive, the trainees are standing by in starched fatigues, freshly blocked covers, and spit-shined boots. The rooms and the trainees are very squared away. Lieutenant Gallagher follows the inspection party around with a clipboard and watches them tear through room after room, including his own. Mattresses are overturned, and the contents of drawers and lockers spilled to the floor. Only three rooms pass, and they are virtually indistinguishable from the ones that didn't. Chief Schultz looks over the destruction in the last room that failed the inspection.

"What kind of pigsty are you running here, Mister Gallagher? These rooms are terrible and your uniforms are not up to par. Hit the surf, sir, all of you."

"Hooyah, Chief Schultz."

Class 228, all starched and spit-shined, heads for the Pacific. Neither Gallagher nor any of his officers can remember any room inspection at the Naval Academy as harsh or capricious as this BUD/S room inspection. Certainly the consequences of failure at Annapolis were not so immediate or severe.

After the barracks and personnel inspection debacle, 228 forms up and runs down the beach to the BUD/S area. The next evolution is IBS surf passage. Ten boats are lined up at the staging area just off the grinder near the Indoc barracks. They are rigged, fully inflated, and ready for sea—paddles and life jackets are all in place. The boats were prepared by the class that morning well before 0500 and the start of PT. Ten boats were prepared, but because of the DORs, only nine are needed.

Their first First Phase surf passage evolution is directed by Chief Taylor. Ken Taylor is an eighteen-year veteran of the teams who is on his second tour as a BUD/S instructor. He has handsome, classic features and an animated, professional manner. Taylor saw action in the Gulf War and has a solid reputation as an operator. He and Chief Schultz seem to be cast from the same mold: short, muscular, and very fit. Both are compact, powerful men who exude confidence and authority. Chief Taylor is a most innovative instructor. The trainees learned the basics of IBS surf passage during Indoc, but nothing has prepared them for the mischievous ways of Chief

Taylor. He makes a game of surf passage, but it's a cold, punishing game. This is their last evolution of the afternoon and their last time in the surf. Taylor works them hard, making them remove their blouses and T-shirts and roll in the sand under their boats.

"Okay, fellows, on the next race, everyone faces aft in the IBS and you have to paddle backward through the surf. Then back in stern first, paddling forward. Ready . . . Go!"

The class fights their way out through the surf and back. The winning crew gets to rest, and the other eight boats line up for another race.

"All right, this time you paddle out, dump boat, and store your oars in the righted boat. Then I want you to swim your boat back through surf. As always, it pays to be a winner. Ready . . . Go!"

Chief Taylor is a very clever tormentor, but each IBS race puts a premium on teamwork. He also blends a measure of humor with the pain, and always looks for ways to reward spirit and leadership. Class 228 will come to Taylor's evolutions with mixed feelings. The trainees know they will suffer, but they will have a little fun as well. They also know that Chief Taylor is scrupulously fair. At 1700, the class secures from the last surf race. Back at the Center, a weary Class 228 washes down its boats and prepares to run to evening chow.

The last evolution of this long and ruthless day is an evening class on surf observation, or SUROBS. After chow the trainees straggle into the classroom, where Instructor Mruk teaches them the accepted way to gauge and classify surf, and shows them how to record the data in the proper format. They get no harassment from Mruk this evening, only information. Tomorrow morning at 0500 they will be out on the beach with Mruk for a SUROBS practical. Each morning thereafter, a swim pair from Class 228 will be on the beach at 0430 to observe the surf conditions and complete a SUROBS report. This report will be used by the instructors for water-training evolutions. If there are discrepancies in the surf reports, or in the wind and tide data, the whole class will pay for the oversight of the reporting swim pair.

Tuesday is not an easy day, but it is nothing like the trauma of Monday.

After PT and the run to morning chow, they are scheduled for classroom briefings through 1000, when they take to the O-course. Two trainees don't make it that far. They DOR before breakfast. One of them is Petty Officer Carreola. He has pneumonia and training is over for him. Losing the senior petty officer is never easy for a class. In the case of Class 228, it's still early in the game and the trainees have yet to gel as a class in First Phase. For Robert Carreola, this is a bitter personal tragedy. He nearly made it through the Hell Week of a previous class. Now he is out of 228. Carreola has a good career ahead of him in the Navy; he is a first class petty officer with an outstanding Navy record. He is only a few credits short of gaining his bachelor's degree in resource management. But at this point, it looks doubtful that he will ever become a Navy SEAL.

The trainees' first classroom evolution on the second day of First Phase is a briefing by the First Phase leading chief petty officer. Chief Bob Nielsen appears different from the other phase staffers. He is tall for a SEAL, about six-two, and slender, with dark receding hair and a push-broom mustache. He looks more like an academic than a BUD/S instructor. Nielsen has a casual manner and a dry sense of humor. He came to BUD/S from the East Coast, where he deployed with SEAL Teams Two and Eight, and saw action in the Gulf War.

"Feet!" Bill Gallagher calls out.

"FEET!" Class 228 responds.

"Drop!" Nielsen intones.

As the members of Class 228 begin to count them out, Chief Nielsen asks that they do so quietly. Golf course, they call it—the trainees count out push-ups in hushed tones. The class continues to push linoleum while Nielsen adjusts the remote control for his presentation slides.

"Okay, take your seats. My name is Chief Nielsen and I'm the phase leading chief. This briefing is to let you know what we expect of you during First Phase. First of all, what's my job here as the leading chief?" He doesn't wait for an answer. "My job is to ensure training is conducted safely and to see that you get quality training. I'm also here to see that the First Phase staff excels at their job." He gives the trainees a crooked smile.

"Some of you may think they excel just a little too much. And finally, I'm here to see that the training goals established by the Special Warfare Center for First Phase training are met."

While Nielsen speaks, the topic headings of his presentation slide into view on the screen behind him. Nielsen cautions them about their dealings with his staff. "Don't try to get one over on us; we've seen it all. You can try, but when we catch you, we'll make you pay.

"All right, let's take a look at the phase schedule. We have you for eight fun-filled weeks. The first four weeks are conditioning—running, swimming, log PT, the O-course, surf passage, and all that. What does this mean?" Again the wry smile. "The first four weeks are a kick in the crotch. It means we're gonna hammer you, right?"

"HOOYAH!"

"Conditioning and cold water is the name of the game. That's our job; that's your job. Week five is Hell Week. The last three weeks, we concentrate on hydrographic reconnaissance and mission planning. This will allow those of you who are still here to heal up a little while we try to teach you something." He clears the screen and brings up the next topic.

"Standards. If you cannot meet these standards, you will be dropped from First Phase. Most of you will be dropped and never return. A few of you will have a chance to come back through with a later class, but don't count on it. So here they are, gentlemen; this is what you have to do—at a minimum. Run four miles on the beach in thirty-two minutes. If you can't do it in that time now, what are you going to do when the minimum times come down in Second and Third Phase? I understand a third of you failed the first timed run; this won't cut it, gents." He calls another line of text to the screen with his remote control. "Two-mile open-ocean swim. Ninety-five minutes before Hell Week and eighty-five minutes after Hell Week. Obstacle course. You guys have the O-course later today, right?"

"HOOYAH!"

"The first time through, you will be expected to do it in seventeen minutes. You can walk that course in seventeen minutes. By the time you leave First Phase, you will be expected to do it in thirteen minutes. Feet."

"FEET!"

"Seats."

"SEATS!"

"Don't be falling asleep on me or you'll wish you hadn't. I'm putting this information out for your benefit. We can always go out on the grinder and do this another way." Nielsen again has their full attention. Several men rise and go to stand in the back of the room. Two of them go for the ice bucket. Before each class in First Phase, one of the trainees is assigned to see that a pail of ice and water is in the back of the lecture room. The two sleepy trainees dunk their heads in the slurry and return to their seats. They'll manage to stay awake for a while.

"Okay, let's talk about academics. You will have to pass a written test; seventy percent is passing for enlisted men, eighty percent for officers. Who're the officers here?" Nine hands go up. "How many from the Academy?" All the hands stay up. "All of you from the Naval Academy?" Nielsen raises his eyebrows in a neutral gesture. This was not the first time, nor the last, that the class officers will be surveyed for their Academy/non-Academy affiliation. "You officers have more schooling and more responsibility, so we hold you to a higher standard. And not just for the written test. We expect you to be leaders in training, understand?"

"HOOYAH!" the class officers respond.

"Hell Week. You'll get more on this later; but for now, let's just say you have to perform and survive. In the past, all you had to do was to survive Hell Week. Now you have to perform as well. You officers and petty officers have to lead. You have to function as boat crews and as a class in Hell Week, okay?"

"HOOYAH!"

Nielsen gives them a doubtful look and scans his notes. "Pool standards. We lose guys out of every class because they can't pass all the pool evolutions. There are four performance tests you'll have to pass. You all learned drown proofing in Indoc, right?" He holds up a fist to cut off the standard response. "Here in First Phase, you'll have to put all of that together to pass the drown-proofing test. You've practiced your knot tying underwater, right? You'll have to do all your knots at fifteen feet. Then there's the fifty-meter underwater swim without fins. Fifty-five yards—kick, stroke, and glide. You do this or you get dropped. And finally, you have to pass a lifesaving practical. You have to be able to handle yourself in the water in this business and be able to take care of your buddy as well."

Nielsen pushes through a standard set of dos and don'ts while in training. Basically, BUD/S trainees are expected to train during working hours and to use their nontraining time to prepare for training. This means preparing their equipment and resting their bodies when not actually engaged in training evolutions. Working hours for a BUD/S trainee are 0500 to 1700—longer if they have to come in for a night evolution, but fourteen hours at a minimum. Chief Nielson touches on safety issues, and the zero-tolerance policy on drugs and alcohol-related incidents.

"Let's talk about the philosophy of getting through training. What's it take to make it through here? First of all, this training is not for everyone. Being a SEAL is not for everyone. A lot of good guys come here and for one reason or another decide that this is not for them. So be it; let them walk away, and let them do so with dignity. You laugh at someone who quits or make fun of a man because he DORs, and we'll hammer you—big time. The cold facts are that at least two-thirds of you sitting here will quit." He steps away from the lectern to one side of the room. "Okay, there's seven rows of you here in the classroom. These two rows will be there on graduation. Maybe a few more, maybe a few less. All the rest of you guys, these five rows, are gonzo—history—back in the fleet. That's reality; that's the way it is. As a class, you may fool us and more of you will be here on graduation day. We'll see. It's really up to you.

"How do you get into these first two rows? Have a positive mental attitude. Pay attention to detail. Take it one day at a time, one evolution at a time. Mentally rehearse things; it really works. Before you go down to tie your knots, rehearse in your mind exactly what you're going to do. Mentally go over it. And you know what? You'll do it. Expect to have weak areas; we all do—drown proofing, O-course, whatever. Work on your weaknesses. If you need help or extra instruction, we'll see that you get it. That's part of our job. Overcome your weaknesses and you can get through this course.

"Now, you've heard this before, but you need to hear it again. Your reputation in the teams begins here. How do you want to be remembered? As someone who just did the minimums and barely got by? That might sound acceptable to some of you right now, but it's not the way we do business in the teams. You want a reputation as a guy who has spirit and can be counted on; someone who gives it his best shot. Who do you want in your platoon—someone who only meets the minimums, or someone who always tries to excel? Think about it. And remember, there's only one person here in this room who knows if you are going to make it through this training—that's you. Think about that, too. Feet."

"FEET!"

"What's your next evolution, Mister Gallagher?"

"The commanding officer's briefing."

"Then I guess you better stand by for the CO."

Nielsen leaves them. Some of the trainees turn and talk quietly among themselves, others bend or stretch to relieve sore muscles. Still others sit back down to get off their feet. As a group, they don't seem to know how to act unless someone is telling them what to do.

"Okay, lock it up," calls one of the trainees, and the class quiets down. It's Daniel Bennett, an easygoing second class petty officer from Alabama. With the departure of Carreola, he is now the class leading petty officer, or LPO. "We've got to pay attention and keep an eye on each other. Nobody falls asleep or we'll all pay for it. If you start to nod off, go stand up in the back of the room. If someone taps you, don't argue; just go stand up."

Bennett has been here before. He DORed with Class 208 on the second day of Hell Week. After two years in the fleet, he's back to try it again. He is a serious trainee, and he has good rapport with the other petty officers. Bennett knows the game; he's like a border collie, quietly moving around the class, offering advice and giving direction.

"Stand by!" yells one of the class door sentries. "Feet!"

"FEET!"

There's a mild commotion and scraping of chairs as the members of 228 get back to their places. A moment later a Navy captain enters the classroom, followed by a half dozen instructors. The instructors take seats in the rear of the class while the captain makes his way to the front of the room.

"Please, take your seats," he says in a pleasant voice, "and carry on."

He regards the class with an easy smile, then drags a chair from one side to the center of the classroom. "I really don't have a speech or any prepared remarks. I just thought I'd take a few minutes and talk with you about training." He has the appearance and manner of Mr. Rogers, and he probably doesn't weigh more than 150 pounds.

Captain Ed Bowen is the commanding officer of the Naval Special Warfare Center. As the CO, he is responsible for all the courses taught at the Center, as well as the East Coast Naval Special Warfare Center extension. There are some twenty-six courses taught at various times at his command, but 90 percent of the money and manpower, and 100 percent of the public attention, are on BUD/S.

"They treating you all right here? Nobody is being too mean to you, are they?" Eyes roll and a murmur runs through the class. "I was an eighteen-year-old seaman when I came through this training back in 1964. I know some things have changed since then, but I'm sure a number of things haven't. It looks like the instructors are still keeping you cold and wet. How many officers in the class?" He counts the hands. "That's a good ratio of boat-crew leaders for this size class. Any from the Academy? All of you? Even better. Academy officers tend to do well here."

Officers at BUD/S have a lower dropout rate than enlisted men. They tend to be older and, as a group, better educated. In 1970, the first Naval

Academy ensigns began to show up for BUD/S directly from the Academy. Because of the highly competitive selection process at Annapolis, they have a history of success in training. However, one Naval Academy ensign from the class quit during the first week of Indoc. He was not injured, nor was it a conditioning or harassment issue. For reasons known only to this young officer, he decided this duty and this lifestyle was just not for him.

"What does it take to be successful in this training?" Captain Bowen continues. "I guess what it really comes down to is this: do you really want to be in the teams? Those of you that do will make it through this course. But you have to want this program—this kind of life. If you want it, then you'll put up with all the harassment those instructors in the back of the room dish out. You'll take it so you can get to the teams." He pauses a moment to frame his words. "I suppose I really have only two pieces of advice for you. First of all, don't give in to the pressure of the moment. If you're hurting bad, which will happen often, and you don't think you can go any further, just hang on. Finish the evolution; finish the day. Think about what you really want; make your decision then—after the evolution or at the end of the day. Secondly, take it one day, one evolution, at a time. Don't mentally DOR because you're looking ahead to all the pain and suffering in the days and weeks ahead. Just focus on getting through the day. Any questions?"

Class 228 looks around warily. BUD/S trainees are not the most forthcoming; anonymity is a virtue in a BUD/S class.

"When I was in training some thirty-five years ago," the captain continues, "the senior instructor got us together and briefed us on training. I remember one of my classmates asking that instructor just what he expected from my class. 'What we expect,' he told us, 'is all you have to give.' I think that still holds true. Yes?"

"Ensign Birch, sir," Birch says as he stands and comes to attention. "We understand that you're the Bullfrog. Could you tell us something about that and your career?"

Bowen smiles self-consciously. "It seems that I'm the last one of my generation of SEALs to quit." In the reception area of the Naval Special Warfare Center is a tall, garish trophy with a huge bronze frog affixed to the top of it. Ed Bowen's name placard is the most current on this statue. "I have been on active duty longer than any other Navy SEAL. Some say I'm either a glutton for punishment or very lucky. I think I'm lucky. I began my naval career as a seaman recruit. I came straight to BUD/S from boot camp. While I was an enlisted man, I made chief petty officer. I was very proud that I made chief in the Navy. Then I had the opportunity to become an officer. I worked my way through the ranks from ensign to captain. And here I am, commanding officer of the Center. One reason I say that I'm lucky is because I broke into the platoons as an enlisted man. Officers are fortunate if they get two or three platoon deployments before they have to move on. I was able to make several operational deployments as an enlisted man and several more as an officer. So I got to see this business from both sides. I'm proud of these," he says, holding one of the captain's eagles on his collar, "but I made chief petty officer in only eight years. I worked very hard to make chief that quickly. As I look back over the years, the decades really, I'm most proud of having been a chief petty officer in the United States Navy."

Bowen says nothing of his combat record, which is legendary in the teams. Aside from his platoon combat deployments, he served with the Provincial Reconnaissance Units, or PRUs, in Vietnam. Ed speaks Vietnamese fluently. His PRU teams were particularly effective and savaged the Vietcong cadres in the Mekong Delta. Whenever the Vietnam-era SEALs gather to swap stories, there is a special reverence for Ed Bowen. He is considered by many as the best jungle fighter ever produced by the SEAL teams—a true warrior. His place in the lore of the teams is not just from his combat record. After thirty-five years in uniform, his character and his commitment as a leader are also legendary.

Many officers and enlisted men who have made a career in the teams have served as a BUD/S instructor or phase officer. Ed Bowen did neither. He was, however, a SEAL cadre instructor. In the Vietnam era, SEAL Team One on the West Coast and SEAL Team Two on the East Coast conducted their own training in jungle warfare. The SEAL teams—there were only these two at that time—assigned a selected cadre of combat veterans to teach the new men about SEAL operations in Vietnam. For close to ten years, the SEALs did little else but deploy to Vietnam and fight in the jungle. Cadre training was intense and very focused; the new SEALs would be in the Mekong Delta and in combat within a few months of their BUD/S graduation.

In 1970, with several tours under his belt, Ed was taken out of deployment rotation and assigned as a cadre instructor at SEAL Team One. The following anecdote, as told to me by Commander Gary Stubblefield (USN, Ret.), former commanding officer of SEAL Team Three, illustrates the character of Ed Bowen.

Early one morning, Ed was bringing his cadre class back from the mountains near Cuyamaca, California. At the time he was a first class petty officer. They had been on a land navigation exercise and patrolling in the mountains the whole night. The entire class of sixteen new SEALs were crowded in the back of a 6X6 canvas-covered truck—bone-tired, cold, and hungry. They lined either side of the truck bed on wooden benches with their weapons and gear piled between them. It was a long, uncomfortable ride back to the team area. As they made their way up the Strand on Highway 75, Ed shouted over the noise of the truck.

"Okay men, here's what we have to do. I want all the weapons cleaned and the gear properly stowed. I know we'll miss morning chow, but we all have to be in dress whites and standing tall for the awards ceremony at zero eight hundred."

There was a chorus of complaints and groans. The students had been up for a day and a half, and were in no mood to get cleaned up to parade for a ceremony.

"Stop the truck!" The usually mild-mannered cadre instructor pounded through the canvas to the cab of the truck. "Stop this truck right now!" The truck lurched to a stop on the shoulder of the highway, causing the packed SEALs to accordion forward on their wooden benches.

"Now you guys listen to me," Ed continued in a quiet voice. "In this business, you will often have to work all day and all night, and then keep going. This is not a profession where you can quit when you're tired or when you think you've done enough. You're a Navy SEAL. We're in this business because we believe in it—because of who we are. If this doesn't set well with you, then make other arrangements. You're still volunteers. You don't have to be in Team One and you don't have to go to Vietnam. But if you want to be in my team and in my cadre class, clean your weapons, stow your equipment, and be standing tall at zero eight hundred in dress whites."

Ensign Stubblefield and the rest of his cadre classmates were standing tall at the designated time in the proper uniform.

Now Captain Bowen sweeps Class 228 with his eyes. "I don't know what else to tell you men, other than to wish you good luck in the days ahead. If you can get through this training, there's a wonderful career ahead of you in the teams. That much I do know." He rises to face the class. "Thank you for your attention."

"Feet!"

"FEET!"

After Captain Bowen leaves, the class remains at attention. When he is out of earshot, one of the instructors barks out, "Drop!"

"DROP!"

"I saw one or two of you clowns nodding off during the captain's briefing. How dare you fall asleep in the presence of a man of his caliber? You guys are gonna pay for this."

They pay dearly. The next evolution is the obstacle course. Before they even get started, the class is sent on multiple trips over the dune berm and into the surf. Between trips, the trainees push 'em out. Times on the O-course are not up to par and the class is sent back out into the surf. Finally they are released for chow. Not all of them go.

Another young trainee has had enough. He goes to the First Phase office and waits for Instructor Mruk. There are tears in his eyes and he is ashamed, but he will not have any more of this. Finally Mruk joins him on the grinder.

"You ready to quit?"

"Yes, Instructor Mruk."

"You sure?"

"Yes, Instructor."

"Okay, ring the bell."

He does not move or give any sign that he heard Mruk. He just stands there, staring down at his feet.

"Hey, c'mon, man," Mruk says gently, "it's tradition. Ring the bell."

Finally the trainee takes the lanyard and, holding the lip of the bell with his other hand so as not to add decibels to his shame, he quietly rings out. Then he walks slowly off the grinder. Sean Mruk has a lot to do and is anxious to get the paperwork started to process this man out of BUD/S. Yet he knows this ex-trainee needs some time alone to get himself together. He watches him for a moment, then goes back into the office.

. . .

Next to Hell Week, the first week of First Phase causes the greatest percentage of attrition. It's as if some of the trainees simply wanted to get to First Phase before they DOR. Somehow, there is less shame in quitting during BUD/S phase training than during Indoc. Much of the first week's attrition comes on the first day, but it goes on all week. The evolutions take their toll on the class. The most demanding are the conditioning runs, log PT, and IBS surf passage. All are conducted with liberal doses of harassment from the First Phase staff. In all evolutions, the winners get a brief break from training and the losers earn more torment. From the trainees' perspective, the punishment handed out by the instructors seems capricious and arbitrary. In fact, these are very well-planned and closely monitored evolutions. This was not always the case.

In years past, there were no specific performance standards. Instructors laid it on their trainees as hard or harder than their instructors did to them. If a man was still standing at the end of training, he was graduated. Trainees were sometimes made to sit in the surf until one or more of their number quit. It has always paid to be a winner, but there were times past when this was carried too far. Trainees were put in a classroom and told that the last two men remaining in the room were winners. In the brawl that followed, bones and skulls were sometimes broken. Now First Phase training is performance based. Leadership and teamwork are stressed along with harassment and cold water. Training is just as hard, just less abusive.

During the first week of First Phase, Class 228 prepares for open-water swimming. For the first time, they don fins in the pool and begin doing laps using the accepted, modified sidestroke. In the teams, they'll swim with any fins they like, but at BUD/S they wear the same standard duck feet that have been used by frogmen since the 1950s. After instruction, critique, and lap swimming, it's harassment time. The trainees are made to lie on their backs with their heads over the edge of the pool. With their masks full of water and heads tilted back, they do flutter kicks. The class did this during Indoc, but now with the addition of the big duck feet, the flutter kicks are much harder. With stomach muscles burning, the men have to sing the BUD/S version of "Take Me Out to the Ball Game":

> Take me out to the surf zone,
> Take me out to the sea,
> Make me do push-ups and jumping jacks,
> I don't care if I never get back,
> For it's root, root, root for the SEAL teams,
> If we don't pass it's a shame,
> For it's one, two, three rings you're out,
> Of the old BUD/S game.

Yet there is reason for the harassment, a purpose to this singing with a face mask full of water. It will help them in Second Phase when they have to breathe underwater from their scuba rigs without a face mask. After a choking, Donald Duck–like version of "The Star-Spangled Banner," they're ready for the open water—almost. Before they muster by boat crew and leave the pool, Chief Taylor drops them for more push-ups. Then he singles out a group of trainees.

"I want to see the senior enlisted man in each boat crew—no officers, just enlisted." While the rest of the class waits in the leaning rest, eight trainees gather around Taylor. "You men are the senior petty officers in each of your boats, right?"

"HOOYAH, CHIEF TAYLOR!"

"Okay, I want you guys to take this on board. The success or failure of your boat crew can depend on you. Your officer is in charge and he gives the orders, but there's a lot you can do to help him. You have to be leaders as well. When he's getting instructions for the next evolution or away from the boat, you take charge and organize the rest of the crew. It's your job to support these officers. If your boat crew has problems or performs poorly, it's a reflection on you as well as the boat-crew leader, understand?"

"HOOYAH!"

"Now, I'm going to be watching each one of you. I expect you to lead by example and to motivate the rest of your crew. Sometimes, an officer is a good boat-crew leader or a poor one depending on the support he gets from his senior enlisted man, understand what I'm saying?"

"HOOYAH!"

"Get back with your boat crews and push 'em out."

After Taylor dismisses them, they leave the pool on the run and head for the eastern side of the base on San Diego Bay.

The first open-water swim is a one-mile bay swim to gauge the relative speed of individuals in the class. This is the one and only time they swim without a buddy. Swim pairs will be assigned by comparable ability, so a fast man will not have to wait for a slow one on a timed swim. As with most evolutions, there are inspections and protocol. The instructors inspect the UDT life jackets and diving knives closely. Both are relics from the past. The inflatable rubber life jackets worn on the chest are identical to the one I trained with in the late 1960s. So is the leather-handled Ka-bar knife. The temperature in San Diego Bay is sixty-six degrees, so the trainees swim without protection. This is their first and only bay swim on the surface. It is also their shortest. All other swims will be in the open ocean and longer than a mile, but they will be allowed wet-suit tops in the Pacific.

Perhaps the most critical evolution of the first week, aside from pure survival, is the fifty-meter underwater swim—fifty-five yards without fins. They have to do this to continue in First Phase. It's an honest fifty meters—no diving start. The trainees must jump in the water, do a front somersault underwater, and begin their swim across the twenty-five-meter pool. After touching the wall, they swim back. The instructors test four trainees at a time. As they turn and head for home, four instructors close in on them, swimming just above and behind. The instructors watch them closely. As they touch the wall, the trailing instructor grabs them by the waistband of their trunks and helps them from the water. A corpsman is there to check each man. All make it but two, who will be retested next week or face being dropped from training.

Friday afternoon of this first terrible week finally arrives. Class 228 has only two evolutions to get through—log PT and IBS surf passage. The trainees are starting to gel as a class. They began the week with sixty-nine men and they are now down to fifty-two. Seventeen men who survived Indoc failed to make it through the first week of First Phase. Those who remain move more quickly as a class; musters are delivered smartly and there are fewer stragglers. For the survivors, log PT is a much smoother evolution than it was on Monday morning. Not easy, but smoother. For those crews who work together and show spirit, the log exercises are manageable. For those who don't, there are trips into the surf and Old Misery. After log PT, they run across the beach to the BUD/S compound to fill canteens and get the IBSs. Chief Taylor is waiting for them as they line up the boats.

"God help me, but I just love IBS surf passage. How about you fellows?"

"HOOYAH, CHIEF TAYLOR!"

"Just a few boat drills and we knock off for the weekend. Piece of cake, right men?"

"HOOYAH, CHIEF TAYLOR!"

"But you better show me something. I can stay out here as long as it takes. Coxswains, front and center."

The boat-crew leaders scramble up to the front of the line of boats and stand facing Taylor. There are now seven boats, seven boat-crew leaders.

"Report."

Each officer in turn comes to attention, salutes Taylor. The chief crisply returns their salutes.

"Listen up for your instructions, men." They lean in to hear him as they know the chief will not repeat himself. "Paddle out beyond the surf zone, dump boat, paddle back in, and line up your boats. When you get back here, I want you to swap life jackets, properly set up your boats, and report back to me. Now, when you swap life jackets, no one can touch his own life jacket while taking it on or off. You have to buddy up, dress and undress each other—learn to work together, as a team. No crewman touches his own life jacket. Questions?" There are none. "You will have thirty seconds to brief your crews. Go!"

The coxswains race back to the stern of the IBSs. They quickly tell their crews the rules of the race. Taylor gives boat leaders a few extra seconds to plot strategy and fire up their crews. His surf evolutions are clever; the crews have to follow directions as well as pull together to win a surf race.

"Ready?"

"READY!"

On the coxswain's command, each crew takes up its IBS, three men on a side holding the boat off the sand by the rope carrying handles. They crouch at this low carry, ready for the sprint into the surf.

"Hit the surf!" Taylor calls, and the seven boat crews charge down the slope of the beach to the surf. The surf is relatively low today. The boats return quickly and all are still in contention. There's a collective scramble as the trainees strip off each other's life jackets and make the swap. While the coxswains race to report to Taylor, their crews dress their boats for inspection. It's a close contest, but there is a winner—Boat Three, Ensign

Will Koella's crew. The other six boats are losers. Boat Three takes a seat on the beach while the other crews, feet on the IBS main tubes, push them out. As winners, Koella's crew gets to sit out the next race.

"All right, I want to see the junior man of each crew." Soon there are six men standing in front of Taylor. They are not nearly so crisp or military-looking as were the officers who directed the boats in the first surf charge.

"You guys are now in charge," Taylor tells them as he moves down the line correcting their posture and showing them how to properly hold the paddle when making a report. "Instead of taking orders, you'll be giving the orders. You're the coxswains. Now, here are your instructions for the next race."

For the next hour and a half Class 228 does surf passage drills. Each time there is one winner and six losers. On one race, Taylor takes the number-two paddlers on the starboard side of each IBS and makes them coxswains. They take the boats out through the surf backward and back in the same way. Winners get a break; losers do push-ups or have to drag their boats over the berm dune and back. The races are spirited, and Chief Taylor likes what he sees. His drills are designed to give a taste of leadership to each crew member and to force the crews to think and work together. He works them hard, but the class likes Taylor and they give him a good effort. They come off the beach in good spirits. One man does not.

At the start of the last race, one of the boats comes down from a high carry onto the head of Petty Officer Shawn Groves and knocks him to the sand. He quickly recovers and rushes to rejoin his boat crew as they head for the surf. But he's walking funny and having difficulty finding his IBS carrying handle.

"Hey, Groves, get over here," Taylor yells at him.

Groves isn't sure what to do. He doesn't want to leave his boat crew, but Chief Taylor is calling to him. He turns and tries to catch up with his boat. Taylor and Corpsman Dan Maclean seem to materialize on either side of the stunned trainee. Taylor pulls Groves aside and sends his IBS ahead without him. Groves again tries to resist this and rejoin his boat crew. Taylor and Maclean gently escort him up to the soft sand. They make him sit, and Maclean begins to ask him some simple questions.

"What is your name?"

"Where are you?"

"Who is president of the United States?"

Groves is clearly dazed, yet he gets most of them right. He wants to get back to his boat crew, but Maclean restrains him.

"What do you think, Doc?" Taylor says.

"Probably just a mild concussion or a compressed vertebra in his neck. Or nothing at all. I don't want to take any chances, though." Two other instructors bring a rigid litter from the ambulance and help Maclean to strap Groves to the board. Maclean wraps a padded collar to Groves's neck and they strap him to the board so his neck, head, and torso are immobile. Another corpsman radios the BUD/S clinic. The wet, bound trainee is then loaded in the back of the 4X4 ambulance for the thirty-second drive to the BUD/S medical facility. The loss of Groves and their delayed charge to the surf means Groves's boat crew gets a bad start on the race. They finish last and have to pay the price for being losers.

One week down, three to go. Then Hell Week. There are no defections on Friday afternoon. Fifty-two trainees, including Groves for now, have survived the first week of First Phase. The second week of Phase One is more of the same. Whether by design or by schedule, the pace is not so intense as week one. On Monday, the four-mile timed run is scheduled at low tide when the trainees can run on flat, hard-packed sand. All but three are under the thirty-two-minute minimum.

On Monday of the second week of First Phase, Class 228 reports to the CCT after morning chow. Only two members of the class have yet to pass the fifty-meter underwater swim. One of them is Petty Officer Mark Williams. Williams is the old man of the class at thirty-three. He's a powerful man from Sacramento who played football in high school and college. Before he came to BUD/S, Williams was a staff sergeant in the Marine Corps. He left his Force Recon company to become a SEAL. Williams comes from a service family. His mother is a lieutenant colonel in the Army Reserve; his father was killed in Vietnam.

As a second class petty officer he, along with Daniel Bennett, is one of the enlisted leaders of Class 228. He is a strong trainee, but has problems in the water. Mark Williams should have been in Second Phase, but he came down with pneumonia during Class 227's Hell Week. He was coughing blood by Wednesday of that week and medically rolled back to 228. During First Phase with Class 227, he passed the fifty-meter swim, but he also passed out as he touched the wall. Now he has to make the swim again. The first deficient trainee passes the swim; now it's Williams's turn.

"C'mon, Williams, you can do it."

"Yeah, man—kick, stroke, and glide."

As his classmates cheer him on, Williams takes a deep breath and drops into the pool. He does his somersault and heads for the bottom, knowing that deeper is better. A key to the underwater swim is a long, precise glide between strokes. Too many strokes use too much oxygen; two few and you can't go the distance. Once again, Williams coasts home to complete the swim, but once more he passes out. The unconscious trainee is quickly hefted from the pool; the corpsmen are on him instantly.

"Did I make it?" he asks as he comes around. The former marine wants to be a Navy SEAL very badly.

"Yeah, Williams, you passed the swim," growls one of the instructors. "Now get over there and start pushing 'em out for scaring us like that."

Williams's problems in the water are not yet over. Each trainee must pass drown proofing before he leaves First Phase. Many blacks who come to BUD/S, like Williams, are men with a heavy muscle mass. They tend to sink like a stone. With hands and feet bound, BUD/S trainees must travel several lengths of the pool and tread water for a period of time. Then, after executing an underwater somersault, they have to "swim" or wriggle to the bottom and retrieve their face mask in their teeth. In two tries at the pool, Williams is unable to pass drown proofing. If he is to stay with Class 228, he will have to pass this evolution.

On Tuesday Groves rejoins the class. After his injury on Friday during surf passage, he was examined by Lieutenant Josh Bell, one of the BUD/S medical officers. He was then taken immediately from the BUD/S medical facility to Balboa Naval Hospital for X rays. He also received a head CAT scan. The tests revealed nothing, but the BUD/S medical staff is very careful with head and neck injuries. Dr. Bell came in on Sunday to reexamine him and adjust his neck collar. On Monday, Groves was held out of training for the day and sent over for additional X rays. All through this, Groves maintained that he felt fine and just wanted to get back with his class. This is not the first injury Petty Officer Groves has suffered in BUD/S. He was here before in Class 226. He broke two ribs just before Hell Week, but tried to gut it out. By Tuesday of Hell Week, the pain forced him out of training, and he was medically rolled from 226 back to 228. This is his last chance to get through BUD/S. Trainees are allowed only one medical pardon. Groves is a solid trainee, and his boat crew is glad to have him back.

On Friday morning of the end of week two, the class is dragging, but just one man has DORed over the past four days. The prospect of a weekend keeps many of them going. At 0450 they muster at the rear of the BUD/S compound and prepare for PT.

"Mister Gallagher."

"What is it, Dane?" This is a busy time for the class leader. He has to make sure that all the overnight chores for which the class is responsible have been done. This includes preparing the IBSs, vehicles, first aid equipment, and classrooms for the day's training. He also has to take an accurate count to the instructor leading PT or suffer terribly for a bad muster.

"That's it for me, sir; I want out."

Gallagher looks up from his clipboard and focuses on Seaman Wesley Dane. "You want to quit?"

"Yessir. I've had it. I'm going to DOR."

"But why now? You've only got one more day before the weekend."

"I know, sir, but I just don't want to do this anymore."

"Hey, Lieutenant, we better get—"

"In a minute," Gallagher snaps, and turns back to his seaman. "Look, Dane, we all have bad days; we all get down. Why don't you gut it out one more day and think about it over the weekend? It'll give you time to rest up—make a better decision."

"C'mon, sir! If we're late for PT, we go into the surf."

"We go in the surf anyway," Gallagher replies. He's back to his classmate. "Dane, we gotta go. Just one more day. How about it? I know you can do it."

"Thanks, sir, but this just isn't for me. Good luck to you and the rest of the guys, sir."

Seaman Dane turns away and walks toward the First Phase office and the bell. Gallagher watches him for a moment, then swings back to the waiting class. "Let's do it."

With Ensign Jason Birch chanting cadence, the class troops into the BUD/S grinder.

"Left! Left! Keep it in steh-hep!"

"LEFT! LEFT! KEEP IT IN STEH-HEP!"

"Two!"

"TWO!"

"Twenty-eight!"

"TWENTY-EIGHT!"

"Two!"

"TWO!"

"Twenty-eight!"

"TWENTY-EIGHT!"

The class halts in front of the elevated platform with Class 226's large gold numbers on it. The trainees are dressed for PT—fatigue trousers, boots, white T-shirts. Each man has a full canteen.

"Class Two-two-eight is formed, Instructor," Gallagher reports. "Fifty-one men assigned, fifty men present, one DOR."

"One DOR—this morning?"

"Hooyah, Instructor."

"Get wet and sandy."

"Hooyah, Instructor."

Another day of misery and it's the weekend. Weekends are small islands in the sea of pain for BUD/S trainees. They have official duties, like standing watches at the Center and preparing equipment for the coming week, but there are no training evolutions. They eat, sleep, and eat again; treat blisters and raw skin; and try to rest battered joints and aching muscles. Often, only the thought of getting to the weekend gets a man through a week of training. BUD/S trainees dread Monday morning like inner-city high school teachers.

. . .

On Monday of week three Class 228 begins rock portage. Rock portage is IBS surf passage with an attitude. The boat crews bust through the breakers in front of the BUD/S compound and head north, just beyond the surf zone. Instead of taking their boats back in across the beach, they wait just off the rock jetty in front of the Hotel del Coronado. While curious hotel guests gather to watch, Instructor Timothy Hickman signals the first boat crew to come ashore. Hickman is a solid, no-nonsense first class petty officer from Boise, Idaho. Like Williams, he was a marine before he became a SEAL. The teams attract men from all services, but most cross-service transfers are from the Marine Corps. Hickman is a veteran of five platoon deployments and the Gulf War. He stands on a pile of boulders the size of Volkswagens while the breakers boil around him. The first boat comes in.

"Bow man out," cries Ensign Clint Burke to his boat crew over the crash of the surf. As the nose of Boat One slams into the rocks, Petty Officer Scott Carson with bow line in hand jumps onto the boulders amid the churning surf and scrambles for high ground. Boat One is the tall-guys' crew. While the rest of Burke's crew paddles furiously to keep the IBS against the rocks, Carson quickly wedges himself into the boulders and wraps the line around his waist.

"Bow-line man secure!"

"BOW-LINE MAN SECURE!" echo Boat One's paddlers.

"Water!" yells Burke as a breaker smashes into the stern of the boat, nearly capsizing them. The back surge tries to carry them seaward, but Carson has a good purchase on his boat.

"Paddles forward!" Burke screams.

"PADDLES FORWARD!"

One man with all the paddles gathered in his arms slips over the bow and begins his journey up and over the slippery rocks. He stacks the paddles on the beach and scrambles back to where Ensign Burke and his crewmates, now out of the boat, are starting to horse the IBS onto the rocks.

"Bow-line man moving!" Carson yells.

"BOW-LINE MAN MOVING!"

While the boat crew fights to hold the IBS, Carson scrambles forward to a new position in the rocks. This is a critical time, and a breaker almost wrests control of the boat from Burke and his men. The trainees, who now wear hockey-style helmets, have been briefed never to get between their boat and the rocks. Rock portage is serious business; several corpsmen are standing by as well as Lieutenant Peter Witucki, the BUD/S senior medical officer.

"Bow-line man secure!"

"BOW-LINE MAN SECURE!"

"Ready!"

"READY!"

"Heave!"

The IBS begins its torturous journey over the rocks toward the beach. Burke sets his men; they call "Ready" and heave the boat forward. All the while, the surf is crashing around them, fighting to reclaim the boat and its crew. Finally the men crest the rocks with their boat.

"High and dry! Bow line over."

"Bow line over!" Carson replies and returns to the boat. He throws the bow line into the boat and helps his crewmates heave the IBS down the rocks to the sand.

"Stop what you're doing," says Instructor Hickman.

Burke and his men instantly stop and wait for the instructor to climb down from his perch atop the rocks.

"That's not bad for your first time," he tells them, "but you have to be quicker. Bow-line man, you have to be more nimble. You left your crew exposed to those breakers for too long. Mister Burke, wait a bit longer after you call 'ready' and make sure your men are in position to lift the boat. Understand?"

"Hooyah, Instructor Hickman."

"You paddlers, get set quickly. If you aren't ready, you have to let your coxswain know that you're not ready, okay?"

"HOOYAH, INSTRUCTOR HICKMAN!"

"You have to move quickly, but remember, three points of contact while you move over these rocks. No balancing acts. Again, not a bad job on your first try. You get a pass this time, but I won't be so easy next time. Now get out of here."

"HOOYAH, INSTRUCTOR HICKMAN!"

The tall guys take their IBS down off the rocks to the soft sand. Rock portage is a mixed evolution for the tall crew. The big men have more brute strength, but pulling the cumbersome boat from the surf over the rocks also requires agility and quickness. Once on the soft sand, the crew restows its paddles and awaits inspection.

"Drop," intones Chief Bob Nielsen.

"DROP!" Burke and company do push-ups with their toes up on the main tube of the IBS.

"Did you pass?"

"Hooyah, Chief Nielsen," Burke replies. Nielsen makes a check mark in his notebook. Crews that don't pass get immediate and more severe attention from the phase leading chief.

"Very well, recover and go see Chief Taylor."

The tall boat crew slings its IBS at the low carry and jogs a short distance to where Chief Taylor is waiting. Taylor then sends the men back out over the rocks and into the surf. Getting back into the surf from the rocks is almost as dangerous as coming in. In order to make a game of it, Taylor times them, urging each crew to try to better the previous crew's time back out over the rocks. Each boat crew must make three successful landings, then drag their boat back out over the rocks and launch it into the plunging surf.

That evening, after dark, Class 228 again paddle their boats north toward the Hotel del Coronado. This time they will do rock portage at night. BUD/S trainees will remember night rock portage like naval aviators remember night carrier landings—with respect and a full measure of terror.

Week three costs 228 one more trainee. He is a medical drop and is sent back to the fleet to heal with a recommendation that he come back and try again. With one week to go before Hell Week, Class 228 is down to forty-nine men.

Week four, the week before Hell Week, is more of the same—but different. There are conditioning runs and PT and surf passage and ocean swims, but each evolution seems to be conducted under a cloud of what is to come.

"If you can't do this now," an instructor barks at them, "what are you going to do when you haven't slept for three days?"

The instructors keep the pressure on, but they are attentive to trainees who may be limping or have other injuries. The First Phase corpsmen make a point of being a little more approachable. At the same time, the instructors are more intolerant of trainees whose negative attitude or lack of motivation seem to be hurting their boat crews. Officers who show poor leadership on an evolution are shown no mercy. The First Phase instructors are subtly taking ownership of the class; the performance of Class 228 is a reflection of their ability to instruct and motivate.

On Tuesday of week four, the class runs across the base to the combat training tank for their lifesaving practical. Lifesaving training at BUD/S is basically a condensed Red Cross senior lifesaving course. Passing the practical exam is a requirement for completion of First Phase. The instructors act the part of drowning victims and the trainees must rescue them. At civilian lifesaving courses, drowning victims struggle to test the technique of the rescuer. At BUD/S, the lifesaving practical is basically a water buffalo rodeo. These are vicious aquatic contests with trainees clamped to backs of thrashing instructor-victims. One trainee comes out of the tank with a bloody nose, and two of them vomit on the pool deck from the exertion. Another, who is recovering from pneumonia, is put on oxygen to recover from his struggle to rescue a recalcitrant instructor. All but three in the class pass the lifesaving practical. At the end of the day, another man DORs, bringing Class 228 down to forty-eight men.

Also, during week four, they have their last two-mile ocean swim. To be allowed to continue on to Hell Week, trainees have to make the swim in under ninety-five minutes. The ocean temperature is now fifty-nine degrees. The trainees wear wet-suit tops, UDT life jackets, masks, and fins. First they swim out through the surf zone to a safety boat waiting a hundred yards offshore, just beyond the breakers. They then swim north past the rocks off the Hotel del Coronado and back—one mile up and one back. After checking in with the timekeeper in the boat, they return through the surf to the instructor on the beach. He checks the swim pairs off to fully account for all the trainees who entered the water. Then he drops them for push-ups.

"Hooyah, two-mile ocean swim."

"Recover and get out of here."

Two by two, they run up over the berm back to the BUD/S compound. As a class they are strong in the water. All are under the pre–Hell Week ninety-five-minute minimum, and all but three pairs are under the post–Hell Week eighty-five-minute time. This is a tribute to Tim King and the Indoc instructors who worked with them on swimming technique.

The pivotal event of week four for Class 228 is pre–Hell Week screening. This consists of performance and medical screening. The most difficult and contentious is the performance screening, which is the work of the First Phase Review Board. Review boards, in all phases of BUD/S training, meet periodically to review individual trainee performance and his fitness to continue training. Aside from the physical performance standards, there is a requirement that trainees must demonstrate teamwork, professionalism, and a can-do spirit. In First Phase, this board is chaired by the phase officer, Ensign Joe Burns, and consists of his First Phase senior petty officers. The First Phase Review Board met once before during week two of Class 228's First Phase training. Their objective at that point was to counsel marginal trainees and warn them of the consequences if they didn't improve their performance. On Wednesday of week four, Ensign Burns convenes his phase review board with a more serious agenda. They must decide who will, and who will not, begin Hell Week with Class 228.

Thirteen men are brought in for phase board review. All have at least one adverse performance chit in their training files. Most have failed to make more than one of the four-mile timed runs, failed drown proofing, or failed the lifesaving practical. Some have chits in their file for leadership or motivational reasons. One man has an unsatisfactory time on the obstacle course. All performance chits are reviewed and signed by the individual trainees, so their sins are well known to all before they get to the board. The files are reviewed by the First Phase board, and the trainees are called in individually. Only one of them is a class officer.

Ensign Burns and his First Phase instructors sit along one side of a long, polished conference table in the newly refurbished BUD/S conference room. The well-appointed interior is in sharp contrast to the rough, serious men seated at the table. It's Instructor Mruk's duty as class proctor to escort each trainee into the room. They are in starched fatigues and spit-shined boots. Each, in turn, stands before this board of inquisitors, green helmet cradled in the crook of his arm, and announces himself "Reporting as ordered."

They are called in by order of the seriousness of their transgressions. The first eight are given a tongue-lashing and asked to speak to their poor performance or lack of motivation. The trainees, knowing that their quest to become a Navy SEAL could end right here, are appropriately contrite.

"We're going to send you into Hell Week," Burns tells one of the initial eight, "but the staff is going to be keeping a close watch on you. You start dragging down your boat crew or whining, and you're history. We don't need crybabies or no-loads in this outfit. It's time to pull your weight or get the hell out, understand?"

"Hooyah, Ensign Burns."

The trainees are also cautioned that if they should make it through Hell Week, they have to correct their performance deficiencies or they won't graduate from First Phase. Not all the trainees are taken over the coals by the First Phase board. One of those is Mark Williams.

"Petty Officer Williams, reporting to the phase board as ordered."

"Williams, you're a good trainee," Burns begins, "but you're going to have to do something about your swimming."

"Hooyah, Ensign Burns."

"If you get through Hell Week, you'll have to pass drown proofing or we'll have to drop you from training. You understand this?"

"Yessir."

"Otherwise, keep up the good work. Now get the hell out of here."

"Hooyah, Ensign Burns."

Five members of Class 228 will not go on to Hell Week. The First Phase board reaches this decision quickly but not easily. The merits as well as the shortcomings of each trainee are debated. Some of the phase instructors are quick to point out where one of the unlucky five did well or demonstrated spirit. Yet most of these trainees are deficient in more than one area. There is a consensus; they will not continue with Class 228. The board has only the authority to remove a trainee from First Phase. They cannot remove him from BUD/S training.

Lieutenant Bill Mahoney, the basic training officer, and Chief Jeff Rhodes, representing Indoc, are sent for. The assembled group now forms the Academic/Performance Review Board, with Lieutenant Mahoney serving as chair. The training of Class 228 has yet to include academic subjects; today this board will only evaluate physical performance, attitude, and potential to successfully continue training. They are also joined by Rick Knepper, the BUD/S curriculum specialist. Knepper is the only civilian and a nonvoting member of this board, but his opinion carries weight. He is a retired master chief petty officer and a former BUD/S instructor. While on active duty, he also served as the Center's command master chief petty officer. The Academic/Performance Review Board decides whether these five trainees will be rolled back to Class 229 or sent back to the fleet.

The First Phase staff and the three new board members again plow through the training records. Now the debate becomes more spirited. An agreement is quickly reached on four of the five. They are to be sent back to the fleet; they can come back at a later time, but they will have to leave BUD/S and reapply for SEAL training. The decision of what to do about Seaman Chris MacLeod is not so easy. MacLeod is by far the weakest member of the class. He has poor upper-body strength, and his lack of stamina has been hurting his boat crew. He is the only trainee to fail the O-course, and he has great difficulty with PT. But MacLeod has guts. He has held back nothing, and the First Phase staff respects him for this. Trainees with heart, but who lack the necessary physical tools, are not easy for the board. They call him back in.

"Seaman MacLeod, reporting as ordered."

"MacLeod," Mahoney begins, "this is the Academic Review Board. Do you know why you're here?"

"Yes, sir. My performance has been unsatisfactory and not up to standards."

"You know that you are no longer with Class Two-two-eight."

"Yes, sir."

"And you know this board is convened to decide whether you will or will not remain in BUD/S training."

"Yes, sir."

"Okay. Why don't you tell us why you're here? Why did you come to BUD/S?"

"I want to stand with the best," MacLeod replies. He is crying and makes no attempt to wipe his eyes. The tears roll off his cheeks. "I want to stand with the best and fight for my country." This declaration is met with a respectful silence.

"Any questions for this man?" Mahoney says, looking around the table for help. More silence. "Okay, MacLeod, you can wait outside and we'll tell you what we decide."

After the tearful trainee leaves, more debate. In the eyes of the senior First Phase staff, motivation and desire trump physical ability, but MacLeod is very weak. Ensign Burns looks down the table to Chief Rhodes.

"Jeff, if we send him back to PTRR, can you fix him?" The Indoctrination Course is part of the PTRR (Physical Training, Rehabilitation, and Retraining) phase at BUD/S. "Can you get him ready for the next class?"

Chief Rhodes remembers MacLeod from Indoc. He is an experienced instructor and knows the limits of what PTRR can and cannot do for a weak trainee.

"Look, Joe, if you want to send him back to us, we'll give it a try, but you want my honest opinion?" Burns does. "We'll break him. He's a good kid, but he just has too far to go. Two-two-nine will class up in seven weeks. There's just not enough time, even with the Christmas break." Rhodes shrugs. "Like I said, we can try and I know he'll try. But I think we'll break him, and it'll take six months to fix the damage. We'll have him here for a year or more."

The review board is looking for a way to keep this man, but Chief Rhodes is not giving them one. There is no alternative; they recall MacLeod to the tribunal.

"Seaman MacLeod, reporting as ordered, sir."

"The board has considered your case," Mahoney tells him. "MacLeod, it is our decision that you will not be rolled back. I'm sorry, but you will be dropped from training altogether."

"You've done a helluva job here, MacLeod," Chief Taylor tells him from his seat at the end of the table. "And you've got nothing to be ashamed of. You've given it your best shot. We all know that. It's just that it's not fair to your boat crew for you to continue with them."

"Chief Taylor's right, MacLeod." Ensign Joe Burns is a hard man, but his tone with MacLeod is gentle. "This training isn't for everybody, and right now it's not for you. Go back to the fleet. Get yourself built up, and then come on back for another try. We'll be here when you're ready."

MacLeod regards them a moment. He doesn't wait to be dismissed; he simply turns and walks from the conference room. The instructors glance at one another uneasily and the meeting begins to break up. Mruk gathers up the training records as the others file out. Aside from the performance standards, the review boards are guided by two principles: what is best for the program, and what is best for the trainee. The design is clear, but the calls are not always easy. Underlying this process are the requirements of the end user—the active duty SEAL and SDV teams. If they allow a marginal trainee to continue on, he may survive Hell Week and make it to the teams. Once in the teams, he could become a weak link in a platoon and cause a teammate to get hurt or killed. Or cause a mission to fail.

MacLeod has choices. The First Phase and Academic/Performance Review Boards have done him a favor. He's bitterly disappointed, but he knows their decision was right—and fair. MacLeod has a degree in chemistry from the University of Maryland. He can go to the fleet, improve his fitness and strength, and return for another try. Or he can put in for a commissioning program and try to come back as an officer. Either way, he now knows what it takes to get through BUD/S. He also knows that he personally has the grit to make it through this training. Now he has to take the time to better prepare himself physically.

Each of the forty-three men of Class 228 who will go on to Hell Week are also carefully screened by the BUD/S Medical Department. They are told to refrain from taking any Motrin or aspirin during the weekend. Motrin or any other pain medication will be given to them as required. Hell Week is going to hurt, they are told; it's supposed to. But they won't be given pain medication until they really need it. They are also told to report serious symptoms, such as coughing up blood or skin infections.

Nearly all of the men in 228 have some injury or ailment. Many have respiratory problems or some fluid in their lungs. Others have cuts or abrasions from rock portage or the O-course. Most are experiencing some tendinitis or joint pain. And a good many have blisters on their hands and feet that are in various stages of healing. The BUD/S medical staff catalogs each trainee's list of afflictions. They will closely monitor these in the week ahead. Everyone in Class 228 gets a heavy dose of antibiotics by injection to help ward off infection. Hell Week will test their immune systems as well as their bodies and spirits. Each trainee is given a careful medical examination, and this exam will yield the last pre–Hell Week attrition for Class 228.

Petty Officer Shawn Groves has an infected ingrown toenail that has responded to antibiotics slowly. During Hell Week, the trainees are wet and on their feet without rest for days at a time. The inability to properly monitor an infection under these conditions is too great a risk; even a seemingly minor infection like this could cause permanent damage before it was caught. Groves is removed from Class 228, and since it is his second medical drop, he will have to leave BUD/S. This is not easy on the medical staff or the First Phase instructors. Groves was a solid trainee with every prospect of becoming a Navy SEAL. He does not accept this decision with equanimity, as did Seaman MacLeod. He is angry and feels betrayed, but the decision stands. If he wants to be a Navy SEAL, he will have to come back and try again after a tour in the fleet.

After chow on Friday morning, the trainees get their phase motivational briefing on Hell Week by Chief Keith Lincke. Chief Lincke is new to BUD/S and First Phase, but a very experienced SEAL with operational time with Teams One and Three—he has seven operational deployments including the Gulf War. This tour at BUD/S will allow him enough time in one place to complete the final year of his degree in information technology. Chief Lincke's presentation is built around his six keys to getting through Hell Week: a positive attitude, teamwork, guts, a never-quit mentality, a belief in yourself, and focus.

"The teams are a fraternity," Lincke tells them, "and everybody there has done what we're going to ask you to do. It's a given that you will be cold, wet, and tired. All the time. Your reputation in the teams will begin by how well you handle yourself when you're cold, wet, and tired. I can promise you that I've been colder and more tired in the teams than I ever was during Hell Week. True statement. Hell Week is to see if you can suck it up and keep going when you haven't slept in a few days and you're freezing your ass off. And remember, you have to do more than just survive; you have to perform."

The new First Phase chief prowls the front of the classroom. This is his first classroom presentation; he's looking for the right words. "It's like this; you've done it all before. Everything we will ask you to do during Hell Week you have done during the last few weeks—run, swim, the O-course, surf passage, all of it. There's nothing new. But anybody can perform when they're warm and well rested. You have to show us you can perform when you're cold, wet, sandy, and you haven't slept for a few days."

Late Friday morning of week four, right after a conditioning run in the soft sand, Class 228 is again addressed by Captain Bowen in the First Phase classroom. This time he doesn't sit, but simply stands in front of the class. He notes that in their four weeks at First Phase, their number has shrunk from sixty-nine to forty-two.

"Everyone here ready for Hell Week?"

"HOOYAH!"

"That's good, because you have a very challenging and difficult week ahead of you. What you are going to experience next week is a test—a very painful test. But it's also instructional. Each one of you is going to learn a great deal about yourself. You're going to find out what you're really made of. During every evolution, you will have a choice; do I give in to the pain and the cold or do I go on? It's up to you. I have no quotas or numbers that have to graduate or must be weeded out. That's for you to decide. But to continue in training and to join us in the teams, you have to do this. It won't be easy. Each one of you must decide for himself just how much you want this program." He silently regards the anxious trainees for a moment. "I'll be there on Friday and I hope to shake each and every one of your hands when Hell Week is secured. Good luck to you."

The class scrambles to their feet and Captain Bowen takes his leave. Instructor Mruk threads his way through the standing trainees to the front of the room.

"Okay, take your seats. I have some word to put out before you break for chow, so I want you to listen up. After lunch you will have time to go to supply and square away any equipment problems, and get back to medical if you need to. Hell Week is scheduled to begin sometime Sunday evening. You will all be back here at noon on Sunday, in this classroom. After that time, you will be restricted to this classroom until the festivities begin. Bring a book, bring some chow, games, whatever. We'll have some videos here for you, and pizza will be brought in late afternoon. It'll be a chance for you guys to rest up as a class and get your heads together." He grins at them. "Time for a little class bonding, sing 'Kumbaya,' whatever. My advice is that you bring lots of chow and eat your brains out. Trust me; you can't eat enough.

"Equipment. This is what you will bring and only what you will bring with you in your seabag. Besides the fatigues you'll be wearing, bring one extra full set and two extra pairs of socks—the new ones you were issued. Bring your swim gear but no canteen belt, canteens, and no knives." Another sly grin. "We don't want you armed for this evolution. Have your name stenciled on everything. Also, bring a set of comfortable clothes— sweatshirt, sweatpants, shorts, sandals. Place these clothes, along with soap and a towel, in a paper bag. Staple the bag shut and write your name on it. For those of you who are still here on Friday, you'll have something to wear when it's over. The same for you guys who are back here before

Friday. The bags will remain here in the classroom, along with any of your personal effects. There will be a twenty-four-hour watch here at all times. No one will bother your gear."

Mruk punches through a laundry list of what they need to do and not do between now and when they arrive at noon on Sunday. As Mruk briefs them, a few in Class 228 start to look around. They are beginning to wonder who among them will DOR and be back in the classroom before Hell Week secures, seven days from now.

"Any questions?" Mruk asks.

"Can we bring blankets or pillows so we can sleep Sunday afternoon?" a trainee asks.

"Bring whatever you like," Murk tells them, "but you guys will be too keyed up to sleep. Just plan to come here with all your gear squared away. Then plan to relax, watch movies, and eat. If you remember nothing else, remember to eat."

After Mruk gives Class 228 their last instructions, the remaining forty-two trainees form up on the grinder to run to chow. A half hour later the classroom is filled with almost as many instructors. Ensign Joe Burns briefs the BUD/S staff on Hell Week. This is an all-hands evolution for the First Phase staff as well as those instructors from Indoc, Second Phase, and Third Phase who are assigned to help. Hell Week is conducted by the BUD/S staff in three shifts. It will be five days of round-the-clock pressure. Every eight hours, a fresh set of BUD/S instructors will come on duty to greet the weary survivors of Class 228. Hell Week has a lot of moving parts. In addition to the twenty or so instructors who are involved, there are various support, logistic, and medical personnel who also play important roles.

Hell Week is a familiar and well-choreographed event, but safety considerations and operational details have to be reviewed and individual duties assigned. There are some sixty-four separate evolutions in Hell Week. Each evolution has a detailed lesson plan, and each has specific written instructions for safety, risk assessment, and supervisory criteria. Each one is designed to contribute to the overall goals of Class 228's Hell Week. Those official, stated goals are:

> STUDENTS WILL DEMONSTRATE THE QUALITIES AND PER-
> SONAL CHARACTERISTICS OF DETERMINATION, COURAGE,
> SELF-SACRIFICE, TEAMWORK, LEADERSHIP, AND A NEVER-
> QUIT ATTITUDE UNDER ADVERSE ENVIRONMENTAL CON-
> DITIONS, FATIGUE, AND STRESS THROUGHOUT HELL WEEK.

The reality is that away from the public eye and the formal U.S. Navy training conventions, these SEAL instructors will create a week of living hell for the members of Class 228 to see if they have what it takes to join this warrior culture.

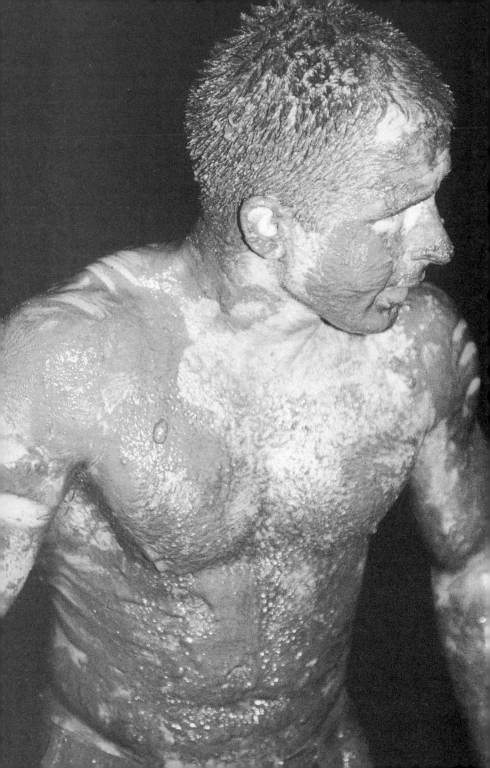

CHAPTER THREE

THE WEEK

O n most Sunday evenings, the Naval Special Warfare Center is bathed in a soft yellow halogen glow. Invariably there is some activity behind the BUD/S compound and around the student barracks as trainees prepare for the next day's training. Not tonight. The area is completely dark and no one is about—no roving patrols, no student movement, no one from the watch section checking the back gates. There is a fluorescent bloom from the quarterdeck, where two Indoc students sit confined to the reception desk. They have been told to remain at their post and to stay away from the glass doors that lead out to the grinder. Next to the barracks, six IBSs have been readied for rock portage. Helmets with attached Chemlites sit perched on the main tube at each paddler's position. Between the chain-link compound fence and the tall beach berm, two large tents wait silently. These will serve as makeshift barracks for the trainees for the next week—where they will be allowed their meager ration of sleep. Inasmuch as Class 228 will have a home during Hell Week, it will be these two canvas shelters.

It is Sunday, 14 November, at 2000 hours. A file of men in dark clothes and bloused boots emerges from the administration complex on the south side of the grinder. The sliver of moon has not yet risen and only a few of the brighter stars have found their way through the light sea mist. It is a clammy sixty degrees—about the same temperature as the ocean. The men all wear ball caps and three of them carry automatic weapons. They move soundlessly across the grinder like a SWAT team moving into position. As they approach the First Phase classroom, light filtering around the shade on the door reveals that the armed men have ammunition belts clipped around their torsos. The leader gives a signal and three of the men break away to make their way down the outside hallway to the side door of the classroom. Other dark forms move into position around the grinder.

Inside, the forty-two men of Class 228 and Instructor Sean Mruk are halfway through *Old Yeller*. They all know it's coming; only Mruk knows exactly when and how.

Since noon, the class has been confined to the classroom, allowed to leave only to make a head call. No one has been allowed to leave for the last few hours. The classroom looks like a Red Cross shelter. The one-arm student chairs are pushed and stacked to one side, and blankets and pillows litter the floor. Each man's change of clothes, identical to what he is wearing, has been neatly stacked in the back of the room. Each item of clothing is stenciled with his name. The brown paper bags with casual civilian gear—for the most part sweat clothes and sandals—are piled in a corner near the chairs. Each bag bears a student's name written in black Magic Marker.

That morning, before the Hell Week lockdown, Chaplain Bob Freiberg held a service for Class 228. It was a voluntary, nondenominational gathering attended by most of the class. Chaplain Freiberg is Baptist by training, but he casts a big tent for the Hell Week class. He read the passage about deliverance from the Valley of the Shadow of Death and led them in the Lord's Prayer. Then he asked God to bless and watch over these young men during the trial ahead. Together we sang "Eternal Father," the standard Navy version:

Eternal Father, strong to save,
Whose arm hast bound the restless wave,
Who bids the mighty ocean deep,
Its own appointed limits keep,
O hear us when we cry to thee,
For those in peril on the sea.

This is followed by verse 17, the one for Navy SEALs:

Lord Father of sea, air and land,
Protect us with thy mighty hand,
For in your cause we do so strive,
Be present as we jump and dive,
Lord keep our SEALs within your care,
That liberty we all may share.

Amen

It's been a long day of eating, watching videos, and waiting anxiously. Some watch the movies, some don't. Some try to sleep while others read. Individually, they move in and out of small groups. Often they gather in boat crews and reaffirm their collective resolve. There is a quiet restlessness in the room. They are a class, but each man has to come to terms within himself about the ordeal ahead. Some are quiet and reflective. Others are talkative and social, wanting to be in the company of others. Stories abound about the start of previous Hell Weeks. Five of the trainees have been here before: Mark Williams, John Owens, Zack Armstrong, Lawrence Obst, and Daniel Bennett. Only Williams, who made it to Wednesday in Hell Week with Class 227, is willing to talk. He roams the First Phase classroom offering encouragement to his classmates.

"You ready for this, man? Hey, it's doable; we just got to suck it up and get it done."

"Thanks, Mark."

"Hey, let's kick ass, guys."

"Right on, Mark."

"How about it, sir. You ready for this?"

Bill Gallagher is among those who wait quietly. "I guess—ready as I'll ever be. Thanks for all your help so far. Good luck, Williams."

"Good luck to you too, sir."

Those uninterested in the diversion of the video wait silently, lost in their own thoughts. The room is warm, close to ninety degrees, and the air heavy with anticipation. It happens quickly. There is a crash as the side door of the classroom is kicked open, the rear door a second later. A hand reaches in and sweeps off the lights. The big yellow dog fades from the screen, and all hell breaks loose.

First there are the whistles—shrill police-type whistles. Class 228 has been told what to do when they hear a whistle. They hit the deck, cross their legs, and cover their ears with the palms of their hands. The six men move in, three from each open door, and the shooting starts.

"Hit the deck!"

"Incoming!"

"On the floor! Get your heads down!"

"Welcome to hell, gentlemen!"

The Mk-43s, a SEAL version of the M-60 light machine gun, begin to bark. The 7.62mm blank rounds don't have the brisance of live rounds, but the noise is still deafening. More whistles, more shouting, and lots of shooting—for sixty seconds, nothing can be heard but the sound of gunfire and shouting. The room is lit by muzzle flashes. The machine gunners step over and around the prone trainees as they do their work, mindful of the stream of expended shell casings from their weapons. They are hot and can cause angry welts if they land on exposed skin. Soon the room is heavy with smoke and the stench of cordite.

"Everybody outside!"

"Move, people! Let's go! Let's go!"

The forty-two members of Class 228 scramble from the previously warm, secure environment that has suddenly turned violent, and break out onto the grinder. More whistles and they fall to the blacktop, covering their ears, heads down. There they are met with fire hoses, more instructors, and more shooting. Barrels have been placed around the grinder, secure receptacles for the artillery simulators. Soon there is the scream and boom of imitation artillery rounds to accompany the shooting. Shouting instructors are everywhere, herding them to the center of the grinder. The class bunches together on the blacktop as they are assaulted by the fire hoses. Then the whistle drills begin.

Fweet! The mass of confused students melts to the grinder. They scoot about on the wet blacktop so their heads are in the direction of the instructor with the whistle—ears covered, legs crossed. They knew it was coming—the shooting, the explosions, the shouting, and the fire hoses. But it's one thing to know it's coming and yet another to be in the middle of it. In some ways, it's more difficult on the five in Class 228 who have been here before. They know how much it will hurt and how long the sleepless days ahead will be. More than one of them envies the relative ignorance of the first-timers.

Fweet! Fweet! They begin to crawl toward the sound.

Fweet! Fweet! Fweet! They scramble to their feet.

Fweet! Back on the grinder—legs crossed, hands over their ears.

"Get your head down, turkey!"

"Don't just lay there; crawl to the whistle!"

"Hey, only five more days of this! Quit now—avoid the rush later!"

"How about a hot shower? All you gotta do is ring that little bell!"

For the next five minutes, they crawl about the grinder, treated to sporadic bursts of machine-gun fire and explosions. Knees and elbows start to abrade on the wet blacktop.

This Hell Week breakout for Class 228 is as effective and successful as it could have been. The breakout evolution is designed to create chaos and confusion. It sets the tone for this difficult and challenging ordeal. The First Phase staff can only vary the standard fare of noise, shock, and chaos so much. The last Hell Week class was ordered into the grinder before the shooting started. This time the machine gunners assaulted the class inside their classroom. Often, the Hell Week class is tipped off about the instructor's method of attack by the brown shirts, former Hell Week graduates.

All students in First Phase wear white T-shirts. After Hell Week and for the rest of training, they wear brown, or olive drab, T-shirts. A crew of post–Hell Week rollbacks in PTRR, all brown shirts, will work around the clock to support 228's Hell Week. They are in PTRR waiting for injuries suffered in training or a previous Hell Week to heal. They will also work tirelessly to covertly help the Hell Week class and, on occasion, to thwart the instructors. This is not just a gesture of sympathy or solidarity. Most of them will join 228, either after Hell Week or in Second Phase. The guys being punished on the grinder are their future classmates. To make sure that Class 228 had no warning, Ensign Joe Burns ordered the brown shirts quarantined to the Center barracks and a guard placed on them.

The shock of breakout has its effect on Class 228. They are confused and disoriented. Many wonder if it is real. For the moment, they are no longer trying to be Navy SEALs, BUD/S graduates, or even First Phase graduates. All they want to do is get through Hell Week. They want to become brown shirts. But first they have to get through Sunday evening.

Breakout is an all-hands evolution for the First Phase staff and the Hell Week instructor-augmentees, which puts the ratio at one instructor for every two trainees in Class 228. Ensign Burns watches the controlled mayhem with apparent satisfaction. Captain Ed Bowen observes off to one side; he lets his staff do their job without comment. Then someone informs Burns that they may be short one of the trainees.

"May be? What the hell do you mean, may be short? Get a count."

The students are ordered to their feet and into a line. "Count off!"

"One! Two! Three! . . ." This will happen often during Hell Week. Until the class stabilizes and boat crews become relatively fixed, they will muster like this. ". . . Forty! Forty-one!"

This is serious. People get hurt during Hell Week—even during breakout, which is a highly supervised evolution. Burns says nothing, but he is clearly unhappy. If a trainee gets hurt during breakout, he'll have to answer for it.

"We got him, Joe," says one of the instructors.

"What the hell happened?" Burns is relieved, but not mollified.

"He got confused coming out of the classroom and ran for the beach. We found him out in the surf."

Burns scowls, wondering how his instructors managed to let a student get to the beach undetected, and wondering what the student must have been thinking out there in the surf by himself. Sometimes the confusion and disorientation works too well.

"Put 'em all in the surf," he says. "We'll sort 'em out on the beach."

The class makes a quick pass into the surf, then is lined up for another count. Back in the soft sand, the whistle drills continue. The wet students worm their way through the sand like a litter of suckling animals, gathering at the feet of the instructor who owns the whistle. *Fweet-fweet; fweet-fweet!* They keep crawling. Then another instructor up on the berm dune or down by the water sounds two blasts and the crawling mass wheels in his direction. They do this for half an hour, rubbing their knees and elbows raw. Then they're back in the water for the next evolution, surf conditioning.

Surf conditioning, surf torture—same thing. First, fifteen minutes immersed in a line, arms linked. This is the maximum time allowable at sixty degrees. *Fweet! Fweet!* They crawl from the surf up into the sand, then back in the water for flutter kicks and games for another ten minutes. Then they crawl out of the water for more whistle drills and back into the water, this time without their shirts.

"J.B., I can't stand this. I'm gonna quit."

Jason Birch watches in disbelief as the man next to him pulls away from his linked arm and begins to stagger through the shallows toward the beach.

"No, wait!" Birch dives for him and misses as a wave knocks him sideways. He rises and tries to pursue his classmate across the wet sand, but an alert instructor steps between them.

"Get back in the water, Mister Birch."

"But, Instructor, he doesn't really want to do this! Honest!"

"You want to quit, Mister Birch?"

"No, Instructor."

"Then get back in the water, sir."

Birch returns to the line of shivering trainees. Up on the beach, the lone trainee approaches Joe Burns. He is the first.

"You want to quit, sir?" Burns doesn't have to call him sir; they are both ensigns. The trainee is shaking so bad he can hardly talk. He nods in the affirmative.

"Are you sure? It's not too late if you go back in the water right now."

"I j-just don't like this shit."

"Very well. Go get in the truck and wait for an instructor to take you back." The ambulance and an extended-cab pickup truck, both with big beach tires, are always close at hand.

In just under an hour and a half of Hell Week, the first man quits—and it's a Naval Academy ensign. He's also a boat-crew leader.

"Go figure," one of the other instructors says quietly as they watch the student officer climb into the pickup. "He was a tough kid—good runner, good swimmer."

Burns shrugs. If he is concerned, he doesn't show it. He cares little about the officer who quit; if he doesn't want to be here, good riddance. But he's worried about the other men out there in the water. When an officer quits, a strong performer like this one, it's not good for the class. Burns's fears are not groundless. Moments later three enlisted men quit. The DORs come in spurts. It's never pretty, but Burns had hoped the first group would not leave for a while. Surf torture on Sunday night is a double-edged sword. The men in the sixty-degree water are cold, but they've all handled this much immersion time before. The difference is that they will be tormented like this again and again for the next five days, with little sleep and without ever getting warm. Just thinking about it can cause a trainee to ring the bell.

The games on the beach continue. For close to an hour they do run-paddle-run. The IBS crews are sent out through the surf line where they dump boat, paddle up the beach a few hundred yards, come back in, and then race down the beach with their boat to the starting line. At 2300, Class 228 trades their IBSs for logs, and they begin log PT—in the surf. The log PT degenerates into more surf torture and three more men quit. Then it's off to the O-course with the boats. The forty-two have now become thirty-five. They run the O-course in boat crews with their boats, hauling the bulky rubber craft over the obstacles. And another man quits. Following the O-course, the class puts to sea and paddles north for rock portage. It's now 0200—2:00 A.M., Monday morning—and Hell Week is six hours old.

The paddle north to Hotel del Coronado is the real first break for the Hell Week class. They are still cold and wet, but once beyond the surf line, there are no instructors yelling at them. The serenity of the night on the water seems surreal. They're like shell-shocked infantry troops between artillery barrages. As each boat reaches the Hotel del, it turns right, paddles shoreward, and crashes into the rocks.

"Okay, uh, bow-line man, out."

"What the hell are you doing, sir?" screams an instructor.

"Paddles forward . . . I mean, keep paddling!"

"Think, sir, what comes next?"

"One's out . . . Two's out."

"Wrong, sir, wrong. If this was a combat insertion, you just killed your entire squad! Hey, you! Yeah, you. How many times do we have to tell you guys not to get between the boat and the rocks? Get this damn boat up on the beach and start pushing 'em out!"

The makeshift, reshuffled boat crews attack the rocks, and most do it poorly. There are still plenty of instructors present, but only about half as many as there were during breakout. Lieutenant Norm Moser is standing by. He or one of the other medical officers will be on hand for all high-risk evolutions. Moser has a unique blend of skills. He is a qualified physician's assistant and a qualified Navy SEAL—a warrior and a healer. After two rounds of rock portage, the IBS crews are sent into the water without boats for more surf torture—flutter kicks, push-ups, and sit-ups in the surf—or worse—sitting in neck-deep water, arms locked and doing nothing.

"Okay," Chief Nielson tells the line of trainees sitting in the surf. "You guys look like you're getting too warm. Take off your shirts."

They're too tired to complain. They simply begin to fumble with the buttons on their blouses. All but one.

"To hell with it; this is bullshit. I ain't doin' it." He rises and walks up to Chief Nielson. Another man joins him.

"Me, too," he says. "I've had enough."

Nielson regards them. Both are strong First Phase trainees. "Are you guys sure? You won't get another chance to do this, but if you want to take off your shirts and get back in the water, I'll let you."

"I'll g-go back if you will," says the second man, clenching his teeth to keep from shivering.

"No way," says the first. "I've had it."

"Me, too, then," and the class becomes two men smaller.

Nielson watches them go with a measure of sadness. "We always give them a minute to think about it and a chance to go back," he tells me. "But they're given this second chance only once." He pauses a moment. "Come to think of it, I can't ever recall a trainee finishing Hell Week who quit— one who quit and then went right back." I asked several other instructors about this. They all remember trainees who quit, thought better of it, and went back, but none who ever ended up making it through.

At 0450, the class brings their boats up to a head carry and begins the run-shuffle across the base for breakfast. At the chow hall, they do IBS drills, mostly overhead IBS push-ups. When they finally bring the boats down to the ground, it's regular IBS push-ups with their feet up on the boats. Once inside the chow hall, the class gets their first rest since breakout the evening before. Well ahead of the rest of the sailors on base, they crowd through the chow line. Two men guard the boats while the rest eat. There are thirty-two of them—ten gone in a little under nine hours.

"Let's go, let's go, people," barks Instructor Terry Patstone. "No coffee or soft drinks and everybody drinks two glasses of water. C'mon, let's go."

At the tables, Class 228 settles down to their first meal. This is their first chance to take stock of what has happened. They will be allowed as much as a half hour with no harassment to eat and drink as much as they want. Over at a table away from the trainees, the night shift is having its breakfast. There are seven of them. Hell Week is a three-shift duty for the instructors, but the night shift has been on duty since breakout. They, too, are tired and tend to their meals, allowing the class to eat in peace.

The class collects at the six-man tables in boat crews. Most of the trainees shovel it in; they're hungry and they've been told to eat as much as they can. A few of them already have the "thousand-yard stare" and have to be prodded by their classmates to eat. Some of them still have a smile and want to talk; others want to eat in silence. Still others sit staring at their plates, hands clamped around mugs of hot water. There is a dark cloud gathering over the trainees; Hell Week has just begun and already they are very cold and very tired. Gallagher breaks away two men who are finished and sends them out to relieve the men guarding the boats. They each leave behind a puddle of sand and seawater in their chairs.

Instructor Terry Patstone, the shift corpsman, calls out the names of trainees on prescribed medication, and motions them over to his table. Chief Nielson gets a cup of coffee and wanders among the seated trainees. He's casual with them, even friendly.

"How's it going, Baldwin?"

"Oh, just terrific, Chief Nielson."

"Really? You look like crap. How you doing, Mister Steinbrecher?"

"Couldn't be better, Chief. How about yourself?"

Nielson ignores the query, smiles, and moves on. It was not an idle question. He saw Steinbrecher limping a little, and this was his offhand way of checking on him.

"Let's go, children," Patstone yells at them, and they begin to push away from the tables. "Recess is over. Boy, are you guys gonna have fun in school today."

The trainees are allowed a quick stop at the Porta Pottis outside; they're too wet and sandy to use the inside toilets. Inside the plastic facilities, they find the handiwork of the brown shirts. The Porta Pottis have been stocked with Snickers and PowerBars stashed along the ceiling ledges. Back at the boats, Instructor Darren Annandono, the leading petty officer of the night shift, is waiting for them. After several sets of push-ups, the class tosses their boats back onto their heads and lines up behind Annandono for the march back to the Center. When on the move, it's an elephant walk. The boats line up bow to stern and the trainees follow the instructor who's leading them. He usually walks at a brisk pace, forcing the trainees to shuffle-trot along behind, banging the boats roughly on their heads. Today Annandono varies his pace, causing the boats to periodically string out, then bang together when they race to catch up.

"Let's go, bow to stern—bow to stern. Close it up!"

"You in charge of this boat, sir? Then move the hell out; you're holding up the parade."

The class pauses briefly at the BUD/S clinic for a quick inspection by the medical staff, then heads for the beach. These medical exams will become more comprehensive as the class gets further into Hell Week. Across the compound in the First Phase classroom, ten former BUD/S trainees sleep on canvas cots. Inside the dim room, the air is rich with snoring and the stench of damp clothing and urine. At the entrance, two former BUD/S students sit at a table and keep a log of all activity. All students who DOR must spend twelve hours in this makeshift dormitory and be cleared by the BUD/S medical staff before they can return to the Center barracks. When one of them has to go to the head, he is accompanied by one of the men on watch. The ex-228ers wear the sweat clothes and sweaters they brought to wear at the end of Hell Week. None had planned on wearing them this soon. Wrapped in Navy blankets, they sleep soundly while their former classmates begin the first day of Hell Week out on the beach.

"All right, fellows, guess what's first on the schedule this fine morning?"

"Surf passage?" offers one of the trainees. The five crews are lined up on the beach under their boats—cold, wet, and sandy.

"Good guess," Chief Taylor replies, "but the wrong answer." Taylor and the day shift have replaced Chief Nielson and the night shift. "We're going swimming. Prepare to down boat—down boat." The five boats drop from the trainee's heads to the sand. "Your swim gear is in the tents just over the berm. Wet-suit tops and hoods. Two minutes; move it, move it!"

The class races to the tents for their swim gear. Inside the tents, there is a fumbling scramble as each trainee finds his duffel bag, strips off his wet clothes, and struggles into his swim gear. The brown shirts help, but there is a great deal of confusion. Back on the beach they line up by swim pairs.

"Too slow, guys. Much too slow. Everybody drop."

Taylor gives them fifteen minutes of PT with the IBSs until they're sweating in their wet-suit tops.

"Okay, gang," he tells them while they are in the leaning rest, feet on their IBSs, "here's the drill. Go through the surf, swim north to the rocks at the Hotel del, and back to here. Safety first—stay with your buddy. Naturally, it pays to be a winner. Line it up, quickly."

Sixteen swim pairs line up. Two instructors from the day shift work the line of swimmers, checking life vests, not that they will need them; the wet-suit tops will keep them buoyant.

"Go, go, go!"

The class lumbers into the surf and trainees groan as they trade the sweat inside their wet suits for cold seawater. At this point, most of them have been awake going on twenty-four hours. Two more trainees decide that this is not for them. They walk back ashore and quit. Heads hung, the two DORs are escorted back to the compound by an instructor.

"Hey, Pat, we can win this thing," Lawrence Obst tells his swim buddy.

"I don't know," replies Pat Yost. "The two jg's are pretty fast." Bill Gallagher and another junior grade lieutenant, a competition swimmer from the Naval Academy, have recorded the fastest swim times in the class.

"No way," says Obst. "Did you see them at the chow hall? They're both draggin' butt."

"Let's go for it," Yost agrees.

Petty Officer Second Class Pat Yost is five-nine and stocky, perhaps 160 pounds. He was a good high school swimmer back in Omaha. Yost is a Naval Reservist who came back on active duty for BUD/S training. Prior to returning to active duty, he was head counselor at the Stanford National Swimming Camp. At thirty years old, he's still a strong swimmer. Petty Officer Third Lawrence Obst, twenty-five, is five-ten, weighs 155, and never swam competitively. But he is a fierce competitor. His classmates call him Otter; he's quick in and out of the water. Obst grew up in Florida and is more accustomed to warm water. He, too, came to BUD/S from the reserves—twice. While in Hell Week with Class 217, he broke his leg during surf passage. On the one-mile swim, most of Class 228 chooses a steady stroke, relishing the comfort of a wet-suit top and the absence of instructors. Yost and Obst open a quick lead on the other swim pairs and finish the swim going away.

"Yost and Obst," Taylor observes as the two struggle back in through the surf. "I should have known. Good job, you guys. Have a seat on the beach. Take a break."

Gallagher and the other lieutenant finish next. The first three pairs get to sit on the beach. As the rest of the pairs make their way ashore, Chief Taylor has them strip off their wet-suit tops and puts them through surf torture.

Taylor continues to chide them. "Hey, fellows, hot showers just over the berm—dry clothes and a warm rack," he offers, but he gets no takers. Just to be fair, he puts the six winners back in the surf, but they don't mind. A little praise from Chief Taylor goes a long way. As the Hell Week class struggles in the surf, five of the previous DORs ring out all at once on the BUD/S grinder. Down on the beach, it sounds like a church bell calling the faithful to worship.

The class secures their swim and climbs back into their cold, wet fatigues. Brown shirts are again there to help out and slip them candy bars. Back on the beach, Instructor "Reg" Register, the day shift's leading petty officer, puts them back in the surf. Then he calls them back out for more run-paddle-run. As always, it pays to be a winner.

After the first race, it's obvious that two of the trainees are having difficulties. One of them is having trouble breathing; the other is throwing up blood. The instructors outwardly show no sympathy, but they carefully watch trainees who may be in physical distress. Chief Taylor calls over HM1 Richard Sprunger, the shift corpsman. Register is also standing by. The man in respiratory distress is sent immediately to medical; the one with the blood in his vomitus says he'll be all right, and rejoins his crew for another race. After the second race, he, too, is sent to medical. Neither man will finish the day with Class 228. The first, Airman Chris Robinson, is certified unfit to continue training after a chest X ray at the base clinic. He has pneumonia and is medically rolled back to a future class. The second is Daniel Bennett, Class 228's leading petty officer.

Bennett is simply too sick to continue and decides to leave training—to DOR. This was Bennett's second try at BUD/S. He and John Owens, also in 228, were here with Class 208. Both made it to Tuesday of Hell Week with 208. When I asked Daniel Bennett if he would be back again, he said probably not. Like most experienced petty officers who come to BUD/S, he has options in the Navy. Bennett is a qualified air crewman and a search-and-rescue instructor. He entered the Navy right out of high school and has ten years of service. Along the way, he earned a bachelor of science degree in criminal justice. He plans to apply for an aviation officer program. But Daniel Bennett left his mark on Class 228. He helped Bill Gallagher to organize the class for Hell Week, and he worked to develop the class petty officers into a solid cadre of enlisted leaders. While he was with 228, he earned the respect of his classmates and the instructors.

When the class comes off the beach and heads across the base for noon chow, they are down to four boat crews.

"Pat, you got it," Gallagher says as they run under the IBS. "Bennett's gone."

"Gone?" replies Pat Yost. He can't believe it. "You're kidding."

"I wish; you're my leading petty officer. Okay, Pat?"

"Aye-aye, sir."

"Cut the grab-ass under there and keep moving," Instructor Register tells them. "Bow to stern—bow to stern!"

Meals are a brief oasis in the middle of the suffering. Before and after entering the mess hall, the instructors put the trainees through PT and boat drills; once inside the chow hall they are given time to eat. After the noon meal, the four boats head for San Diego Bay. They launch on the eastern shore of the Amphibious Base, dump boat in the bay, and paddle for Fiddler's Cove, the Amphibious Base's marina, two miles south of the main base. During these paddles, the Hell Week class has some respite from the instructors, but it's still a race and it always pays to be a winner. Once at Fiddler's Cove and after another dunking, the trainees take their boats to a head carry. They jog across the sand spit and the Strand Highway to the Pacific. Chief Taylor halts them at the surf line.

"Ready to down boat—down boat." The trainees heave the boats off their heads and catch them by the carrying handles, careful not to bounce them on the sand.

"All right, gang," Taylor continues, "let's everybody get wet and sandy. I don't want to see one square inch of flesh or green material that's not covered with sand."

The trainees jog into the knee-deep surge and topple over into the water. Then they return to the soft sand and flop around until they look like cake doughnuts. Then Taylor has them do surf passage races. Winners get to sit for awhile. The sun is out and Taylor has them sit in a boat-crew file, bob-sled fashion, and lean back with faces up to work on their tans. Losers have to do surf laundry. They take off each piece of clothing, down to their tri-shorts, wash them in the surf, and neatly fold them on the hard sand. Hell Week is the first time the trainees are allowed to wear tri-shorts—black, Speedo-type nylon tights that come down to just above the knee. Tri-shorts help to combat what the trainees call crotch rot—the chaffing of their genitals and the inside of their thighs. Once a losing crew has done their laundry, they take a surf plunge and get dressed for the next race. It's not a bad evolution. Chief Taylor has a knack for keeping trainees cold, wet, and engaged.

Taylor, Register, and the rest of the day shift work the class under the watchful eyes of the shift officer in charge, or OIC. The shift OICs, with exception of Ensign Joe Burns on the evening shift, serve primarily as safety observers and seldom get involved with the mechanics of Hell Week. The day shift OIC is Lieutenant Phil Black. He is a Second Phase officer and the world's tallest SEAL. The height cutoff for BUD/S training is supposed to be six feet, six inches. Black was able to slump a little during his screen-

ing test and get into the program. He's six-foot eight. He has an easy smile
and lets his shift chief do his job. Apart from his primary job as safety officer, he is also responsible for the Hell Week log. This official record of Hell
Week training is passed from shift OIC to shift OIC.

After boat drills and surf laundry, the class takes their boats at a head
carry and follows Register two miles back up the beach to the BUD/S compound. Once there, they park the boats on the beach, then Taylor orders
them to remove their fatigue blouses. They line up on the beach.

"Every week at BUD/S you have a four-mile beach run. Hell Week is no
different. What's the First Phase cutoff time, Mister Gallagher?" Taylor
demands.

"Uh, thirty-two minutes, Chief."

"That's right, fellows, thirty-two minutes, and it pays to be winner.
Ready, GO!"

Twenty-eight white shirts head north along the beach toward the Hotel
del Coronado. As they pass the rocks, the class is badly strung out. A few
tourists on the beach watch with fascination and concern as these obvi-
ously tormented young men straggle past the hotel.

Three vehicles accompany the Hell Week class at all times. One is the
ambulance. The other two are extended-cab pickup trucks, one blue and
the other white—Big Blue and Great White. Near the North Island fence,
the trainees round Big Blue and head for home. Most are moving at little
more than a jog.

"What'd Chief Taylor mean," gasps one trainee to his running mate,
"thirty-two minutes?"

"Beats me. Maybe . . . maybe this is a graded run."

"No way," says the first runner. Then he adds, "You really think so?"

For one of them, it doesn't matter. If it's a race of any kind, Otter Obst
will try to win it. And he usually does. It's not often that a trainee makes
the thirty-two-minute cutoff in Hell Week, but Obst does easily. Chief
Taylor is at the finish line with Stephen Schultz, the evening shift chief petty
officer.

"H-T-Three Obst," he gasps as he runs past them. "H-T-Three Obst."
Hull Technician Third Class Obst has at least three hundred yards on
the next trainee. The two CPOs exchange a grin; they like a good effort
and they really like Obst.

"Not bad, Obst, not bad," Taylor says, looking at his watch. He turns
to two of the brown shirts. "Morrison, Luttrell. Take this man up to the
compound and find him some dry clothes."

The two brown shirts guide the Otter over the berm. Behind the BUD/S
clinic there is a laundry facility where the brown shirts wash and dry the
Hell Week class's shirts, socks, and fatigues. Clothes from those who DOR
are cycled into the rotation as fatigues and T-shirts become ripped or lose
buttons. While Lawrence Obst sits on the beach in dry fatigues, Taylor
surf-tortures the rest of Class 228.

"Good run, Obst."

"Thank you, Chief Schultz." Schultz slips him a candy bar. "Thanks
again, Chief."

Schultz doesn't reply. He wanders out to where Taylor is working the
others in the surf. He watches for a while, then relieves Taylor in mid–surf
torture. Ensign Joe Burns takes the Hell Week log from Phil Black and the
evening shift takes over.

"Let's round them up, Tim," Schultz says. "Time to start across the base
for the chow hall."

The four IBSs leave the center in elephant-walk file, following Instructor
Timothy Hickman at a brisk pace across the berm dune. They cross the
Strand Highway to the main portion of the base. Hickman gives them a
brisk round of boat drills and sends them into the chow hall.

"Eat well," he tells them. "Tonight you're going to need all your
strength."

To survive Hell Week, a trainee has to do two things: take the punishment being dished out, and get past thinking about the punishment to come.
Often, the latter will break a man quicker than the former. Hell Week lasts
five days and five nights, but most SEALs will tell you that Monday night
of Hell Week was the most miserable experience of their life. The trainees

in Class 228 know what's coming. The brown shirts and trainees from previous classes have told them what to expect. They all fear Monday night.

"Come Tuesday morning," one instructor tells me, "we will pretty much have what we want out of a class. From then on we try to keep them moving and keep them from getting hurt."

The Hell Week class goes into Monday evening having had little rest and no sleep for the past thirty-six hours. The men have been cold, wet, and tormented for the last twenty-four. They still have four nights and four days ahead of them—an eternity. As they eat their evening meal, they think about this. For three of them, just thinking about it causes them to get up from the table and DOR. One of them is another Naval Academy ensign. Class 228 began First Phase with eight officers, all Academy men. Now six remain.

After chow, four boats and twenty-five trainees head for the combat training tank (CTT) for a quick hygiene inspection. They strip to their trishorts and stand in the decontamination station, a tubular, awninglike affair that serves as a car wash for BUD/S trainees prior to entering the pool. It's a miserable, cold-water treatment, but they've all done it before. The class is in the decon station for only a few minutes—a few minutes in the cold mist with time to think. Two more DORs.

From the CTT, the four boats elephant-walk a few hundred yards to the SDV piers, also called the steel piers by the Hell Week classes due to their construction. This pier complex served SDV Team One until the team relocated to Hawaii. The tide is low. Just off the quay wall, there is a floating steel caisson served by a steep metal brow. Burns tells the trainees to take off their boots, then sends them down the ramp to form in a line along the edge of the steel float. He gives them a few moments to think about what's in store for them. Another man DORs.

"Everyone in the water," he yells from the top of the brow, and the twenty-two remaining members of Class 228 splash into the dark waters of San Diego Bay. Instructor Dan Maclean, the shift corpsman, checks the water temperature—sixty-six degrees. He relays this to Joe Burns. Burns checks his watch; he knows the immersion tables by heart. He tells them to spread out and tread water. After about ten minutes of treading water, he tells the trainees to take off their fatigue blouses and toss them up onto the steel deck. It makes little difference temperature-wise, but undressing in cold water makes them feel more vulnerable and cold. One of the brown shirts collects their blouses and takes them to the top of the quay wall. After another ten minutes Burns calls, "All right, out of the pool and back up on the shore." The trainees numbly hoist themselves from the water and file up the ramp, hugging their shivering bodies for warmth. Most can't stop their teeth from chattering.

Instructor Hickman gives them back their shirts, leads fifteen minutes of calisthenics, and then sends them back into the water. Burns checks his watch; they get fifteen minutes this time.

"You guys having fun?" Burns yells to them.

"You bet, Mister Burns."

"C'mon in, the water's f-fine."

Joe Burns grins. He likes it when tired, cold trainees show a little spunk.

"Cap-tain Bow-en!"

"HOOYAH, CAPTAIN BOWEN!"

Bowen makes his way down the ramp and joins Burns, who is now on the steel float.

"Evening, sir," the First Phase officer greets him.

"Evening, Joe," Bowen replies, returning his salute. "How we doing?"

"Hard to say. They're feeling pretty sorry for themselves right now. We'll see."

Bowen nods. He knows about Monday night. He kneels and splashes his hand in the water.

"Yep, feels like bathwater to me." He regards the class for a long moment. "You guys hanging in there?"

"HOOYAH!" comes the weak response.

"Carry on, men," he replies, and heads back up the brow.

They hooyah him again as he leaves. Bowen joins the medical officer and Chief Schultz on the quay wall. There is a tense feeling among those gathered to watch the class during the steel piers evolution. This is a fragile time for Class 228. None of them want to see any more DORs, but it's not in their hands. The evolution has to run its course, and 228 will have to get through it, just like Class 227 and all the classes before them. Burns again checks his watch and the class continues to tread water.

"Bill, I'm cold. I'm gonna quit."

"What?"

"I've had it. I'm gonna quit. You going with me?"

Gallagher stares at him; he can't believe it. It's his swim buddy, the other lieutenant in the class. Like Gallagher, he's a fleet officer, surface warfare qualified. And a Naval Academy graduate.

"You coming?"

Adam Karaoguz, a durable, no-nonsense second class petty officer, is close enough to catch the exchange. He doesn't mince words. "Let the sonuvabitch quit if he wants," he says to his class leader, "but you stay right here." If Gallagher had any thoughts of joining his swim buddy, Karaoguz quashes them. The tall officer pulls himself up onto the float, leaving Gallagher and Karaoguz behind. Burns is waiting for him.

"You want to quit, sir."

"Yes, Ensign Burns."

"You sure?"

"Yeah, I'm sure," he says without hesitation.

"Go on up there and see Chief Schultz." Burns turns his back on him and looks at the trainees in the water. He doesn't like quitters—officer quitters even less. Class 228 is down to five officers. Then he again checks his watch. Fifteen minutes: no more, no less.

The trainees get ten minutes more PT on the quay wall, shed their shirts and socks, and get another ten minutes in the water. After another round of PT, they are again sent down the ramp to see if anyone else is thinking about quitting. Instead of ordering them into the water, Burns calls them back up to the quay wall. They are told to climb back into their wet clothes and to fall in on their boats. The brown shirts pass among them with cups of hot chicken broth. Most of the trainees are shaking so badly they can scarcely hold a cup with both hands, let alone guide it to their mouth.

"Oh, man," says Seaman Brendan Dougherty. "I never tasted anything this good in my life." He turns to a brown shirt and trades his empty cup for a full one.

"Mister Gallagher, get over here."

Gallagher steps over to where Joe Burns waits for him by the ambulance.

"Mister Gallagher, I know you've lost a lot of guys in the last few hours, but that happens in Hell Week. Don't let it get to you."

He nods. "Understood."

"You going to quit?"

"No way, Ensign Burns. No way I'm going to quit."

"Then step it up a notch, sir. This class needs you to take charge. They need you to lead these men. Get with it, okay?"

"Yes, Ensign Burns. I'll do my best."

Gallagher rejoins his classmates, and tries to control his shaking enough to drink some broth. He thinks about what Burns has just said and resolves to do better. But his confidence is badly shaken. He never believed so many would quit so soon. Some of them he thought would never DOR. And his own swim buddy; he was the best swimmer in the class.

"Okay, fall in by height and count off," Chief Schultz tells them. They mingle and try to get in a line. "Too slow, too slow. Drop."

After several sets of push-ups, Schultz gets them in a line by height, cuts them into three boat crews, and sends them to their boats. Hell Week is a little more than twenty-four-hours old and the class has been cut in half.

The three boats are ordered to proceed on to Turner Field on the eastern portion of the Amphibious Base. This evolution is a Hell Week boat-crew Olympics of sorts referred to as Lyons' Lope. Lyons' Lope is another antic-ipated, dreaded evolution of Hell Week. It's named for Scott Lyons—the same Vietnam-era SEAL and former First Phase officer who spoke at Class 225's graduation. The crews race around Turner Field with and without the boats on their heads. Back in the water without boats, the crews form caterpillar-like daisy chains and stroke back and forth around the eastern end of the base. Sometimes the human chains use IBS paddles, sometimes they paddle with their hands. The water temperature away from the steel piers is a little colder, but the trainees are now fully clothed and have on their life vests. As the human centipedes paddle close to the shoreline, one of the taller men in each chain is able to touch the bottom and propel the crew along due to the low tide. The trainees think they are having one over on the instructors, and that warms them. In reality, Chief Schultz and his crew know exactly what they're doing. If the boat crews are trying to cheat a little, it means they're working together. The instructors won't call them on it unless it's blatant. It takes about forty-five minutes to complete Lyons' Lope. The winners are the tall crew led by Clint Burke.

"I'd say that was a pretty good race, Chief Schultz," Joe Burns says within hearing of the trainees. "What do you think?"

"I'm not so sure. I think Mister Burke's crew cheated on their last run around the field. I don't think they stayed on the road the whole way. I think they cut across the grass."

"Cheated?" Burns does his best to sound incredulous. The semicoherent trainees hang on every word. "Chief, I'm shocked. But if you think there was foul play, then I guess we'll just have to do it again. Line 'em up. Coxswains, get over here."

"But Chief, we didn't cheat," Burke protests, quickly adding, "on the run, I mean." He's like a grade school kid being wrongly accused of a playground infraction. "Honest, we didn't cut across the grass."

"I'm sorry, sir," Schultz says in a show of sympathy, working to suppress a smile, "but it's out of my hands."

Burke, Gallagher, and Ensign Will Koella are now the boat-crew leaders. Schultz again briefs the three boat crews on Lyons' Lope and they race off once more around Turner Field.

One man is unable to continue, Seaman Miguel Yanez came into Hell Week with a partial shoulder separation. He was offered a medical rollback, but he wanted to try to stay with his class. Now he's in a great deal of pain, and he knows he's hurting his boat crew. He goes to Instructor

Maclean, who sends him off to the Center clinic. Joe Burns gives him a pat on the back as he gets into the ambulance. It's interesting for me to watch the different ways men leave Class 228. For some, it's a curt nod from the shift chief and a simple formality for the shift OIC. Others, like Yanez, are escorted from the field with honor. The instructors saw Yanez as a team player who played with pain. His classmates hate to see him go. So does his boat crew, even though he was holding them back. The staff wants to afford a man like this every opportunity to get through training. Yanez's shoulder will need time to heal. He'll be rolled back to a future class; he'll get another chance.

Ensign Burke's crew, Boat One, again wins Lyons' Lope, and the three crews move on to the CTT for pool games. Time in the pool is a blessing for the class; the water temperature is in the high seventies. At the pool, Ensign Burns has them swimming relay races, then involves them in a diving contest from the one-meter platform. They are graded on backflips and belly flops. Winners get a few moments in the locker room, where it's warm; losers go to the decon station for a cold shower. After one of the decon sessions, Will Koella signals for the corpsman.

"Instructor Maclean, I think you better have a look at Ensign Birch. I think he's in trouble."

Maclean nods. He had been watching Birch for a while, noticing that he occasionally ran in the wrong direction on Lyons' Lope. Now he was having trouble in the pool.

"Mister Birch, get over here."

Jason Birch pads over to him. Maclean asks him a few questions and gets gibberish for a reply. Birch's tightly muscled body is shaking all over, but then so is Koella's.

"I got it, sir," Maclean tells Koella. "Go on back with the class." Koella leaves them.

"Mister Birch. How old are you?"

"H-how old am I?" Birch replies. "W-why do you want to know that?"

"How old are you, sir?"

Birch forces a smile. "Y'know, I should know that. H-how old are you, Instructor?"

While Birch ponders the question of his age, Maclean leads him to the ambulance parked outside the CTT. He puts the trainee inside and proceeds to shove a temperature probe up his rectum. A moment later, the digital readout flashes 89.5 degrees. Maclean disconnects the probe from the monitor, not from Birch. Next, the corpsman pricks Birch's finger for a quick blood sugar reading. It's low, as Maclean suspected it would be. The ensign's temperature is dangerously low, and he doesn't have the fuel to stoke the furnace. He gives Birch a tube of glucose to suck on.

"How is he?" Chief Schultz, seeing them leave the pool area, had followed them to the ambulance.

"He's a cold puppy," Maclean replies. "Call medical and tell them I'm on the way." Maclean speeds across the base for the BUD/S clinic while Jason Birch sucks the plastic tube of glucose flat.

At the BUD/S clinic, Lieutenant Pete Witucki is waiting for them. They help Birch from the ambulance; he's still talking gibberish. They quickly plug him into the clinic monitor, but he's not gaining much ground. His body temp is 90.1. They begin to slowly immerse Birch in the clinic hot tub that's kept on standby at 98 degrees for this very purpose. First, just his pelvis and torso. Dr. Witucki immediately starts an IV of warm saline and again checks his blood sugar; it's still low. The oral glucose takes a while, so Witucki begins to push dextrose through the IV. By the time his limbs are fully immersed, Jason Birch is sleeping soundly and there is a huge smile on his face.

"How are you feeling?" Witucki asks him as he prods him awake.

Birch comes awake with a start, then realizes where he is. "I feel great," he says with a broad grin, then admits, "I can't believe it; I'm warm."

"You're 98.6. Ready to go back?"

"Do I have to?" Birch replies, still grinning.

"It's up to you," says Witucki, watching him carefully. Many are not able to face the cold after finally getting warm.

Birch doesn't hesitate. "Yes, sir, I'm ready to go back."

Ensign Birch is put in a dry set of clothes and one of the clinic corpsmen drives him back across the base. Class 228 is running relay races on Turner Field and is now being hounded by the night shift. The underground sprinklers are on, and the trainees run through the cold rain with their shirts off.

"Well, if it isn't Ensign Birch. Welcome back, sir."

"Thank you, Instructor Patstone."

"Are you nice and warm?"

"Yes, Instructor Patstone."

"And dry, too?" He fingers Birch's fresh fatigues.

"Yes, Instructor Patstone."

"Why don't you just trot over to the bay and get yourself wet and sandy?"

Birch heads for the bay. Since there is very little sand on the bay side, he rolls in the mud. Once back to Turner Field, he strips off his shirt and joins the relay races in the sprinklers. After the races, the class falls back in on the boats for IBS drills.

"I could sure use a dip," announces Instructor Ron Rector. "Any of you guys got some snuce?"

"Sure, Karaoguz does," replies one of the trainees. Karaoguz glares at him, but his classmate is too goofy from exhaustion to understand what he's done.

"Excellent," Rector says politely. "Do you mind?" Adam Karaoguz pulls a round tin of snuff from his blouse and offers it to him. "I just need a small pinch," Rector continues as he carefully takes some. "You can have the rest—all of it—right now."

The class continues with IBS and whistle drills. It's another half hour or more before Karaoguz has a chance to spit out the mouthful of tobacco. At 0200 Class 228 starts running with the boats on their heads. This evolution is called the Base Tour. They will run around the base for the next two hours with only two water breaks, one to drink and one to get wet and sandy. For many in 228, the Base Tour is the worst they will suffer during this long and punishing night. More than a few will call this the worst night of Hell Week. During the IBS tour of the base, Petty Officer Mark Williams is pulled from his IBS and probed. He registers 90.5 degrees and is sent to medical to be thawed out. The rest of the class keeps running under the boats. Williams is able to rejoin the class for breakfast. It's Tuesday morning, and twenty men from Class 228 are there to greet Chief Taylor and the day shift when they come on duty.

Tuesday is one long day of beach games, surf passage, run-paddle-run, and dragging the boats over the O-course. Always, it pays to be a winner. Chief Taylor is everywhere—pushing them, flying into mock fits of rage, challenging them to do their best. When they put out and show spirit, he rewards them. When they finish a race last or start to feel sorry for themselves, he comes down on them. The day shift has a special treat for losers. In the back of Great White is an IBS full of ice and water. Losers or trainees who show poor spirit are sent for a quick dip through the cold slurry. Most of them have now been up for over fifty-six hours. They're in a mental fog, yet none of them wants to disappoint Chief Taylor. The losers take their licks, ashamed that they didn't do better. Clint Burke, with the Otter and some of the taller men in Boat One, wins most of the competitions. Bill Gallagher, in Boat Two, and Will Koella, with the smurfs in Boat Three, fight it out not to be last.

Late that afternoon, Mark Williams DORs. Few in 228 are more respected or better liked than Williams. That goes for trainees as well as the First Phase staff. He's with Boat One, and he's starting to hold them back. It's Tuesday afternoon, and he's having trouble breathing due to fluid in his lungs. This is his second Hell Week and he's having the same problem.

"Anything we can do for you?" Taylor asks him. Williams is surrounded by concerned instructors. They want Williams to stay, but it has to be his choice. He shakes his head, thanks them for their concern, and walks off the beach. HM1 Sprunger, the shift corpsman, accompanies him over to BUD/S medical. Since this is his second consecutive Hell Week, Williams will have to leave BUD/S.

After evening chow, the three boats do their elephant walk back to the

Center and to medical for a hygiene check. To one degree or another, most of them have swollen knees and ankles. Many are starting to develop a bald spot on top of their heads from the boats. Ensign Chad Steinbrecher is held at the clinic; his knees are badly swollen and he can barely walk. The previous night and day of walking under the boats have almost made a cripple of him. He stays in medical, but he's not happy about it. Ensign Will Koella is not much better, but able to stay with his classmates as they launch their boats for the paddle to North Island Naval Air Station.

The night's drill will be IBS cache and E&E—escape and evasion. After the two-and-a-half-mile paddle to North Island, they cache the boats and are divided up into pairs. Chad Steinbrecher clears medical and rejoins the class. The trainees are sent at a run north along the beach for a half mile to the main lifeguard tower on the North Island recreational beach. From there they have to make their way back to the boats and trucks while avoiding the instructors who are out looking for them. It's a grand game of hide-and-seek. This is another traditional Hell Week evolution, and the evading pairs all have their own ideas on how to beat the instructors.

Brendan Dougherty and Seaman Grant Terpstra hatch a glorious scheme to get dry and warm. They sprint over to the bachelor enlisted quarters, an out-of-bounds area, and make for the laundry. Confident no one will be there at that time of night, they plan to strip down and dry their clothes. But a woman is there doing her laundry, so their plan is foiled. But since they're out of bounds, they're relatively safe from the instructors. They walk south across the North Island base golf course and sneak up close to the boats. There they are able to hide and take turns dozing until the recall.

Gallagher and Karaoguz do a low crawl across the sandy backshore away from the beach. They, too, decide to walk back across the golf course, but they get caught. The instructor pretends to buy Gallagher's story about not understanding boundaries, and he lets them go. Yost and John Owens are caught in one of the parking lots near the beach. They are ordered across the beach and into the surf. When they get to the waterline, they drop down and begin crab-walking south along the beach toward the boats. There they are able to hide until the recall. Most of the trainees have daring stories of outfoxing the instructors, but for the most part, Chief Schultz and the evening crew simply turn a blind eye. As long as the trainees make an attempt to evade and don't get too far out of bounds, they let them go. However, one pair really does get one over. A white pickup rolls slowly along the road that parallels the beach and stops near two not-so-well-hidden trainees.

"Hey, you guys want a lift?" Seaman Dan Luna and Airman Zack Shaffer don't move, unsure how to respond. "C'mon, jump in the back. It's okay, we're not the bad guys."

It's a pair of U.S. customs agents on patrol who decide to help the BUD/S trainees. Luna and Shaffer look at each other and shrug, then scramble into the back of the pickup. One of the agents covers them with a blanket and hands them a couple of sandwiches. A thermos of hot coffee follows. The customs agents continue their patrol and deliver the two trainees to a spot near the boats shortly before the end of the evolution. Luna and Shaffer arrive at the IBS cache a bit less haggard than their classmates. It's not the first time American servicemen have been aided by friendly partisans while crossing enemy-held territory.

Every night except Monday night, the trainees are allowed midnight rations, or midrats. Tonight it's field rations, known as MREs (short for meals ready to eat), and hot broth. Again they are given time to eat, and allowed to eat as much as they want. By the time Ensign Burns hands the Hell Week log to Warrant Officer Randy Beausoleil, the trainees are almost dry. The demons of the night shift, as Class 228 calls them, immediately put them in the water.

"It's part of the process," Chief Nielson says. "If they're warm and dry, we get them wet. If they're cold and wet, we warm them up. Since we usually pick them up after midrats, we become the bad guys and get them wet."

Nielson is more philosophical than Taylor or Schultz, the other two shift CPOs. "How do you organize the shift?" I ask him. "How do you decide who's going to harass the trainees and how?"

"I get the shift together before we go on duty and we talk about who's going to do what—who will be in charge of each evolution."

Every Hell Week evolution, from the E&E exercise to IBS rock portage, is conducted from an approved Navy training plan. Each instructor must be certified before he can be in charge of an evolution. To earn this certification, an instructor must first observe the evolution, and then conduct the evolution under the supervision of a certified instructor.

"Who becomes huggers and who becomes haters is something we sort out among ourselves. Usually, it follows the personality of the instructor and their level of experience. It just isn't in some guys to be a hard-ass. It doesn't work for them. And it's not easy to be mean. The haters have a more difficult job and they work a lot harder. Overall, we try to be consistent. If the trainees do it right, we give them a break; they do it wrong, we hammer them. Sometimes getting hammered is preplanned—just part of the evolution."

After a short period of surf torture, the three boats begin paddling south from North Island for Silver Strand State Park, some six miles down the coast. The trainees have quickly learned that when they are paddling, they don't have to put up with harassment from the instructors. If it's a long paddle, they have a chance to dry out. Except for the pain of not being a winner, the three-boat regatta has little incentive to make the paddle swiftly.

Nielson, Instructor Annandono, the night shift LPO, and Warrant Officer Beausoleil roll along the beach in Big Blue. Instructor Patstone follows in the ambulance. Nielson looks at his watch and then at Beausoleil. Beausoleil, the night shift OIC, is a quiet former enlisted man who is in charge of PTRR and the Indoctrination Course. He saw action in Panama. For the most part, he lets Chief Nielson run the shift. The trainees are taking their time on the paddle south, probably even taking turns trying to get some sleep. The instructors don't necessarily mind this, but they're starting to fall behind a very strict schedule.

"Call 'em in?" asks Nielson.

Beausoleil agrees. "Call 'em in."

The trainees are called to shore just south of the Hotel del—no more paddling. They now have to run with the boats bouncing on their heads trying to keep up with a fast-walking instructor. The composition of the boat crews, which continually changed as the class shrunk, now has a new look. Ensign Clint Burke—at six feet, five inches—is now a smurf. The crews are normally sorted by height and to evenly distribute the officer and petty officer leadership. The shorter crew has survived well. Four of the original seven smurfs—Harry Pell, Dan Luna, Zack Shaffer, and Zack Armstrong—are still aboard. But Boat Three was falling behind Boats One and Two. With the big officer in the rear and the smaller men forward, the boat now has the forward lean of a classic hot rod. The smurf boat is also suddenly very competitive in the boat races. For the moment, the race is to stay up with the long-striding Annandono as he walks them south along the water's edge. Terry Patstone tailgates the third boat with a laugh box held to a loudspeaker. The penalty for being last is the shrieking laugh track that is played over and over again at full volume.

Upon arriving at the state beach, four miles south of the Center, the three boats cross over the Strand Highway to the San Diego Bay side and the mudflats. Trial by mud has been a part of Hell Week since the days at Fort Pierce in the mangrove swamps of the Florida coast. First, the trainees are directed to build a fire. The ambulance, Great White, and Big Blue are parked facing east so their headlights play across the fine, silty goo that collects in this part of San Diego Bay. The mudflat games begin. There are boat-crew races, wheelbarrow races, relay races, leapfrog races, fireman's-carry races; races where the trainees crawl on their stomachs; races where they wriggle along on their backs. They make mud angels, on their stomachs, facedown. This is dirty work, but relatively harmless. However, John Owens does a head-plant so deep in the mud that he needs help from another trainee to pull him free before he smothers or breaks his neck.

Winners get a few moments by the fire; losers race again. The stench and taste of the brackish silt cause a few to bring up their midrat MREs. No matter how tired they are, the trainees always compete, trying for a break from the misery or to earn an extra bit of warmth. At first, this seems like mindless harassment, but BUD/S is a sorting process to identify those who have a will to win—to win under any conditions. The Vietnam-era SEALS recall the mudflats as training wheels for combat patrols in the rice paddies and mangrove swamps of the Mekong Delta. Bill Gallagher and Adam Karaoguz finish one of the footraces in a dead heat. But Instructor Annandono declares Gallagher the winner and sends him to the fire.

"What?" challenges Karaoguz. "Hey, I won that race."

Annandono directs him back to the starting line for the next mud sprint. "This is bullshit!"

"Say what?" Chief Nielson steps from behind the muddy trainee and confronts him. Nielson has his hands in his pockets and speaks quietly.

Karaoguz doesn't back down, but his tone is more respectful. "I said this is bullshit, Chief."

"Really?" He regards Karaoguz a moment. "Come over here."

Adam Karaoguz came to BUD/S from the USS *Tarawa* (LHA-1), where he was a second class boatswain's mate. He grew up in upstate New York and is a first-generation Turkish-American. Karaoguz is one of the better runners in the class, but otherwise an average performer. His strong suit is his durability; he's very tough. His division officer on the *Tarawa* claimed, "If there's anyone on this whole ship who can make it through SEAL training, it's Adam Karaoguz."

Nielson takes Karaoguz over to a fresh, untracked plot of mud for some individual attention. Soon the trainee is breaststroking, duckwalking, and burrowing through the silt. After a few minutes of this both of them are laughing. Karaoguz can handle whatever is asked of him, willingly and often with a grin on his face. He's an ideal Hell Week trainee; the harder it gets, the stronger he gets. Nielson knows this and approves. Both tormentor and tormented understand their roles.

"Go get a swim buddy," Nielson tells him. Karaoguz pulls Pat Yost from a relay race, and soon the two of them are doing Eskimo rolls—somersaults with each man holding the other's ankles. They look like fudge brownies with arms and legs.

Mud games last an hour and a half. The class is then sent into deeper water to wash off enough of the mud so they can get into the chow hall. Following the wash down, they paddle north along the western shoreline of the bay to return to the Amphibious Base.

After breakfast, it's back to the Center for hygiene inspection. The Hell Week class has been checked morning and evening by the medical staff, but now the clinic medical officers are inspecting them very closely. In spite of the antibiotics they received before Hell Week began, their immune systems are struggling. By Wednesday morning, most of them have been up for three full days with no sleep. The two doctors and their very capable physician's assistant are alert for a host of problems, not the least of which could include an outbreak of flesh-eating bacteria.

The medical inspection is a gauntlet of sorts—much like what happens when a race car comes in for a pit stop. First the trainees strip to their trishorts in the outside shower at the Center barracks. Here they wash off the top layer of mud and dirt. The brown shirts pack their wet clothes off to the laundry and the trainees move on to the inside showers. After they get spritzed with a disinfectant, they scrub themselves down with antiseptic scouring pads. They get a brief taste of hot water, followed by a cold shock as they stand before hall fans to dry off. They then pad over to the clinic, where they queue up to be inspected by one of the three medical officers. Along the way, the brown shirts take every opportunity to slip them a candy bar or a wedge of orange.

The medical officers are meticulous and quick. They inspect their hands, feet, and genitals, and carefully listen to their chests. All the while, they ask questions. Some trainees will admit to problems and others won't; often the docs have to be detectives as well as physicians. Instructor Patstone is on hand with each trainee's chart of medication history. Some continue with prescribed antibiotics; others will now begin to take them. Patstone notes any dosage changes. A few of the trainees are allowed Motrin, but the medical staff does not dispense it freely.

After they leave the exam room, the trainees pause to swab their crotch and groin areas with a vitamin A&D ointment. Most pull on one of the available cloth penis socks that will help with the sand and chafing. They leave the clinic through the side door, where two brown shirts are waiting for them. One at a time, the trainees step through an ice-water bucket in their bare feet and take a seat on a picnic table. One of the brown shirts sprays their feet with a disinfectant, another swabs them with a topical silicon gel, and they're done—good to go for another round. Next to the picnic table is a line of milk crates, one per trainee with his name on it. Each has a change of dry clothes; for a brief moment, they are warm and in dry clothes. But just around the corner is an instructor from the day shift ready and waiting with a water hose to get them wet. Next is a trip across the beach and into the surf. Then a roll on the beach and 228 is again cold, wet, and sandy.

. . .

Wednesday morning means the day shift, Chief Taylor, and beach games. There are nineteen of them left; five officers and fourteen enlisted men. Ensign Steinbrecher has pneumonia, and is sent across the base for a chest X ray to see how bad. Seaman Chris Baldwin is running a fever. Both clear medical and are able to rejoin the class, but Steinbrecher now has problems with his lungs and his legs. Wednesday afternoon brings something new and different to the weary trainees—a sleep period.

How much sleep a class gets and when it gets it varies from Hell Week to Hell Week. Class 228 will be given a total of five hours of scheduled sleep during its Hell Week. After noon chow and a full hour of run-paddle-run, Chief Taylor sends the trainees to the one remaining tent for their first sleep period. The second tent is no longer needed and has been struck. The brown shirts are waiting to slip them a candy bar and help them to their cots. Inside the tent, the air is damp and heavy with stale sweat. Some fall asleep immediately. Others have fought to stay awake so desperately, their bodies will not turn off. They simply lie on their cots staring mindlessly at the canvas ceiling. A few sit and doze, or walk around, afraid that if they give themselves over to sleep, they will lose the courage to get up and keep going.

The brown shirts are led by Ensign Eric Oehlerich and Petty Officer Sean Morrison. They do what they can to help the Hell Week class. Oehlerich was a Naval Academy classmate of the four ensigns in 228; Morrison is a former marine. Both successfully completed Hell Week with Class 227 and will join Class 228 in Second Phase. They encourage their future classmates and tell them that they're doing well—to hang in there and not give up.

Oehlerich and Morrison are assigned to the day shift to help with Hell Week, but they work around the clock to support 228. The previous night they swam out to intercept the three boats as they paddled north to North Island. They delivered bananas and candy bars in Ziploc bags to the Hell Week class. The chow was appreciated, but it was the show of support and the idea of getting one over on the instructors that really cheered the men of 228. In reality, very little gets past the instructors. Brown shirts slipping treats to the Hell Week class is as much of a BUD/S tradition as cold water and sand. Many a future SEAL conducted his first special operation in clandestine support of a Hell Week class.

While 228 sleeps, or tries to, the instructors leave them alone in the care of the brown shirts. For those who are awake or struggling to stay awake, Seaman Marc Luttrell, a corpsman striker and a brown shirt, is there to help. Luttrell works with them to stretch and massage their legs to avoid cramping. For some, the problem is with their hamstrings and hip flexors. These muscles have been worked constantly for three days and now convulse with inactivity. The first sleep period lasts an hour and forty-five minutes.

Fweeeeet! A long whistle breaks the silence. "Let's go! Let's go! Time to hit the surf!" It's Instructor Hickman with the evening shift.

Inside, some trainees simply rise and stagger to the tent opening. Others bolt upright, wide awake but totally confused. It takes a few moments for them to break through their dazed condition to figure out where they are. Once reality sinks in, they drag themselves from their cots to shuffle after their classmates. Still others need to be called back from the dead. With assistance from the brown shirts, they rise like zombies, unsure of what's happening, but somehow knowing that they must be up and moving. The brown shirts help them move toward the door and prod them along. "C'mon, you can do it. Once you get moving you'll be all right. Hang in there; you're gonna be fine."

"Come on sleepyheads, time for a little dip. Let's go!"

Like baby loggerhead turtles, they scramble across the sand and into the surf. Some literally crawl up the berm and down the other side to the water.

Trainees have been known to quit when sent into the water after a sleep period. All nineteen members of Class 228 get themselves into the surf. Hickman surf-tortures them for fifteen minutes—no quitters. They fall in on the boats and take them to a head carry for the run to chow.

After the evening hygiene inspection at the CTT, they have pool games—and warm water. Joe Burns takes over from his shift petty officers and directs 228 in a game of king of the hill, or king of the IBS. The trainees fight to see who can stay in the IBS and who gets tossed over the side. More often than not, Clint Burke is the king. He's bigger than his classmates and a growing force in 228's Hell Week. The class is slowly dividing into those who have the strength and drive to perform and those who are just hanging on. Often this is a simple matter of who is eating and able to keep it down, and who cannot. But the water is not cold and it's competition—a good evolution for Class 228.

After pool games, the class dresses and rigs the boats for land travel. They're soaked and cold from a good dousing in the CTT decon area. Chief Schultz quietly approaches each of the boat crews.

"You guys did a good job during pool games. We got a long night ahead of us. I want you to stay focused and work together."

He slips each boat-crew leader a handful of candy. Each crew thinks they have joined Schultz in getting one over on Ensign Burns and the rest of the staff. It's part of a good cop–bad cop routine. Schultz has not misled them. They do have a long night ahead. Soon they are back across the base and following Ensign Burns south along the beach. He doesn't walk fast, but he keeps walking for about four miles to Silver Strand State Park and back. Burns literally walks their legs off; they can barely stand by the time they get back near the Center. They've been walking for four hours. This walk south on the beach was a last-minute change. The Hell Week schedule called for them to carry the boats around the base on what is known as the Treasure Hunt evolution. Boat crews are given clues from one destination to the next. They must solve the riddle and lug the boats to and from a series of checkpoints. But Burns is concerned about some of the leg and knee problems in the class. Racing around the base, with its curbs and uneven ground, is an invitation to further leg injuries. He elects a beach walk—a long beach walk. The boat crews can barely stand, but at least there are no injuries and they've had time to dry out.

"Ready to down boat," Burns commands. "Down boat." The trainees gratefully heave the boats from their heads to the sand. "Rig for surf passage." The trainees take their life jacket straps and loop them down under their crotches to secure them in place. They take their places by their boats with paddles in hand, knowing what is next.

"Hit the surf!"

After a half hour of surf passage, the boats are back on their heads and they're doing the familiar elephant walk back across the base for midrats. Meals have become a dreamy hiatus in an existence of cold and pain. But midrats mean that Instructor Patstone is back, along with the dreaded night shift.

"Two glasses of water," Patstone tells them as he walks among the seated trainees. "At least two glasses of water or we all drop for push-ups. You, sir, drink—eat!"

The class continues to segregate itself into eaters and nibblers. Clint Burke, Pat Yost, Lawrence Obst, Adam Karaoguz, and Chris Baldwin lead the eaters. Bill Gallagher, Will Koella, and Brendan Dougherty are among the nibblers. Patstone tries, but he can do little to change these patterns. The eaters continue to shovel it in while the nibblers barely get enough to keep them going; ultimately, the nibblers struggle to perform.

After midrats they are back on the beach near the Center for the evolution called Surf Camp. Chief Nielson sets them to digging a large pit on the beach. Pell, the former marine, is made to walk sentry duty around the beach dig with his paddle shouldered like a rifle. When the pit is finished, they are instructed to build a large roaring fire nearby. After some miscellaneous beach games and surf torture, they gather back near the fire. Next the boats are placed over the large sandpit and the nineteen trainees crowd into this beach burrow. They are allowed ten minutes of rest under the boats, ten seconds by the fire, and two minutes in the surf. It's a hideous, abusive sequence—dozing under the boats, a fleeting pass by the warm fire, then a plunge into the now fifty-seven-degree water. They do it again and again. At 0400 they begin their second sleep period.

The instructors again leave the trainees alone. Some of them cuddle together in the pit and sleep like a warren of opossums. Others, remembering the pain of waking up from a sound sleep, doze lightly and try to keep from going down hard. Many simply stretch and walk about, trying to keep their leg muscles and hip flexors from seizing up. Even the ones who remain awake hover on the ragged edge of consciousness. Some are beginning to hallucinate—to see things that are not there.

Patstone rouses them after an hour and forty-five minutes—first by sounding the siren from the ambulance, then the laugh box on the loudspeaker. Again there is confusion, then acceptance; they are back in hell. The groggy trainees tumble from the sleeping pit and into the surf. Again, some of them have to crawl, but they do it.

Back under the boats, they struggle across the base to the chow hall for breakfast and back to the Center for morning hygiene check. The medical staff gives them a thorough inspection. This is the last full-on medical class inspection until the class secures from Hell Week tomorrow afternoon. Ensign Steinbrecher is again pulled from the class—knees and lungs. The other eighteen men cross the base to CTT for pool games.

The warm water in the pool somewhat revives them. Chief Taylor has them doing IBS races in the pool, but with simple, very specific instructions. And it pays to be a winner. For one of the races he selects a junior man in each crew to be the boat-crew leader. He tells them that they must have their boat crews paddle one length of the pool using only their hands. On the return trip they all have to be in the water, but they can paddle using only their feet—and every man must have a hand on the bow line. The three young coxswains return to their boats to brief their crews, and the race is on. Only one boat crew remembers to hold onto the bow line on the return trip. The other two, in an effort to win, kick from the sides of the IBS while holding onto the carrying handles.

"Okay, we have a winner," Taylor announces, "Boat Crew Three." The men in Boat Two, which arrived first, can't believe it. "Boat Three came in last, but they followed the rules; they all had a hand on the bow line. Boat Crew Three, take five in the shower room and warm up." The hot showers are running to heat the room, but the trainees are not allowed in them. "Boat Crew One and Two, start counting 'em out."

While Boat Crews One and Two do push-ups with their feet on the spray tubes of their boats, Boat Crew Three jogs off to get warm. The two losing crews finish their push-ups and are sent to the decon area for a cold shower. Ensign Steinbrecher again clears medical and joins the trainees in pool games. He can hardly walk, but he can manage as long as he's in the water.

"Saddle up and rig for land travel, fellows," Taylor tells them. They dress quickly and get the boats up on their heads. "Fall in, bow to stern," he says, then walks them over to Turner Field. Turner Field is also the base soccer field. Taylor lets them choose teams and the Class 228 World Cup soccer match begins. It's a surprisingly hard-fought and intense game. The trainees are groggy and half-dead on their feet, but they're still competitors. Some have played soccer before and some haven't. Spirit counts as much as skill. Steinbrecher can't run, but he's a tenacious goalie. A few of them have good soccer skills, but none can match Seaman Chris Baldwin. Baldwin's father was a petroleum engineer and Baldwin spent much of his childhood in the soccer-mad Middle East. Soccer is his game. He's everywhere, taking out classmates with vicious slide tackles and shouting in Arabic. The fact that Baldwin speaks Arabic was unknown to the instructors and most of his fellow trainees. It seems as if Chris Baldwin thinks he's back on a soccer field in Saudi Arabia. The active soccer game and the warmth of the California sun give Class 228 a chance to dry out.

After the noon chow, the trainees walk the boats back to the beach near the O-course. The next evolution is stretch PT. Chief Taylor puts them through a quick regime of serious stretching exercises, then some not-so-serious ones, like eye-openers and eyebrow stretches. It's Thursday afternoon of Hell Week. Chief Taylor is keeping them moving and keeping them amused. On the berm further down the beach from the class, two young women watch the trainees from a safe distance.

"Yost!"

"Yes, Chief Taylor."

"Take a swim buddy and go check out those two girls down the beach. Make sure they aren't someone's girlfriend in the class."

"Got it, Chief."

He grabs John Owens and they shuffle down to where the two girls are sitting.

"You don't know any of the guys in the Hell Week class, do you?" Owens asks. The girls eye the two trainees with caution. They look like refugees from a soup kitchen.

"No," one of them answers. "Is that a problem?"

"Would you like to?" Yost asks.

"I'm not too sure," she replies with a smile. "You guys look awful."

"But we clean up real good," Yost persists. "What's your name?" She tells him, and he and Owens run back to the class.

"You guys took long enough," Taylor says. "What's the deal?"

"Just a couple of tourists, Chief. They never heard of SEALs or BUD/S training."

While Yost and Owens join the class, Taylor considers the next evolution—beach games. He turns to his lead brown shirt. "Mister Oehlerich."

"Hooyah, Chief Taylor."

"What was the beach game that you disliked most during your Hell Week?"

"Hide-and-seek, Chief. No question about it."

"Hide-and-seek, huh? Why's that, sir?"

"Uh, well, you find a hiding place, but you cramp up while you wait for the instructors to find you. Then when you get caught, you get surf-tortured."

"Is that right?"

"Honest, Chief." Eric Oehlerich is not a big man, about five-nine, but he is a tough one. He was one of the strongest trainees in Class 227 and a class leader. In Second Phase, a classmate dropped a scuba tank on his hand and broke it. Now he will begin Second Phase with 228.

"Okay then, we'll play hide-and-seek."

Taylor calls the class in and explains the rules. The instructors will stay on the beach side of the berm while the trainees hide in the backshore between the berm and the Strand Highway. The staff will then try to find them. The backshore area in question is a storage area for pilings, wooden shoring, stacks of pallets, and large culvert piping. The trainees scatter among the debris and hide as best they can. Soon Taylor and the other instructors are walking casually about looking for them.

Oehlerich remembers hide-and-seek from his first Hell Week. It was one of the easier beach games and a chance to stay dry. He thinks he put the hustle on Chief Taylor, and Taylor allows him to think so. The class put out during pool games and soccer, and Chief Taylor had planned all along to give them an easy beach game. But it still pays to be a winner. As the trainees are found, they are sent over the berm to another instructor for whistle and surf drills. Only three of them—Zack Shaffer, Grant Terpstra, and Pat Yost—are able to remain undiscovered. Their reward is that they get to stay dry. Yost, as the class leading petty officer, is a visible member of Class 228. Shaffer and Terpstra are both junior enlisted men and both airmen—quiet, solid trainees who attract little attention to themselves. As the class got smaller, they simply continued to perform and survive—really only noticed by the instructors because they remained while others quit.

After noon chow, the class is sent to their tent home on the beach for their third and final sleep period. Even though their bodies are desperate for sleep, most of them fight it, not wanting to suffer the agony of waking up. Some lie down only to rest, but sleep claims them immediately. Others sit on the side of a cot and doze fitfully. The brown shirts are there, doing what they can. Adam Karaoguz, who has hidden cans of snuff all over the base, can't find any when he needs one most. Morrison gives him a dip. Brendan Dougherty bums a cigarette from one of the other brown shirts. Even though he smokes, he is one of the better runners in the class. Dougherty attended the Coast Guard Academy, but it didn't work out for him. Now he wants to be a Navy SEAL. He and Karaoguz sit on a cot and stare into space like a couple of tramps in a train yard, enjoying their tobacco.

A few BUD/S trainees go through Hell Week, take what comes, and never consider quitting. Pat Yost, Adam Karaoguz, and Otter Obst seem to be like that. They know what they want and will pay the price. Unless they get hurt, they'll make it or die trying. But most trainees, at one time or another, become weary enough to question their stamina and their ability to endure this training. This may cause them to ask if they really belong here. A few experience a real personal crisis. Is this what I really want to do? Is it really worth all the pain and the cold and the lack of sleep to be a Navy SEAL? Some get past it, some don't. For Bill Gallagher, it was the steel piers on Monday night. He's wanted to be a SEAL since he was in junior high school. Last Monday he decided he would pay the price. For Clint Burke, it is Thursday of Hell Week.

Like many of the others, Burke refuses to sleep during the last sleep period. He lays in his cot and tries to relax. Burke has the ideal build for a BUD/S trainee, much like John Owens or Zack Armstrong, lean and well-proportioned, only there's six feet, five inches of him. He's now half mad from lack of sleep, his hip flexors are frozen, and his whole body seems to be in convulsions. By the end of the hour and a half sleep session, he's laying in his own urine and wondering how he can possibly go on. He has nothing left. He hasn't thought of quitting, but he doesn't feel he can go any farther. Clint Burke has committed the cardinal sin of Hell Week; he's feeling sorry for himself.

Burke almost didn't graduate from the Naval Academy. During the summer following his second year at Annapolis, he was caught trying to pass a phony ID in a bar. But he didn't go quietly; he was taken into custody by the police only after a lengthy foot chase. For this, Clint Burke was expelled from Annapolis. He enrolled at the University of North Carolina, but it was not right for him. He had unfinished business in the Navy. With help from friends, professors, and the Navy lacrosse coach, a contrite Clint Burke was allowed back into the Naval Academy a year after his expulsion. Annapolis is a four-year school, period. A very few are allowed an extra year for academic reasons. Most five-year graduates are Mormons who are allowed a year off for missionary work. Clint Burke got a rare second chance at the Naval Academy. During the first four days of Hell Week, he has been a tower of strength. Under the boat, he has been awesome. Now he's not sure he has it anymore.

"Let's go, girls, time to rise and shine." It's Instructor Getka on the bullhorn. "Swim call, swim call. Everybody in the pool."

This is a defining moment for Ensign Clint Burke. It's either curl up in the fetal position and give in to the pain, or peel himself from the cot and keep going. I'm not sure I can do this, he tells himself, but if I have to go, it's full speed or not at all. He lurches from the cot and bursts through the tent flap. Running through the pain, he races up the berm and past his classmates toward the surf. Instead of wading out, he gallops into the waves and plunges in. Once out of the surf, he sprints back to where the instructors are waiting.

"Hooyah, Instructor Getka!"

Getka regards the big trainee. "Get your boat crew and rig for land travel, Mister Burke."

"Hooyah, Instructor Getka!"

Burke runs off to organize his smurfs. Getka glances at Joe Burns and Chief Schultz. The three instructors exchange quiet nods of approval; none suspect that just a few moments earlier, Clint Burke was close to giving up.

The two-mile round-trip to chow is agony, and the trainees stagger under the boats trying to keep it together. In the chow hall, they try to encourage each other, but many begin to slump into their food trays.

"C'mon, man, stay awake."

"Hang in there, we're almost home."

"Hey, it's almost Thursday night. It is Thursday, right?"

"Thursday! We get through tonight and it's done."

After a wash down at the clinic and a quick hygiene check, they begin the Around-the-World Paddle. Everyone in the class is battered, but Ensign Chad Steinbrecher is in the worst shape. He cannot bend one of his legs due to a knee the size of a football, and he still has fluid in his lungs. He begs the doctors to let him continue. Since the remainder of Hell Week will, for the most part, be in the boats rather than under them, he joins his boat crew for the big paddle.

The Around-the-World Paddle is, by tradition, the last major evolution in Hell Week. The trainees must take their boats into the surf at the Naval Special Warfare Center, then paddle up the Strand, around the northern end of Coronado, and back down San Diego Bay to the Amphibious Base. Many will remember this as the longest night of their lives. But lurking deep in the fog of their semiconsciousness, they know it's the last night. This sense of knowing that there will be an end to their pain and suffering is almost too delicious to think about.

They enter the water about 1930, just after sundown. As they begin the paddle north, they are dry. The three boats stay together and make steady progress. Bill Gallagher's crew in Boat Two takes turns—five men paddle while one man dozes in the middle of the boat. Sometimes they doze while paddling. Pat Yost falls asleep in mid-stroke and tumbles into the Pacific. Bill Gallagher grabs him as the boat coasts past and hauls him back aboard. Adam Karaoguz has managed to procure a fresh tin of snuff. This one came from one of the potted plants in the chow hall.

"You guys want a dip?"

"What th' hell," Gallagher replies, "let me have some of that."

Everyone has some. A few have tried it before, but only John Owens is an occasional user. For Gallagher, Steinbrecher, and Fireman Matt Jenkins, it's their first chew. The first-timers get an immediate buzz from the nicotine. Soon they are all as alert as squirrels, and Boat Two surges ahead. They may be talking nonsense, but they're wide awake and paddling.

About 2200, the instructors call the boat crews in to shore along the North Island NAS beach. Joe Burns and the evening shift check them out, and the brown shirts give them water and hot broth.

"Keep stroking, men," Chief Schultz tells them. "Stay focused and work as a team."

"HOOYAH, CHIEF SCHULTZ!" they yell, and they're back under way.

The little flotilla rounds the rock jetty that marks the entrance to San Diego Bay and paddles east toward the lights of the city. Across from the northern end of North Island, Oehlerich and Morrison again swim out with bananas and bags of candy bars. "I'll have to be very hungry," John Owens will later say, "to ever eat another Snickers bar. But they were great at the time." Things are going well—too well. At 0130 Friday morning, near the North Island pier, the instructors again call them in for midrats. Only this time it's Instructor Patstone and the demons of the night shift.

Patstone hails them through the bullhorn. "Dump boat!"

"Asshole!" someone screams back. It's Petty Officer Zack Armstrong in Boat Three, standing up in the IBS, yelling at the top of his lungs. He's half mad from lack of sleep.

"Dump boat," Patstone calls back.

Soon there are trainees and candy bars bobbing around the overturned boats. Once ashore, they build a fire and set up a mini surf camp. For being caught with candy bars, the trainees are made to eat their MREs sitting in the bay. Then it's the Chief Nielson treatment—ten minutes to doze, ten seconds by the fire, and two minutes in the water. After an hour of this, they are again paddling east for San Diego.

Patstone yells on the bullhorn, "Dump boat!"

Armstrong responds in Boat Three, "Asshole!"

They tumble into the water, flip the boats, pull themselves back aboard, and keep paddling. By 0300 they have cleared the north end of Coronado and the air station and are paddling south. By 0400 three of the smallest crafts in the Navy pass one of the largest as they stroke by the USS *John C. Stennis* (CVN-74), a 1,092-foot, 98,000-ton aircraft carrier.

"Uh-oh," says John Owens as they near the Coronado Bay Bridge. "We got some trouble coming. There's some buildings up ahead. Hey, Mister Gallagher, watch out for those buildings."

"Huh," Gallagher replies, half asleep. "What're you talking about?"

"The goddamn buildings, sir. We're gonna run right into 'em." Gallagher tries to ignore him. "Sir! Hang a right at this intersection or we'll hit 'em."

Owens tries unsuccessfully to alert the others in Boat Two of the imminent collision with the buildings.

"Just keep paddling, John," Yost tells him, too tired to explain to Owens that the buildings he sees are only the lights from the bridge and that his mind is playing tricks on him.

They make it to the boat ramp at the Amphibious Base shortly after 0500. There is still no sign of dawn as the exhausted trainees rig for land travel and take the boats to a head carry. The chow hall is only a few hundred yards from the boat ramp at Turner Field. For the men under the boats, it seems like several miles.

"Ready to down boat—down boat."

"Ready to up boat—up boat."

Patstone works them from low carry to head carry, up and down, until it appears that another cycle or two of this might bury one of the crews under their boat. Finally he gives them a last "down boat" and they begin to square away their boats in anticipation of chow. A few of them start to unbuckle their life vests, and Patstone is back on them.

"Did I tell you to get unrigged? Did I?" The class stands numbly by its boats. Some of the trainees feign coming to attention, others just stare at their tormentor. "You people just don't listen, do you? Push 'em out."

The reaction is immediate but slow. They struggle into the IBS push-up position. Ensign Steinbrecher can barely walk. He has to drape himself across the cross tube and wriggle out to where only his boots are on the rubber. But he can still do the push-ups.

"Ready!" groans Bill Gallagher.

"Ready!" replies the hoarse chorus.

Gallagher begins to count them off, and is answered in staccato fashion. There is not much left in their arms, just a slight bending at the elbow and a bobbing of heads.

"No, no, no!" Patstone appeals to them. "If we can't do them together, we'll just keep starting at the beginning until we can."

They wait, swaybacked, until Patstone finishes and Gallagher again calls for the count. After several more tries, they manage to count together, but the push-ups consist of a bobbing of heads.

"Okay, people, we've got a busy day. Get those life jackets off and let's get to chow. What day is this, Darren?" Patstone inquires of Instructor Annandono. "Is this Wednesday or Thursday?"

"C'mon now, Instructor Patstone," Annandono says in mock seriousness, "don't fool with them. It's Thursday."

The men of Class 228 know it's Friday. They talked about it on the Around-the-World Paddle. Yet they're vulnerable to anything someone tells them, even if it's unreasonable. They're starting to have memory lapses. While standing, they can drift off for a few seconds, and when they snap back awake, it takes them a moment to reconnect.

"It's about my turn," says Jason Birch. "I'll stay with the boats."

Gallagher stares dully at him. "J. B., didn't you stand guard last time . . . or was it the time before?" They both shrug; neither really remembers.

"I'll take the first shift with you, sir," says Adam Karaoguz. It's settled, and the other seventeen shuffle off to chow.

There is undisguised pity on the faces of the food service workers as the trainees stumble past.

"Eggs? Pancakes? Hash browns?"

Decisions like this are hard, and require energy and concentration. Most just nod and take what's given to them. They queue up at the drink dispenser, for there is immediate warmth there. Most take several cups of hot water. When they reach the tables, they immediately wrap their hands around a cup for warmth. Some pause to dump in packets of hot chocolate mix; others simply sip and blow at the hot water. Soon the eaters begin to eat and the nibblers begin to nibble. Outside, the two sentry-trainees stand guard.

"Hey, sir, look at that."

"Yeah, what." Jason Birch is going from boat to boat in a clumsy attempt to square away the life jackets and paddles.

"I think I see some light."

"No way."

"No shit, sir. I think that's dawn over there."

Birch stares to the east for a long moment. They don't really have a clear view from here because of the buildings.

"Maybe," Birch concedes, "just maybe."

"You want a dip, sir?"

Birch grins through cracked lips. "Naw, man, I don't want a dip."

"Snickers?"

"Yeah, I'll have a bite of Snickers."

Inside, Patstone has gone from hater to healer. He lays out his portable dispensary and starts checking names against his list.

"You guys who need meds, get over here."

Some of them respond and make their way over to where the corpsman is dealing out pills. Others, Patstone has to seek out. Either they have forgotten they were on medication, or they don't care at this point. But Patstone tracks each one down, and carefully notes the individual dosage in his log. Terry Patstone is an energetic first class hospital corpsman from Maine. He has ten years in the teams, and is one year away from his bachelor's degree in organizational behavior. If the members of Class 228 were to vote on which instructor they fear the most, it would be Instructor Terry Patstone.

"Lots of water. Two full glasses at a minimum. Gallagher, drink. Luna, drink. I want to see those glasses empty." Some of the men don't have two water glasses on their tray. "You either drink it or we'll put you back into it, right now—your choice." This rouses Ensign Koella and Seaman Pell, and they return to the mess line for water. "It doesn't matter," Patstone tells the other students seated at the tables, "you're all going back in the water."

Gallagher pushes back from the table. "We gotta relieve J. B. and Karaoguz. Who's finished?"

Both Owens and Yost are still eating. As soon as they hit the table, they cram in food as fast as they can. Their mess trays are a disaster, like those of two preschoolers.

"We'll get it, sir," says Yost. He and Owens jam in another mouthful of food and head for the door. Soon Jason Birch and Adam Karaoguz are seated before piles of food. Birch picks at his tray; he's a nibbler. Karaoguz shovels it down. Warrant Officer Jim Locklear, who has relieved Randy Beausoleil as OIC, escorts his coffee cup over to the seated trainees. A few of them snap awake at his approach.

"Okay, men, we have some time to kill this morning before we go through the O-course. Now, I'm going to give you a choice. We can do a base tour with the boats, we can do surf passage, or"—he pauses for effect—"door three—a mystery evolution. What'll it be?"

There is a stumbling, semicoherent discussion among trainees on what they should choose. It's an important topic and they try to focus, but no one is thinking clearly.

"Base tour—we don't want to go back into the water."

"Yeah, but I'm not sure I can carry the boat anymore. Paddling is easier." Some of them seem totally baffled by the idea of making a choice; others drift off in the middle of a sentence.

"Okay, if that's the way you want it—door three. We'll go get wet and sandy, carry the boats through the O-course, and then do surf passage." The assembled students accept the verdict like a death sentence. But none question it.

Patstone buttons up his medical kit. "Let's go, people. Forks down." He carefully watches Birch and Karaoguz to make sure they've had a chance to eat. "You think you can hang out at the chow hall all day. We've got a full day ahead of us."

Outside, Pat Yost and John Owens totter on the edge of sleep as they stand a loose parade rest by the boats.

"Friday, right, John?"

"Yep, it's Friday. Wanna go drinking tonight?"

"I wanna get through the day. Hey, John, if something happens to me, you gotta take over as LPO; you're the next senior petty officer. Remember that."

"Ain't nothing gonna happen to you, Pat," says John Owens. "We started this thing together and we'll finish it together."

Chief Nielson arrives ahead of the others, and shares a joke with the two men guarding the IBSs. He senses these two could do another two days of Hell Week if they had to. Patstone and Locklear arrive with the rest of the class. After some light boat drills, they head across Turner Field into the growing dawn. Patstone puts them in the bay and makes them dump boat, then sends them paddling south toward Fiddler's Cove. They're right on schedule for the last day of Hell Week.

The three weary crews head down the bay, each boat trying to maintain a stroke count. Some fall asleep paddling and have to be roused by their crewmates. But gradually, as the dawn swells to daylight, each is becoming more aware that this is Friday, the last day. It's a powerful concept for the nineteen survivors of Class 228—Friday. When they go into the fog for a moment and snap back out, it's still there—Friday.

"It really is Friday, right, man?"

"Damn straight—last day."

"I can't believe it. Friday."

"When do you think they'll secure us?"

"Two-two-seven got secured about one-thirty."

"I heard it was noon."

"Noon? You think they'll secure us by noon?"

At Fiddler's Cove, Chief Taylor and the day shift are waiting for them. Two boats are tied for the lead while Clint Burke's smurfs are trailing badly.

"Okay, who's it gonna be?" Taylor yells across the water. "Who's gonna be the winner?"

Once again, the competitive fires are banked. This time it's Fireman Jenkins who steps up in Boat Two. "Hey, we can win this one. C'mon, guys, let's go for it!" Matt Jenkins is the youngest man left in the class— an eighteen-year-old from New Hampshire. He has often been a source of frustration for the older members of his boat crew, but today he takes charge. They pick up Jenkins's stroke and Boat Two surges ahead. On the beach inside the cove, Taylor is all smiles. Nothing pleases him more than a good race—winners and losers.

"All right, it's Mister Gallagher's crew. Good work, men. Why don't you gents have a seat over there while I attend to these other guys."

Taylor drops the other crews for push-ups, then sends them back out on a boat race around the mooring buoys in the cove. Soon all three boats are racing from the inner shore of the cove out to the buoys and back. These are Taylor's races, Taylor's rules. He chooses a new coxswain each time and gives them specific rules for the race—which buoy they must round, and how, before returning to the starting point. Between races, Chief Taylor checks his watch. He has to have them across the highway to the demo pits by 1000.

"How they doing, Ken?" One of the instructors from Third Phase who will work the demo pits later that morning has come early to watch.

"I think what we have left are good to go. A couple of them are real studs—watch this. Hey, Obst, get over here."

Obst, who is sitting out a race with his winning crew, jumps to his feet. "Hooyah, Chief Taylor."

"Take a swim in the Great White."

The Otter climbs quickly to the back of the pickup and dives into the IBS full of ice water. He emerges from the cold plunge and leaps from the truck to stand before Taylor.

"Okay, get back with your crew."

"Hooyah, Chief Taylor," he says with a grin. Neither the ice water, nor Taylor's apparent lack of a reason for sending him into it, seem to bother Obst. "See what I mean?" Taylor says to the other instructor. "He's one tough kid."

They finish a few more races, then Taylor gets them moving down the sand road that leads westward from the cove across the Strand. Once across the highway, they park their boats by the entrance to a small chain-link compound. So Sorry Day is about to begin.

So Sorry Day has its origins back in the early days at Fort Pierce, where the first demolition trainees were exposed to explosives and simulated combat conditions. They were forced to crawl under barbed wire and through mud while live explosions were set off around them. The half-pound blocks of TNT that used to create the explosions for So Sorry Day at BUD/S have since been replaced by artillery simulators. In deference to the local ecology and the seabird population on the Strand, TNT is no longer used. Even so, as Class 228 crawls into the demo pits, they are about to be treated to an evolution laced with noise, gunfire, and tradition.

Demo pits is a misnomer. The "pits" is a single oval hole dug into the sand that is served by several culverts. The pit measures perhaps a hundred feet on the long axis. During Hell Week, seawater is pumped into this hole to a depth of six or seven feet. The man-size culverts buried into the berm that surrounds the pit allow the trainees to crawl into and out of the hole. Across the length of the oval, two nylon lines have been strung. One is six feet off the surface of the water and another six feet above that.

The trainees begin their journey into the demo pits by crawling under a field of barbed wire just inside the gate. Their vision is cut by thick smoke from smoke grenades, which also produce a strong stench of sulfur. Artillery simulators on either side of the field of barbed wire start their whistle and boom. Then the Mk-43s begin to bark. So Sorry Day is under way. Class 228 approaches the end of Hell Week just as it began, with plenty of shooting and explosions. The noise is not so bad as it was in the enclosed grinder of the BUD/S compound, but the smoke adds another element to the chaos. Two blasts on the whistle, they crawl on their bellies; one blast, they cover up—more shooting and explosions.

For the better part of an hour, the students crawl under barbed wire, through smoke, and in and out of the pit by way of the concrete culverts. A thick layer of scum has formed on the surface of the pit from the reaction of the seawater and the freshly dug sand. The students are past caring or questioning as they half swim, half slither through the pit, occasionally shouting encouragement to each other. They are fairly sure that the end of Hell Week is not too far off. Yet they are very, very tired, and not thinking clearly. The only thing that they do know is that they have to keep moving and do what is asked of them, whatever that may be.

Finally, the remaining nineteen trainees are lined up on one side of the pit, immersed to their necks. One man at a time, they mount the two ropes, standing on the lower line and hanging from the upper line. They have to tell a joke or a story while they try to make their way across the pit. Two of the brown shirts pull on straps tied to the upper line in an attempt to shake the suspended trainee loose. While his classmates cheer him on, the man on the two lines fights to stay aloft. It's a short struggle for most; the brown shirts make sure that no one gets as far as the halfway point. But a few get close. Harry Pell hauls his feet up to the top line and is able to inchworm his way down the line. Clint Burke, because of his height and tenacity, comes within a few feet of the center marker. If just one of them makes it, the brown shirts have to get wet and sandy. They don't particularly like dumping their future classmates off the lines, but it pays to be a winner—always.

As the last of the Hell Week class is dumped into the water, the instructors present—some twelve of them—line up on the far side of the demo pit. There is a ceremonial presence to this line of instructors, and the students sense the magic moment has arrived. It's time to secure! Hell Week's over! As quickly as their spirits soar, they come crashing to earth. It's only a hoax—a trick to get their hopes up—a test to see if they can keep going. The ruse works. They are clearly discouraged, but the members of 228 manage to answer the whistle call and crawl out of the pit.

"Let's hit the beach, men," Taylor yells at them. "Time for . . . you guessed it—surf passage!"

The trainees are allowed a quick lunch of cold MREs, then Taylor sends them on boat races into the surf. There is no wind and the day is relatively warm and sunny. The three boats are greeted by only two to three feet of spilling surf. Even so, two of the poorly crewed boats manage to slew sideways and overturn. Yet the boat crews grimly go through the motions—the stronger men helping the weaker ones and trying to manufacture spirit. Obst, Baldwin, Burke, Yost, and Karaoguz are still strong; they do their best to motivate their classmates. Others are not. Airman Alexander Lopez and Ensign Will Koella have knees so swollen they are unable to run and can walk only with great difficulty. Ensign Steinbrecher is effectively a cripple; he can still paddle, but can only stagger after his crew when they bring the boats from the surf across the sand.

"Cap-tain Bow-en!"

"HOOYAH, CAPTAIN BOWEN!"

Bowen has a few words with Joe Burns, then walks down among the students and their boats. Class 228 stands a little taller now that the commanding officer is among them—partly out of respect and partly because they think, just maybe, he will deliver them from their misery.

"Carry on, men," he tells them before he heads back over the berm. "You're doing a terrific job; keep up the good work."

They hooyah him again and watch as he disappears over the beach. Once again their hopes of relief are dashed. Ensign Joe Burns steps over to where Otter Obst is standing beside his IBS.

"You know, it's like I told the CO, we have to keep going." He looks at his watch. "Hell Week has to run for a certain number of hours or it's not official. Since we got a late start Sunday evening, we have to stay out here until late afternoon."

Obst receives this information stoically. He may be stronger than most of his classmates, but he knows he can't keep this up too much longer. Burns's comments start him to thinking. *Maybe, just maybe, we do have several more hours ahead of us. But I'll not quit—not now, not ever.*

"Okay, fellows," Chief Taylor tells them, "let's leave the boats here and do a little surf conditioning. Everybody in the pool."

Taylor sends them into the surf. They are starting to lean on each other, and two trainees have to help Chad Steinbrecher into the water. They resemble stiffly animated rag dolls. Taylor has them lay in the surf and begin a series of flutter kicks. He watches them carefully, professionally, with no sense of pity for their suffering. He knows it's a hard business, one that demands hard men. Burns walks over and says something to Taylor.

Taylor nods and sends Class 228 out to deeper water to let some of the sand drain out of their clothing from lying in the surf.

This is Ed Bowen's first class at the Naval Special Warfare Center and his first Hell Week. Hell Week is secured in accordance with the wishes of the commanding officer. In times past, visiting admirals or other dignitaries were allowed to secure Hell Week. Captain Joe McGuire, Bowen's predecessor, would muster the class on the BUD/S grinder with a roster of those who began Hell Week and read the Hell Week class list aloud. If a man was still there he would answer, "Present!" If the man had quit, the whole class would roar "DOR!" This is not to be Ed Bowen's way.

"Hell Week is something between the instructors and the students. It's my view they should finish the process together."

"Is my presence here appropriate?" I asked Ed before he left the beach.

"I don't see any problem, Dick," he told me. "You've been out here with them for most of the week."

Chief Taylor calls them in from the ocean, and Joe Burns motions them to gather around him.

"Okay, men. The next evolution is . . . well, there is no next evolution. Hell Week is over; you're secured."

There is a pause while the survivors of Class 228 take this announcement in. At first they suspect this is some sort of deception; they wait a moment for the other shoe to drop. Burns just looks at them and smiles. The trainees know Ensign Burns might try to trick them, but he would never straight-out lie to them—not like this. "Congratulations," he adds. "You guys did a helluva job. I'm proud of you."

"It's over?"

"Really—no bullshit?"

"Hey, man, it's over!"

"Oh, God! Oh, dear God!"

"That's it! We're secure!"

"We did it! Sonuvabitch, we did it!"

"It's really over—we're really secure!"

"Yeessss!"

Some grasp their deliverance quickly—for others it takes a few stunned moments. Slowly, the nineteen members of Class 228 begin to hug each other and hoarsely cheer their survival and fellowship. Some, like Zack Shaffer, are in shock and just stand there with a goofy grin on their faces. A few weep with joy that the torment and the cold are over. Bill Gallagher drops his head a moment, crosses himself, then goes about shaking each of his classmate's hands. "I never," Gallagher will later say, "in my wildest dreams, would have thought that it could hurt that much, or I could be that cold. And I never thought I could have taken that much punishment. I still don't believe it."

Joe Burns quiets them down and motions them in closer. "All right, guys, I want you to take a minute and think about this. No matter what you do in the future, remember this moment; you men just finished Hell Week. Few men are able to do what you just did. Whether you stay in the Navy or get out and run a latte stand—whatever—never, never forget this moment or what you achieved here this week. When things get tough in life, this will be your benchmark. Others will quit, but you won't. Because if you can do this, you can do anything, right?"

"HOOO-YAAAAAH!"

He again quiets them down. "Okay, we know you're tough. Now we're going to see if you're smart and technically proficient. There's still a lot to do; you have the rest of First Phase ahead of you. Then, pool comps in Second Phase and weapons practicals in Third Phase. You need to stay focused on training and keep this in perspective. Hell Week is just a speed bump in BUD/S—an important step, but only one step. You'll have a few days to rest and heal up, but you have to be ready to start back at it on Monday. But today you guys can stand tall and be proud. Whatever happens, never forget what you accomplished here this week."

Sean Mruk and many of the other First Phase instructors are there to congratulate them. "Good goin', guys," Mruk tells them as he shakes each man's hand. "There's beer and snacks on the bus." Then he adds with a grin, "Well, maybe some snacks."

They're still wet, cold, chafed, and battered, but the sure knowledge that they made it through Hell Week carries the ragged band of trainees back over the rise of the beach to the demo pits. Those who can still walk help those who barely can. It's a scene from the Bataan Death March, only these men know they are survivors. As they make their way around the chain-link fence surrounding the demo pits to the waiting bus, a surprise and an honor await them. Along with Captain Bowen, the commanding officers and command master chiefs of the West Coast SEAL teams are lined up, waiting to shake their hands.

"Congratulations."

"When you finish BUD/S, come on over to Team One."

"Tough Hell Week from what I hear; you guys should be proud."

"SEAL Team Five is looking for a few good men."

"Good job; well done."

Soon they are on the bus, heading north on the Strand Highway for the Center. They are terminally weary but, for the moment, no longer sleepy. They made it; it's really over! True to his word, Sean Mruk has candy bars and sodas on the bus for them. Once back at the Center, Class 228 makes its way along a familiar route through the showers and around to where the three medical officers are waiting for them. Three by three, they parade nude before the medical examiners. The medical team carefully scrutinizes them—checking here, poking there, asking questions. Some are given antibiotics and vitamins. Most are pronounced battered but basically sound. Ensigns Steinbrecher and Koella and Airman Lopez are sent into the treatment room. Outside, between the clinic and the Center barracks, each man finds his milk crate with dry UDT trunks, a fresh new pair of fuzzy socks, and—best of all—a brown T-shirt with his name on it. It's only a cheap military T-shirt of a particular color, but it is everything—they're brown shirts.

The trainees sit basking in the sun, eating candy bars and waiting for the last of their classmates to finish their treatment. Then they move as a class along the grinder to the First Phase classroom. There are nineteen chairs arranged in the front of the room. The temperature is uncomfortably high—unless, of course, you just finished Hell Week. On the arm of each desk are two sixteen-inch pizzas and a large bottle of Gatorade. A few in the class are beginning to fade as they shuffle into the class, but the aroma of the pizza revives them.

"Okay, heroes," Mruk says as they file in, "have a seat and dig in. As soon as Doctor Witucki gets here and gives you your medical briefing, we'll drive you back to the barracks and tuck you in." Class 228's proctor steps from the podium and retrieves a slice of pizza from one of his students. The Otter offers me a piece and I accept. It's lukewarm, drenched in grease, and wonderful. A few moments later, Lieutenant Peter Witucki enters the room and stands in front of the class. They regard him through puffy eyes and continue to shovel in pizza.

Witucki, Josh Bell, Norm Moser, and the clinic corpsmen get to know the students as well as any of the instructors. They examine them prior to Indoc and certify them fit to leave BUD/S at the end of Third Phase. Their responsibilities are medical, not military, but they become attached to their patients. A great deal rides on their judgment, so their job is both a medical and an emotional one.

"I know you guys are dying," Witucki begins, "but stay with me for a bit longer, then we'll get you out of here. Tomorrow morning, I want to see you all back here at zero eight hundred—eight o'clock, got that?" There is a muffled, pizza-clogged round of hooyahs.

"Good. Now your job today and for the rest of the weekend is to sleep and eat. You'll be surprised what food and rest can do in just a few days. I know some of you have some problems we'll have to deal with, but we'll take a good look at them tomorrow after you've had some rest. When you get back to the barracks, get into bed and try to sleep on your back. If you can, keep your feet and hands slightly elevated from your torso. This will help the swelling. Drink lots of water. Take two bottles to bed with you, one full of water and one empty. Believe me, you're not going to want to get up for a head call. And try not to get the bottles mixed up.

"There will be a watch posted at the barracks to see you're not disturbed. They will check on you every hour between now and tomorrow morning. If you have a problem, have the watch call us. Either myself or one of the other medical officers will be on call. If it's an emergency, call nine-one-one, but don't go to a civilian doctor unless you have to. They don't know what you've been through. If they see you looking like this, they'll admit you to the hospital immediately, and we won't see you for a week. Got that?" Another weak round of hooyahs.

After Lieutenant Witucki leaves them, Mruk gives them a few more minutes to work on their pizza, but he's running out of time. Some of them are already drifting off to sleep.

"Box up what you have left and take it with you. It'll taste great cold later on tonight, guaranteed. Grab your clothes in the paper sacks over by the wall. I'll give you a few minutes to pull on some sweats or whatever clothes you brought. Then we gotta get moving."

Some quickly pull on the clothes they left in the classroom last Sunday. Others simply board the bus with a box of pizza under one arm and a bag of clothes under the other. Mruk drives them over to the barracks. Only two flights of stairs stand between Class 228 and their rooms, but they seem like Mount Everest. As they file off the bus, Mruk hands each of them a cold bottle of beer. Most of them will not even remember drinking it, or how they got from the door of the bus to their beds. It is Friday, 19 November, and Hell Week is over for Class 228.

CHAPTER FOUR

Beyond the Week

<hr />

"Here they come," muses Lieutenant Josh Bell. "We call it the walk of the living dead." Dr. Bell and medical staff watch from the door of the BUD/S clinic.

The members of Class 228 slowly make their way down the access road from the Naval Special Warfare Barracks to the Center. It is 0800 on the Saturday after Hell Week. They are dressed in sweat clothes or shorts. Some wear sandals; others, shower shoes. Most walk like wranglers, slightly bowlegged to relieve the chafed skin on their inner thighs. Those who had trouble walking on Friday are only a little better on Saturday morning. One of the brown shirt rollbacks has a van and delivers the less ambulatory to the clinic. All of them are stiff and their faces are puffy. Most of them slept twelve to sixteen hours straight. Others were up gimping around the barracks at various times in the night, unable to sufficiently release enough tension to get any sustained sleep. At the Center clinic, they once again strip for a complete medical inspection. The medical officers look for any signs of flesh-eating bacteria, but if they haven't seen it by now, they probably won't. They also look for pneumonia or other respiratory problems. Those trainees who finished Hell Week strong are the

ones who show the most immediate improvement. The trainees with cellulitis and iliotibial band tendinitis, or IBT, are in the worst shape. The
most common cellulitis is an infection between the layers of skin in the legs
and around the knees. When acute, it causes bloating and discoloration.
IBT is an inflammation of the long tendon that runs the length of the femur
to the knee, and is very painful. All of the trainees are hurting to a degree,
some just more than others. All of them have healing to do if they are to
resume training on Monday.

After the medical exams and another round of medications, the men set
off for breakfast—their first sit-down, civilian meal as a class. Marie
Callender's in Coronado offers a group discount for the survivors of Hell
Week. Class 228's table is set up and ready when they arrive. Each finds a
place at the table, some with the assistance from a buddy to get from a
standing to a seated position. The ones who were able to eat during Hell
Week are still in the best condition. They tear into their meal. After down-
ing a large farm-style breakfast, including a side of pancakes, they order a
second round of the same, inhaling everything on their plates. The class
nibblers eat well, but not as much. It will be a few more days before their
systems can tolerate large amounts of food at one sitting. Most have to
improvise to hold a fork with clublike hands and swollen fingers that don't
yet respond normally. After breakfast, they return to the barracks to begin
a routine of sleep, food, more sleep, and more food. Those who have not
yet called their families to let them know they made it, do so before crawling off to bed. Throughout the weekend they take long, hot showers,
and the thought of ever going back into cold water causes them to shiver
involuntarily.

Hell Week is a curious and unique event. I'm not sure I understand it
much better now, having just watched it, than when I went through my
Hell Week some thirty years ago. I do know that it changes a man forever.
Future challenges and many of life's triumphs are now calibrated by this
experience. For a few souls, Hell Week is their zenith, and they have a difficult time getting past it. For them, making it through Hell Week is the
end goal. But for most BUD/S trainees, it is a learning experience and
becomes a powerful engine for future physical and mental growth.

When Draper Kauffman first began to train the Naval Combat Demolition Units (NCDUs) in the summer of 1943, he visited the Naval Scouts and Raiders training camp that shared Fort Pierce with the NCDUs. He took their eight-week physical conditioning program and compressed it into a single week of training. This first week was called "Indoctrination Week," but it quickly became known as Hell Week. The theory behind this grueling initial week was to weed out the weak candidates early on and train those who remained. Since then, Hell Week has been moved from the first week to several weeks into training.

This train-the-best, discard-the-rest philosophy was not the only legacy of Draper Kauffman. Kauffman and his officers went through the first Hell Week with their NCDU enlisted volunteers. The idea that officers have to train and suffer with their men, especially suffering on this scale, is unique in American military service. Today, officer trainees, like SEAL platoon officers, have to lead while under pressure, and have to suffer the same hardships as their men. SEAL work is a harsh, physically demanding business. If an officer is to lead from the front, he needs to be, at a minimum, as physically capable as the men he expects to follow him.

The history of Hell Week is a microcosm of the history of the teams. The Navy SEAL is quite young—just shy of his fortieth birthday. His evolutionary cousin, the Navy frogman, has yet to turn sixty. Both the frogmen and the SEALs were born out of necessity, as was Hell Week. The slaughter of young marines on the beaches of Tarawa in 1943 underscored the need for beach reconnaissance prior to amphibious landings. Volunteers for this dangerous work had to be recruited and trained quickly. Hell Week quickly became the crucible—a way to quickly find the right kind of men for this task. Those who went ashore the following year to clear the beaches at Normandy for the D-day invasion suffered terrible casualties. On Omaha Beach alone, 52 percent were killed or wounded. The NCDUs were consolidated into Underwater Demolition Teams, or UDTs, shortly before the end of the war. As UDTs, these first American frogmen saw action across the Pacific as U.S. forces fought their way to Japan. Later in Korea, they served with distinction, raiding coastal targets and performing critical hydrographic reconnaissance prior to the landings at Inchon in September 1950. Throughout the war in the Pacific and the Korean War, the Navy frogmen were defined by Hell Week.

January 1962 marked the commissioning of SEAL Team One in the Pacific Fleet and SEAL Team Two in the Atlantic Fleet. Training SEALs, like training frogmen, demanded a rigorous Hell Week. The new SEALs focused on duties that included unconventional warfare, operational deception, counterinsurgency, and direct-action missions in maritime and riverine environments. During the Vietnam War, SEAL direct-action platoons and adviser teams compiled an impressive record of combat success despite the fact that even at the height of the conflict, there were never more than 500 Navy SEALs on active duty. At any given time, there were seldom more than 120 SEALs deployed in the combat zone. Since Vietnam, changing missions and increased operational tempo prompted the UDTs to be redesignated as SEAL Teams and SEAL Delivery Vehicle (SDV) Teams. Today, Naval Special Warfare forces also include Special Boat Units and Squadrons. The combatant crewmen who serve in the Special Boat Units experience a demanding training regime, but only SEALs undergo BUD/S and Hell Week. Hell Week and the making of Navy SEALs have become more formal and more structured since my time with Class 45. Then, BUD/S training served a UDT/SEAL community of less than 1000. Today there are currently just under 2,000 Navy SEALs. But from what I saw with Class 228, neither the training nor Hell Week has become any easier.

There was a time at BUD/S in the early 1970s when Hell Week was discontinued. The Vietnam War demanded a higher output of young men for the SEAL teams, so, in a top-down move, the Navy canceled Hell Week. But the gatekeepers remained at BUD/S. Any slack previously afforded the students after Hell Week was quickly taken up by the instructor staff, especially in the Second and Third Phases. BUD/S graduation numbers changed little. According to some veteran instructors, after Hell Week was reinstated, the post–Hell Week pressure and physical demands remained, and BUD/S training became that much more difficult.

Hell Week, and all of BUD/S training, is a work in progress. If Hell Week has changed over the years, it's only been a refinement of the basic theme. In 1969, Class 45 went through its Hell Week in Little Creek, Virginia. Today, I remember the Sunday evening breakout as a shocking mix of noise, smoke, harassment, and confusion. There were fire hoses. We were made to crawl through water and mud after we were driven from our barracks. We were cold and wet all the time, but Chesapeake Bay was not so convenient to the training compound as the Pacific Ocean is to the current BUD/S training area. If I slept four hours during those terrible five days, I was lucky. Many of the evolutions were the same. As did Class 228, we carried the boats everywhere on our heads. One night we ran all night and another night we paddled from sundown to sunrise. Clearly, there is better medical supervision and treatment today, but this capability also allows current BUD/S instructors to safely take the trainees a little closer to the edge. Since each of the sixty-some evolutions in the current Hell Week are tightly scripted, they are continually adjusted in small ways to make them more challenging and effective.

I was often asked, "How did this Hell Week compare to yours?" It's not an easy question: it was a long time ago, a different coast, and, back then, I was in the arena—not a dry, warm observer. Having undergone a winter Hell Week on the East Coast, I enjoy a certain status among SEALs; during my Hell Week, the nighttime temperatures dipped well below freezing. The freshwater ponds and estuaries often had a crust of ice on them. "How did you deal with water as cold as that?" an instructor asked me. "It was different," was my best answer. Water that cold is devastating; you go from miserable to numb very quickly. We were never in for more than a few minutes at a time; immersions were quick and very painful. I'm not so sure that twenty minutes at sixty degrees is any easier than two minutes at thirty-two degrees.

How did I handle it? I'd like to think I was like Adam Karaoguz, Pat Yost, Otter Obst, and Clint Burke—strong performers, able to rally their boat crews. Or that during those long, grim nights, I could always produce a grin like Jason Birch or John Owens. I do remember the training officer, a mustang like Joe Burns, saying, "You're secured," and how sweet it was. Perhaps all I can be sure of at this point is that I didn't quit. I never considered quitting; it was somehow not an option for me. Better still, I was able to take what I learned in Hell Week and apply it to other challenges in my life.

As Hell Week has evolved over the years, so have the young men who come to BUD/S. It can be argued that the current raw product is less ready for this kind of punishment and discipline than previous generations. Today's BUD/S students are clearly stronger and more athletic than those in the past. It's obvious that many who arrive at BUD/S have logged more than a few hours in the weight room. But life in these United States is good—and often soft. On balance, the feel-good generation may be less prepared mentally for the crucible of BUD/S than their predecessors. And where do they come from, these young men who volunteer for such punishment? Adjusted for population density, most of them come from smaller, inland communities. It seems the calling of a maritime warrior is less attractive for those who live on the coasts or in a large city. Perhaps small towns in mid-America, because of lesser economic opportunity or a greater patriotic feeling, send more of their sons off to serve their country.

BUD/S training is lengthy, expensive, dangerous, and difficult. Far fewer trainees graduate than are reassigned back to the fleet. So just what makes a successful BUD/S trainee? And since Hell Week has the largest share of attrition in BUD/S, what does it take to get through it? Psychological profiling is now a part of the BUD/S process, but this screening is designed only to weed out those with pathological tendencies. Other tests have been developed that have a high degree of predictability for success at BUD/S. But since there are no absolutes in predicting who will or will not make it, they are used as guides to influence training rather than as screening tools. BUD/S instructors and curriculum specialists say that most classes break out something like this: Perhaps 10 or 15 percent of those who arrive simply do not have the physical tools to make it through the training or Hell Week; they cannot meet the performance standards or they break down physically. There is another 5 or 10 percent who, unless they break a leg or are otherwise seriously injured, will make it no matter how much they get beat. These are the trainees, like Adam Karaoguz and Lawrence Obst, whom you will have to kill or incapacitate if you want to remove them from the training. But the other 75 to 85 percent are up for grabs. If this large percentage of trainees can find it within themselves, or are properly motivated, they can make it; they have the physical tools. Why more of them don't is a question that Ed Bowen wrestles with daily.

One thing is clear: the instructors still have great power and influence. The skill with which they mete out punishment and approval, to individuals and to the class, has a tremendous bearing on the outcome. A large percentage of Class 228, like those classes before them, are led through or driven from training by their BUD/S instructors. It's a challenging time, both physically and emotionally, for trainees as well as staff. What's at stake for the individual trainee is the personal goal of a young life. For the instructors, it's the future composition of the SEAL teams and the character of this warrior culture.

DORs. What makes one man quit and another of similar physical ability go on? Is this elaborate, tradition-bound process the only way to find out who has grit and who does not? Does it tell us who will stand tall in a firefight in some developing nation and who will come up short?

"Do you ever take bets on who will make it and who will not?" I asked several BUD/S instructors. "Who will DOR and who will not?" None said they did.

"Let's just say we get surprised a lot," said one veteran First Phase instructor. "We get surprised when someone we hardly knew was even in the class is there at the end of Hell Week. Other times, a strong, motivated trainee packs it in before midnight on Sunday. You were out there, Mister Couch; you saw it happen in Class Two twenty-eight."

So I asked some trainees who DORed. Often it was difficult for me to ask, and even harder for them to answer truthfully. Usually, I found them at a quiet moment away from the BUD/S compound, a week to ten days after they left the class.

I would usually begin by asking, "How're you doing?" or, "What are your plans?"

"I'm going back to a ship for a while," said many of the junior enlisted men. "I'll get myself in better shape and then I'll be back." A few of them admitted that at that time they lacked the maturity and focus it takes to get through BUD/S. Most of these who vowed to return said they underestimated the program—that they were insufficiently prepared. Many of these men do come back. Perhaps they will be like John Owens and Zack Armstrong, and return in a few years to succeed and even excel during Hell Week. Naval duty, both aboard ship and on shore, has a way of growing boys into men—helping them to sort out what they really want in life. My guess is that a few of these men will be back, but not as many as say they will.

Some men DOR because they have minor injuries or are sick. Being cold, wet, and exhausted is an invitation to pneumonia, and many were in the early stages of it. But this can also be said of the ones who make it through. Many said, "I lost my motivation," as if it were a pair of reading glasses they had simply misplaced for a moment. Others, even after the rigors of Indoc and First Phase, were still intimidated by the whole process. Hell Week turns the pain meter up several notches. The trainees think, "Another twenty weeks of this!" and they DOR. Quite a few of them, though they passed the screening test and read the BUD/S pretraining literature, learned about SEALs in the movies. They have given little thought to BUD/S or life in the SEAL teams. Certainly none of them have ever been made to hurt this much for this long. They thought of BUD/S training as fraternity hazing or boot-camp-like harassment; they simply didn't bargain for this much punishment. Very few trainees see this business for what it really is—a long and painful road to a warrior culture, one with ongoing physical demands and hardship as a way of life. They don't fully understand the SEAL saying "Training is never over" until they're in it. Some also questioned their suitability for this warrior calling, which entails the taking of human life, and they realized this profession was not for them. I once asked a highly successful attorney friend of mine why he was so good at his job. "Most guys with law degrees just want to be lawyers," he told me. "They don't really, and I mean really, want to practice law." I think it's the same with BUD/S trainees. A lot of them would like to call themselves SEALs, but perhaps not so many of them are prepared to do the work of Navy SEALs.

The most tragic of the DORs are those who somehow allowed themselves to be trapped by the expectations of others. These are good men who have a history of success and are not, by nature or practice, quitters. This is especially true of the officer trainees. Competition for billets at the Naval ROTC units and at the Naval Academy is intense. I've had more than one midshipman tell me that it's harder to get a billet at BUD/S than to get through BUD/S. In the case of Naval Academy midshipmen, Class 228 aside, the statistics bear this out. Their success at BUD/S is nearly the same as those going to flight school. It's a given: the grads with orders to Pensacola become Navy pilots, and the grads with orders to Coronado become Navy SEALs. "Hey, wow, you're going to be a SEAL," their Annapolis classmates say. "That's really cool!"

This is an easy conclusion to reach; the BUD/S graduation rate for the Annapolis men is very high. There have been years when the Naval Academy sent sixteen new ensigns to BUD/S and all sixteen graduated. But too often, the respect is given before it is earned. This respect is very seductive for a motivated, success-orientated, and sometimes naive twenty-two-year-old. It completely drowns out the little voice inside that cries, "Do you really want to be a Navy SEAL?" When they get cold, wet, and sandy, the voice gets louder and harder to ignore. Finally, they have to confront themselves, and this often leads to a fierce inner struggle; are they quitting because it's hard, or are they quitting because this calling truly is not for them? Is this honest or dishonest? Are they, perhaps for the first time in their life, a failure—a quitter? This is a complex, emotional Rubicon for these young men to cross. For many, it becomes a serious personal crisis, and they leave BUD/S badly shaken and often bitter.

I talked with most of those who DORed from 228, yet I only heard one man say what all those who surrendered during Hell Week must have felt: "I just got so damned cold I couldn't take it anymore, so I quit." But why one man quits and another will go on, no matter how hard it gets, is still a mystery. It was the same in 1969 with Class 45.

I think one of the strongest motivators for all of us who make it to the teams is the desire to belong. In the case of the young men fighting their way through BUD/S, it is the desire to belong to an elite group—to become a warrior. Those who succeed have high expectations of themselves, and they want to associate with others who share those expectations. They want to be the best, and they want to serve with the best. I also think success at BUD/S is based on intelligence, or at least the ability to think ahead and to clearly visualize one's personal goals. Hell Week is a mental gauntlet as well as a physical one. Those who have a clear goal of where they are going, and know why they're going there, are less likely to surrender mentally to the physical pain.

Perhaps as I watch Class 228 in the coming weeks, I'll learn more about those who chose not to quit. As Joe Burns so eloquently put it, Hell Week is only a speed bump in BUD/S training. There were two things I did notice as I watched Class 228 finish Hell Week. They were also true in Class 45 some thirty years ago. First, small men seem to get through the training easier and in larger numbers than big men. Clint Burke is an exception. The second has to do with tattoos. With Class 228, success in BUD/S and in Hell Week was inversely proportional to the number of tattoos on a trainee's body. Almost a third of the men who began with Class 228 had tattoos. Some were extensive. All but a very few of these trainees were gone by the end of Hell Week—and those who survived, such as Clint Burke, John Owens, and Pat Yost, have small ones. Perhaps this is not too surprising. Many young people get tattoos because they yield to peer pressure, or because they lack self-confidence or a strong personal identity. These are not traits I saw in the men who finished Hell Week.

For the nineteen survivors of Class 228, the Monday after Hell Week is like the first day of a new school year. They have new status; they're now brown shirts. They have new classmates with the addition of eleven new trainees from PTRR—one officer and ten enlisted men. Class 228 is now back up to thirty men. Most of the new additions are medical rollbacks from Classes 226 and 227. A few were rolled back from previous classes for not meeting performance standards.

The issue of phase rollbacks for medical and performance reasons has always been a contentious issue at BUD/S. At times, there have been more trainees assigned to PTRR than in any of the three regular training phases. At other times, a rollback for any reason was rare. Under the guidance of Ed Bowen, the phase officers have been directed to afford their students every opportunity to meet phase performance standards—the minimum swim, run, and O-course times and to meet the academic requirements. If they don't, there are no rollbacks. A trainee who fails a standard or graded evolution is sent back to the fleet or, in the case of a solid trainee with a single weakness, to the beginning—day one in Indoc. A student who is performing well and becomes sick or legitimately injured will be considered for a medical rollback.

The final three weeks of First Phase are devoted to hydrographic reconnaissance and the mechanics of cartography. The business of hydrographic reconnaissance goes back to the Navy frogmen of World War II. It's a lead-line-and-slate operation. Individual soundings are taken manually by a line of swimmers and recorded on Plexiglas slates. BUD/S trainees perform noncombat, administrative surveys during daylight and at night in a simulated tactical situation. These soundings, along with surf and beach observations, are used to generate nearshore hydrographic survey charts, complete with standard nautical chart references and symbols. The first week consists mostly of classroom work, then the men take to the water to get their soundings and draw their charts. This work is not just a chapter in history for the BUD/S trainees. Deployed SEAL platoons do this work routinely for amphibious force commanders. In 1993, SEALs made hydrographic surveys of the beaches and harbors in Somalia before U.S. military units moved ashore. More recently, beaches in the Adriatic were surveyed in support of contingency planning for military operations in Kosovo. Whenever there is a potential for the Marines to go ashore, or whenever the U.S. military feels there may be a need to secure a beachhead to move supplies inland, SEALs are called to perform a hydrographic survey.

During the first week of this training, the men have PT sessions on Monday and Wednesday. These are light sessions with a great deal of stretching, especially on Monday. The new additions to Class 228 are fresh, and the instructors send them out to get wet and sandy often. By the end of the week, everyone is getting wet and sandy, and there is a normal ration of push-ups salted in with the classroom evolutions. Now that the trainees are past Hell Week, whenever they drop for push-ups, they drop for sets of thirty.

On Monday of the second week, there is a four-mile timed beach run. Those who make the thirty-two-minute cut get to jog easy and cool down. Those who don't—and this includes about half the recent Hell Week class—head into the surf for remediation. It still pays to be a winner. For one of the rollbacks there is no remediation; he is sent to the Phase Board and dropped from training. He was rolled back from 227 because of poor run times, and for him, there is no next week to try for a better time. Also on Monday, one of the original members of Class 228 decides he has had enough; he DORs. He had struggled during Hell Week, yet he made it through to Friday. "Why don't you hang in there a few more days?" the First Phase instructors tell him. "The end of First Phase is only two weeks away." But he's had enough; he wants no more cold water and punishment. He is also very weak from Hell Week and doubts that he will be able to meet the run and swim times. That leaves twenty-eight in Class 228— including eighteen of the originals.

The classroom evolutions are divided up among the First Phase staff, but the trainees see a lot of Instructor Mruk and Chief Nielson. And Instructor Terry Patstone. He's followed them into the classroom from Hell Week. Once the mechanics of the process are covered, the class takes to the water for practice hydrographic recons, first by day, then at night. In preparation for these outings, the class officers conduct the operational briefings and are responsible for the execution of the hydrographic survey.

During the second week, the class is surveying a section of the beach on the San Diego Bay side of the Amphibious Base. The water temperature has dropped to fifty-seven degrees in the bay. The swimmers are cold, but they have wet-suit tops and hoods. Instructor Patstone is in charge of the evolution and watches them from the shore. They are doing a perpendicular combat recon, in which the swimmers make their way shoreward from deep water, take soundings along the way, then retire back to the boats waiting offshore. Patstone feels they are not moving fast enough. He calls them in to the shore, makes them strip off their wet suits, and has them redo the survey. An hour later, the class comes out of the water a second time—and they're chilled to the bone. Petty Officer Sean Morrison, the medical rollback from Class 226 who was so active in 228's Hell Week, is probed and sent to the clinic to be warmed up.

"Chief Lincke said we'd be colder in the teams than we ever were in Hell Week," says Pat Yost, "but I didn't expect it to happen two weeks after Hell Week."

During the critique of the evolution, there is a change in Patstone. The intensity is there, but now he's a teacher.

"Okay," Patstone begins. "On balance, you guys did a good job. I hope you now understand that you have to pay attention and move quickly when you're on a combat recon." A collective shiver runs through the class as they think of their afternoon in the bay. "Get in, get the job done, and get the hell out. The task unit commander needs that information. The longer you're in the water, the greater the risk to the mission. And for you officers, the sooner you get your men out of the water, the less they will be at risk. Let's start from the beginning. Mister McGraw, you gave a good hydro brief." Ensign Matt McGraw is the new officer in the class, a medical rollback from Class 227. "But when you do your mission overview, give it to them in English and keep it short. Forget about all the big words in the Patrol Leader's Guide. You want your guys to see the big picture and understand the objectives of the mission. Then they will better understand their individual assignments when you get into the details of your briefing, okay? See what I'm getting at?"

McGraw does; they all do. Patstone can teach as well as he can torment. He walks them through the entire evolution, praising them and offering a list of "do betters"—ideas on how they may have approached an aspect of their survey differently or more effectively. Members of the class really want to hate Patstone, and he's given them good reason, but it's hard. Patstone is like a tough old Jesuit in a parochial school, roaming the isles of the classroom armed with a ruler. He can strike at any time, for any reason or no reason—highly unpredictable. But he cares and he knows his business. The trainees know this. They respect and even like Patstone, but they also still fear him.

. . .

It's the last week of hydro and of First Phase—another pivotal week. All the days at BUD/S are long; Tuesday of the last week in First Phase is one of the longest. Most nights, the trainees spend more time in the cold water than they do sleeping. On this Tuesday morning, they run the O-course for time after morning PT. They have a four-mile timed run on the beach in the afternoon. When not on these physical evolutions, the class prepares its charts from the previous night's survey and readies its equipment for the coming night's work. The men were up well past midnight on Monday conducting a parallel recon in the bay. This is a hydrographic reconnaissance in which the swimmers swim parallel to the beach to get their soundings—some men in deeper water, some along the shore. Tonight it's another parallel recon, only it's in the ocean. The surf is about eight feet, and the swimmers in the surf line get pounded. Ensign Joe Burns makes the swim with them. It's dangerous at night in that kind of surf, and he's worried about his students. He also loves big surf.

The last week of First Phase is also the last week of training for three of the original members of Class 228. Airman Alex Lopez never recovered from the cellulitis he developed in Hell Week. He has struggled on the O-course and never made a run time after Hell Week. If he wants to be a SEAL, he'll have to come back and try again. If he does, he knows he has what it takes; he made it through Hell Week.

Ensign Will Koella, like Lopez, never fully recovered from Hell Week. On the last timed four-mile run, he holds nothing back, but he cannot make the cutoff time. He, too, is dropped from 228. Unlike enlisted men, officers have only one shot; they are not allowed to return after time in the fleet. And under the current policy at BUD/S, there are no performance rollbacks, no time to heal and join up with the next class. Will Koella led his boat crew through Hell Week, but he will not go on to Second Phase with them. He's bitterly disappointed.

For four years at Annapolis he dreamed of becoming a Navy SEAL. He fought for and won one of the coveted billets at BUD/S. Now he's out. But Will Koella never quit. Some other branch of the Navy will get a good man, trained at Annapolis and tempered in a BUD/S Hell Week.

Ensign Chad Steinbrecher also can't make the run. But he now has full-blown pneumonia and is declared medically unfit to continue training. The fluid in Chad's lungs buys him a medical rollback to Class 229. And that's often the harsh reality at BUD/S. Two good men, both Annapolis graduates: one of them has the chance to keep his dream alive; the other will have to find another dream.

The lines have to be drawn somewhere. This means the medical officers and the phase boards must make some very difficult calls. These lines, within a narrow range, shift from year to year and commanding officer to commanding officer. For the most part, a young man's fate at BUD/S is in his own hands. For those very close to the line, it can seem arbitrary, unfair, and even cruel. But then so is the business of special operations and combat.

. . . .

On Thursday, when the class musters for training at the dive tower, the men are treated to something novel—warm water. The dive tower is a fifty-foot vertical steel cylinder filled with clear, heated, eighty-two-degree fresh-water. This is a training evolution, not a graded one; the instructors joke with the trainees as they prepare for the tower evolution. First the trainees dive to thirty feet and tie three of their knots on a jackstay. Then they make a fifty-foot dive and tie a single knot. Many in the class have never been this deep, and the fifty-footer is a real confidence builder. Patstone is there checking each man as he breaks the surface.

"I feel fine!"

He checks their eyes to make sure they can focus on him. If there is any doubt, he tells them to say it again.

"I feel fine, Instructor Patstone."

On Thursday afternoon there is another tradition—the Monster Mash. It's a race of sorts, and the last physical evolution of First Phase. And it still pays to be a winner.

The trainees line up on the beach behind the Center compound by the climbing ropes. They're in T-shirts, fatigue trousers, and boots. The race has a staggered start with a thirty-second interval between each contestant. First they all have to eat one of the jalapeño peppers that Joe Burns brought especially for the occasion. The officers also have to take a swallow of jalapeño juice. Then they're on the course. First they run down the beach and negotiate half of the O-course. Then they head back up the shoreline to Gator Beach, where they strip to their swim trunks. They toss their clothes in the back of Great White and keep running north, around the rocks, past the Hotel del to where Big Blue is waiting for them. Their swim gear is in the back of the pickup. They quickly jock-up in wet-suit tops and fins, and swim south around the rocks to Great White. Then it's out of the water, swap the swim gear for boots and fatigues, and run down the beach to finish the O-course. At the Slide for Life tower, there is a pail of eggs on the top platform and a bucket on the sand below. If they can drop an egg into the bucket, they get to subtract two minutes from their time. After the O-course, it's back to the starting point, up the climbing ropes, do four sets of thirty push-ups, get wet and sandy, and it's over.

There are instructors scattered over the course, and if they catch a trainee cheating, they drop him for push-ups. Sometimes they drop him even if he isn't cheating. The trainees cut corners where they can, and not all of them get caught. It pays to be a winner, or at least not the loser. When it's over, the wily John Owens is declared the Monster Mash champion. The loser, the man with the slowest time, is Jason Birch. He has to drink the Monster Mash grog—the last of the jalapeño juice, which has been laced with pepper and hot sauce. Ensign Birch chugs the grog and manages one of his broad, easy smiles before he deposits the libation back onto the beach.

Friday, the last day, features course critiques and individual trainee evaluations. The trainees are asked to rank their classmates one through twenty-five; the instructor staff does the same. Then each man is called in before an informal gathering of instructors in the First Phase office. For the most part, these are positive and upbeat performance reviews.

"Where do you think you excelled?"

"What are your weaknesses; what do you think you need to work on?"

"Good job . . . Stay focused."

"You know you have to work on your run times, or you won't make the Second Phase cutoff, understand?"

"You're done with First Phase, but don't let up."

"Congratulations. Keep up the good work."

"Don't forget to give us a thorough critique of the phase," Joe Burns tells them. "We can't hurt you anymore, so if you have a bitch, I want to know about it. Your opinion counts."

Petty Officer Pat Yost is rated first among his peers and at the top by the instructor staff. Mid-afternoon on this Friday, the twenty-five weary trainees, including fifteen of the originals who began Indoc together, gather up their gear and head across the grinder to the Second Phase classroom. It is December 10. Class 228 is still three weeks away from the halfway point in their twenty-seven-week Basic UDT/SEAL course.

Let the games begin! Class 228 waits at the Combat Training Tank for Instructor Reno to arrive on the first day of BUD/S training. Of the men in this photo, only one graduated.

The men of Class 228 learn they're going to be cold, wet, and sandy until the day they graduate. Airman Harry Pell on the beach during Indoc. Pell, a former Marine Corps officer, was one of the many former marines in Class 228.

Boat drills begin with the boat-crew leaders getting their orders. Petty Officer Lawrence Obst, nearest the camera, listens carefully.

Below: The IBS is an awkward craft, best suited to training and torturing SEALs-to-be. The members of Class 228, under their boats, struggle with the extended-arm carry.

Rock portage is a dangerous evolution. Here, the bow-line man and the first two members of the crew are already out and trying to hold the IBS steady.

Clint Burke leads Adam Karaoguz across the Burma Bridge. Big men like Burke (who's 6'5") often have trouble on the O-course.

Bill Gallagher, Class 228's leader from start to finish, threads his way through The Weaver obstacle.

Drown proofing. SEALs and SEAL trainees must learn to be comfortable in the water. Here, trainees bob for air.

For Navy SEALs, water is a refuge, not an obstacle. Trainees are taught to swim with both their arms and legs tied.

Push 'em out! Instructor Reno and Class 228 at the edge of the surf.

Chief Ken Taylor surf conditions—or surf tortures, depending on your point of view—Class 228 during Hell Week. Water temperature: 60 degrees.

Jason Birch pulls while the other members of his boat crew push as they run their IBS through the O-course. Cold, wet, and without sleep, a boat crew must perform as a team.

Class 228 does IBS sit-ups on the beach during Hell Week.

Even the strongest are challenged. Clint Burke shows the strain on Thursday night of Hell Week as he arrives at the chow hall. Note the bald spot on the top of his head from carrying the IBS.

Zack Shaffer waits by his IBS for the next surf passage race.

Zack Armstrong tucks into an MRE during Class 228's Hell Week. This was Armstrong's second Hell Week. Few men can do once what he did twice.

Trial by mud. Top to bottom, left to right: Will Koella, Harry Pell, Zack Shaffer, Zack Armstrong, Clint Burke, and Jason Birch—three officers, three enlisted men.

Wash down on the way to medical/hygiene inspection. Faces visible from front to back: Brendan Dougherty, Bill Gallagher, and Clint Burke.

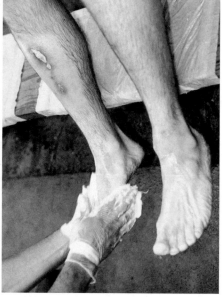

The price of days on the run with no sleep. Here a trainee gets a foot lube after his medical inspection, then quickly goes back into Hell.

"You're secure!" The nineteen men from Class 228 who made it through to the end of Hell Week.

Those who didn't make it. The green helmets from Class 228 and the BUD/S bell. Each helmet represents a DOR—drop on request.

Dan Luna demonstrates that "the only easy day was yesterday" as an instructor leaves him in a leaning rest. The weight belt and tanks weigh nearly 80 pounds.

Jocking-up in Second Phase. Left to right: Zack Armstrong, Clint Burke, Pat Yost, Jason Birch, and John Green.

Jason Birch awaits his turn for pool comps in Second Phase.

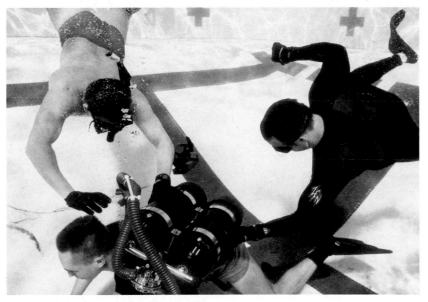

Two Second Phase instructors attack Matt Jenkins during pool competency testing. The trainees call it pool harassment.

The Wall of Shame. These 228 trainees will get a second chance to pass pool competency. If they fail, they will leave BUD/S.

This combat swimmer is geared up for a practice underwater ship attack wearing a Draeger LAR V Scuba. Day and night, members of Class 228 dove the Draeger and made mock underwater ship attacks.

"You cannot just aim; you must hit." Bob Ekoniak, A.K.A Instructor Ikon, coaches Bill Gallagher and Matt Jenkins at San Clemente Island on the use of the M-4 rifle.

Young warriors in the making: Adam Karaoguz and John Owens on San Clemente Island, ready for battle. Note the boom mics from their waterproof Saber radios.

Even in Third Phase, the trainees still have to "push 'em out." Now, though, they're expected to drop for 50 push-ups. Marc Luttrell (left) and Tyler Black are nearest the camera.

Matt Jenkins and Warren Conner carry two haversacks of C-4 to the beach. They're about to load it onto submerged obstacles for the underwater beach shot.

Top left: Charges set, Eric Oehlerich, Casey Lewis, John Owens, and Adam Karaoguz emerge from the surf. The det cord is for the backup electric firing assembly.

Bottom: Fire in the hole! Class 228's underwater shot goes high order.

Top right: Seaman Casey Lewis checks his equipment in preparation for Class 228's final battle problem on San Clemente Island.

The men of Class 228 as they listen to their graduation address by Captain Dick Couch. In a few minutes they will ring out of BUD/S and head for the teams.

Friends now! Adam Karaoguz and Class 228's First Phase proctor, Instructor Sean Mruk, on graduation day.

The last of the originals from Class 228 graduate. Left to right: Sean Morrison (began with Class 227), Chris Baldwin, Grant Terpstra, and Miguel (Yanny) Yanez. All graduated with Class 230.

CHAPTER FIVE

INTO THE SEA

ake your seats, gentlemen. Welcome to Second Phase. My name is
Steve McKendry and I will be your class proctor. Do you have a
report for me, Mister Gallagher?"

Gallagher rises. "Hooyah, Instructor. Thirty-six men assigned, thirty-six
men present."

Class 228 has been reconfigured, just as it was after Hell Week. And
once again, eleven men have been added to the class—this time, two officers and nine enlisted men. Most are rollbacks from Class 227. The rollbacks are like replacements for battlefield casualties in 228's war of
attrition at BUD/S. The character of the class changes with each of these
augmentations. Since the class must function as a unit, these new men will
have to meld quickly into the group. Gallagher and Yost organize the class
into six boat crews, with one of the six class officers to head each crew.
There are no boats in Second Phase; it's an accountability convenience.
When Gallagher asks for a count, his boat-crew leaders answer: "One's
up . . . Two's up . . . ," and he can quickly report the status of the class.

McKendry is one of the junior instructors in Second Phase and no older
than some of the senior petty officers in Class 228. He is a very fit man

with a calm intensity. He looks young, with choirboylike good looks and a soft manner. McKendry deployed with SEAL Team Two and served with Special Boat Unit Twenty before coming to BUD/S. Like many BUD/S instructors, he is finishing his college degree in his spare time. For McKendry, it's computer science. He consults his notes for a few moments, then speaks in a quiet, measured voice.

"Most of you have just completed First Phase. Some of you have been here before and are back for another try at this phase. You are all the same class now, Class 228. Let me tell you what I expect—what you will need to do if you want to successfully complete Second Phase.

"First of all, I like being an instructor here. This may sound strange, but I even liked being a BUD/S student. I think you need to like this business to be successful at it. At least, that's how I see it. Let me tell you what I don't like. I have little tolerance for anyone who sandbags it—does just enough to get by or cuts corners. That may have been tolerated to some degree in First Phase. Not here. We don't cut corners underwater. You cut corners here and it can get someone killed, your swim buddy or possibly yourself." He pauses a moment. "I also have little patience for those who lack spirit. You get through this training as a class. If you aren't contributing to your class spirit, then you're holding your classmates back— you're sandbagging it." He again pauses a moment to regard the class. "And what I will not tolerate at all is being late for watch or missing watch. This is a duty you have to perform. If you're late, it shows you don't care about your classmates—your future teammates. Miss a watch or show up late and I'll see you out of here. Is that clear?"

"HOOYAH!"

"Now, you've all been around here long enough to know the rules, but for the record, let's make sure. Mexico is off-limits; stay away from the border. Alcohol. If you are involved in any alcohol-related incident, no matter what the provocation or circumstance, you will be removed from training. Is there any question about that?"

"NEGATIVE!"

"Good. Let me tell you something about myself. I don't drink. I used to, but I don't anymore. I had a couple of 'almosts.' You know the kind of thing I'm talking about—things that almost get you into a whole lot of trouble. I decided that if I kept drinking, sooner or later it would cost me something very valuable. So I quit. You all can do what you like, but don't let alcohol come between you and accomplishing your goals here at BUD/S.

"You have duties and responsibilities here in Second Phase, more so than in First Phase. In addition to the vehicles, medical equipment, diving equipment, charging bottles, and all that, you are responsible for the phase status boards. The rollbacks know about the collateral duties and can help you with the office chores. And don't forget the cartoon. Every day we want a new cartoon in the Second Phase office. It better be well drawn and it better be funny. Now, your Second Phase training will have a Christmas break. We shut down training for the Christmas holiday. Don't lose your focus over Christmas.

"It goes without saying that we expect you to show respect for the staff and for the chain of command. I expect you to have respect for your class-mates as well." Again he studies his notes. "The performance standards from First Phase will not be good enough here. The four-mile-run time will have to come down to thirty-one minutes. Swim times in open water: two miles in eighty minutes. Your obstacle course times will start at eleven minutes, but after pool comp week you'll have to do the O-course under ten and a half minutes. You all know the policy about performance roll-backs—they don't exist at BUD/S anymore. Meet the standards or you're history."

He gives them a shy smile. "I tend to like physical conditioning, and if you're having a problem, I can help. Especially with the runs. I'll work with you and help get those run times down. This also goes with any problem you may have, training-related or personal. Let me know and I'll help. I know two of you guys are married. So am I. This business can be hard on a spouse, but you have to stay focused on training. Any of you can call me anytime, day or night—weekends, anytime. I'm here to help you get through this training. Questions?"

There are none.

. . .

Friday night, the last day of First Phase the class holds their end of First Phase party. It's basically the same venue as the class-up party after Indoc, only there are fewer of them to celebrate. Some of the trainees find a stack of pallets nearby and build a fire on the beach. They were up most of the previous night and worked late that afternoon following Instructor McKendry's Second Phase briefing. The elation of leaving First Phase is giving way to weariness. They'll have one evening to celebrate, and those who don't have watch will have Saturday free. Sunday will be devoted to preparing their rooms for inspection on Monday and attending to their collateral duties in the Second Phase spaces. And they have to repaint their helmets. The green helmets are no more; the white 228 numerals will adorn blue helmets for Second Phase.

The new First Phase graduates begin to gather shortly before 1800. They sit around in small groups and drink beer or hard cider, and talk about training. Those who remain in Class 228 have won a major battle, but the outcome of the war is still to be decided. Each of them understands this.

"It seems like no matter how far you get in this business," Bill Gallagher remarks, "you still have a long way to go. In some ways, it's gone by quickly, but I'm getting so tired of the long days. Thank God for the weekends."

The original fifteen members of 228 are now a minority in their own class, but the class leadership remains with Lieutenant (jg) Bill Gallagher and Petty Officer Pat Yost. They are still the senior officer and senior enlisted members of the expanded class, but had that not been the case, they would remain the class leaders. By tradition, they retain these positions as legacy of their unbroken training record.

Among the new men are Ensign Eric Oehlerich and Ensign John Green. Oehlerich came to BUD/S from the Naval Academy, where he was a classmate of Jason Birch and Clint Burke—Class of '99. Naval Academy graduates from the same year group are spread over several BUD/S classes. Oehlerich came to the Naval Academy from Whitefish, Montana, where he had to choose between Annapolis and the U.S. Alpine Ski Team. Oehlerich is a strong BUD/S trainee, a leader in Class 227 until the accident that broke his hand. For the last two months, he has endured the purgatory of PTRR, waiting to begin Second Phase with 228. John Green has been in PTRR with Oehlerich, healing from stress fractures in his shins. Green is a linguist and a Harvard graduate. He speaks seven languages—eight counting English—and is fluent in Arabic and French.

The twenty-five recent First Phase graduates know their new classmates; they've all been around BUD/S for a while. For the 228 originals, many of the new men were the ones who helped them during Hell Week. Among the most welcome of the new faces is Seaman Marc Luttrell. Luttrell's goal is to become a SEAL team corpsman. He, too, is recovering from stress fractures. Luttrell is a legacy; his father, Danny Luttrell, was a Vietnam-era frogman. Dad expected that Marc would come into the family business after he graduated from college. It was with mixed feelings that Danny learned his son had enlisted in the Navy to become a SEAL.

"I heard too many stories about the teams when I was growing up, Dad," he told his father. "Now it's my turn to follow my dream."

Marc's younger brother recently flew out to Coronado to visit his brother and to meet with the BUD/S medical officers. Recovering from a badly broken femur, he wanted to see if it would prevent him from also coming to BUD/S. As soon as he graduates from college, he, too, will enlist and follow his brother and father to BUD/S.

The party starts slowly, but soon gathers momentum. Most of the men in Class 228 have had little alcohol for several months. A cup or two of beer from the keg and they begin to loosen up.

John Owens is still basking in his victory at the Monster Mash. "You know," he tells his classmates, "I think that evolution says a lot about a man's character and his ability to deal with adversity. A guy who can handle the Monster Mash is a real stud." Owens is wearing a gaudy belt buckle that his classmates presented him for winning the Monster Mash.

"What are you talking about?" sputters Otter Obst, always the competitor. "You cheated; I saw you. You ran completely around the high wall."

Owens sips his beer and pats Obst on the shoulder. "It's okay, son. You've done well in training and you're going to do just fine in Second Phase. But . . . you came in second on the Monster Mash. Otter, that makes you a loser. Hey, a nice guy and all that, but a loser."

"Yeah, right—I'm a loser." Obst rolls his eyes. He knows Owens is the last person to take himself seriously, but Obst is a competitor. He hates to lose under any circumstances.

"Hey, Otter, why don't you just call me 'Champ'." Owens looks around with an easy grin. "Y'know, that has a nice sound to it—John Owens, champ."

"I can't stand this," the Otter replies. "I'm going for another beer."

"How do you feel about heading into Second Phase?" I ask Owens.

"I'm kind of looking forward to it, actually. Maybe we won't be so cold in Second Phase. I'm really tired of being cold all the time."

"Are you serious?" says Zack Armstrong, who joins us. "Second Phase is dive phase. We'll be in the water. The water's cold."

"I know that. I'm talking cold like in Hell Week cold or hydro cold."

Armstrong nods. Both of them remember the hydro recon in the bay when Instructor Patstone sent them back out without wet suits to finish.

Owens and Armstrong are solid, archetypal BUD/S trainees. Both are about five-nine, 155 pounds. Neither has the bulk nor the impressive physique of a Hollywood SEAL. Both are hard as nails. John Owens is from Fort Lauderdale; Zack Armstrong is from Thornton, Colorado, just north of Denver. During Hell Week, they could always muster a smile, and they always had time to help a classmate when things really got bad. They've been here before. Owens joined the Navy after two years of college; Armstrong, right out of high school. Both first came to BUD/S from Navy boot camp. Both DORed from a previous class—

THE WARRIOR ELITE • *185*

Owens with Class 208, Armstrong with Class 212. After a tour in the fleet, they are back as second class petty officers—more mature and very focused.

When I asked him about it, Owens downplays his strong motivation to be a Navy SEAL. "I just want to do something special before I get too old—ah, no offense, sir," he quickly adds with a grin. "When I was here before, I don't think I had the right attitude. I didn't want it bad enough. Now? Well, now I'm here, ready to give it my best shot. If my best shot isn't good enough, so be it; I'll move on and not look back. But this time I'll know I held nothing back. I won't quit, though. If they want me to leave, they'll have to drag me out of here."

When he was in Class 212, Zack Armstrong DORed after Hell Week. His knees were swollen and he simply couldn't pass the run times. He gutted it out as long as he could, but quit just a week before the end of First Phase. This was Armstrong's second Hell Week. Few BUD/S trainees who survive one Hell Week have the courage to come back a second time. BUD/S lore has it that one man did it three times.

"I've been really curious to know," I ask him. "Which Hell Week was the hardest?"

Armstrong is on his second beer and gives me a lopsided grin. "It's hard to say; they both really sucked. But I think this one was a little easier. It's a stronger class—better organized—and we seem to catch less heat from the instructors for the little things. Also, I think these First Phase instructors were more positive than when I was here before. There was nobody here then like Chief Taylor. You don't want to disappoint a man like that."

"You guys like Taylor, don't you?"

"Yeah, he's a great role model and you can trust him. As long as you put out, he'll do his best to help you get through."

"About Hell Week. How did you feel about having to do it a second time?"

Armstrong just shrugs. "I had no choice. Along about Monday night I said, 'Hey, this really hurts.' But I just told myself that I did it once and I can do it again. Now all I want to do is get this behind me and get to the teams."

"No third Hell Week?"

"No way."

A few of the First Phase instructors arrive, led by Sean Mruk. He's almost as glad to have Class 228 gone as they are to be out of First Phase. Class proctors work hard; they come in very early and often stay into the night to work with their class. Mruk will get a week off from BUD/S, partial compensation for all the extra hours he put in with 228. Then he will be back as a regular instructor for the next class. As he was with Class 227, he will be one of the haters in First Phase for Class 229.

Class 228's First Phase party attracts some other graduates. The SEAL Tactical Training class had their graduation that afternoon. STT is a three-month advanced training course that serves the active SEAL and SDV teams. New BUD/S graduates attend this training soon after they return from Army Airborne School. The West Coast STT training is conducted by Naval Special Warfare Group One for SEAL Teams One, Three, and Five and SDV Team One. Group Two sponsors similar training for SEAL Teams Two, Four, and Eight and SDV Team Two. Since the STT graduation was earlier that afternoon, many of them have been at McP's, so they have a good start on Class 228. McP's Irish Pub in Coronado is the unofficial West Coast SEAL watering hole, similar to The Cutter in Virginia Beach for the East Coast teams. STT is an intense and challenging course, and a milestone in qualifying for the SEAL Trident pin. Nonetheless, these soon-to-be SEALs remember what it was like to finish First Phase. Everyone is talking shop, swapping Hell Week and training stories. The officers tend to seek each other out. Since a majority of them are from the Naval Academy, they all know each other. They form a kind of executive, junior officer Mafia. But their BUD/S affiliation transcends the Academy connection. Ensigns McGraw and Green move comfortably among the Annapolis men. The STT-Annapolis grads are anxious to know why so many of their alumni in 228 quit in Hell Week. It's a small community and there are few secrets. The STT officers have already heard about Clint Burke's strong performance in Hell Week, and they want to know more about it. Chad Steinbrecher and Will Koella are also there; they are no longer in 228, but their gritty performance in Hell Week earned them the privilege. They congratulate the First Phase graduates and bravely accept the condolences of their former classmates.

"Hey, Captain Couch," Bill Gallagher says as he beckons me to join them, "we heard that when you went through training, there were no billets to BUD/S directly from the Naval Academy. None at all?"

"That's right. The few of us from the Boat School who came to BUD/S had to do a tour in the fleet, just like you did, Bill. In my case, I was discouraged from the highest level."

"Sir?"

"Well, it's a bit of a story."

"Hey, sir," says Chad Steinbrecher as he hands me a cup of beer, "that's what we're here for. Let's have it."

"As you guys know, Admiral Draper Kauffman is the founder of UDT and the Navy frogmen. He was also an Academy graduate. He was not commissioned in the Navy due to his poor eyesight, so he went to Europe and served in France and England prior to our entry into World War II. In England during the Blitz, he became a demolitions expert. In 1941, the Navy called him home to active duty. After the casualties on the beaches at Tarawa, the Navy sent then–Lieutenant Commander Kauffman to the east coast of Florida to solve the problem. At Fort Pierce, Kauffman began to train men for demolition work on landing beaches. So he was the first Naval Academy man in the teams. And we're all the descendants of those first frogmen trained by Admiral Kauffman at Fort Pierce.

"In spring of 1967, I was a first class midshipman just a few months from graduation. Boy, did I want out of there." This gets a round of chuckles. "That April my company mates and I were required to attend a reception at the home of the Academy superintendent. You guys have to do that as firsties?" I get a round of knowing looks and grimaces. "Then you know the deal. We had to remain there for an hour, and we all kept an eye on our watches. When it was my turn to meet the admiral, he asked, 'Mister

Couch, what will be your choice on Service Selection Night?' I replied, 'A destroyer out of Japan to begin with, sir. But as soon as I can, I'm going to go to UDT.' Well, the great man put his arm around me like he was my dad and says, 'Son, you're regular Navy. You have a wonderful career ahead of you in the fleet. You can be a destroyer man, an aviator, or a submariner, but there's no future for you in underwater demolition. That's not why you're here at Annapolis.' He had a deeply tanned face, thick glasses, and rows of combat decorations. For me, it was like talking to God. 'Thanks for the advice, sir,' I told him, 'but I'm going to do it anyway.' He smiled, I smiled, and he moved on to talk with one of my classmates. Well, guys, that superintendent was none other than Rear Admiral Draper Kauffman."

"You mean *the* Draper Kauffman tried to talk you *out* of going to BUD/S?"

"You're shitting us, sir."

I shrug. "That's the way it was then. Most of us were told it was career suicide. The CO on my ship endorsed my request to BUD/S, 'forwarded, not recommended.' How many of you came to BUD/S from the Class of Ninety-nine?"

"Sixteen," replies Clint Burke.

"The same from my class," says Gallagher. "How many in your class got to the teams?"

"Seven of us from the Class of Sixty-seven. Only one, Admiral Ray Smith, is still on active duty."

"Did you ever talk to Admiral Kauffman again?" Will Koella asks.

I shake my head. "No, but he did sign my diploma from the Naval Academy. I have it at home."

Unlike the trainees at the Indoc party, the members of Class 228 here tonight look much less like a group of college students. Collectively, there is little attempt to be trendy; the dress is more conservative. It's colder than it was just eight weeks ago at the beginning of First Phase. Most of them wear jeans or shorts, sneakers, and sweaters or sweatshirts. The STT graduates have not yet earned their Tridents, but many of them wear their ball caps with team logos. Only Harry Pell shows up in different attire. Pell is a biker, and he turns out in black leather and a head scarf. Few take notice, but one of the STT grads makes a comment about the little guy in the Zorro outfit. "Hey, he was in my boat crew during Hell Week," Zack Armstrong tells him. "He pulled his load and then some." End of discussion.

A spirited debate breaks out between two members of 228, one of the new men and one of the originals, as to who had been wet and sandy last. They decide to settle the issue by seeing who can get wet first. They disappear over the berm and return a few moments later, soaked to the skin. The two men get a fresh beer and go stand by the fire to dry out.

Seaman Chris Baldwin is his usual talkative, affable self, and with the addition of Ensign John Green to the class, he now has someone to speak Arabic with. Jason Birch wanders about with a Coke in his hand and his familiar grin. He's like a man running for office. At one time or another during training, everyone in 228 has received a helping hand from Ensign Birch. He makes sure he spends a few minutes with each of his classmates, old and new. Clint Burke and Bill Gallagher pull on their beers and talk with Ensign John Cremmins, who is at SEAL Team Three. Cremmins just finished STT. Cremmins and Burke were classmates at the Academy until Burke took his year's leave of absence. Pat Yost is at his ease, but he's still the leading petty officer. When he sets down his beer and begins to change the keg, Dan Luna and Tyler Black are right there to help him. Dan Luna is one of the quiet originals from 228. No one noticed him until he was still there at the end of Hell Week. Black is an affable prankster who grew up in Tyler, Texas, and always has a mischievous grin. A medical rollback from 227, Tyler Black is an anomaly at BUD/S—he's chubby. But while he doesn't look like a BUD/S trainee and is never at the head of the pack, he always gets the job done. His classmates call him "D-8," a reference to the largest bulldozer in the Caterpillar line of earthmovers.

Courtesies between the officers and the enlisted men are carefully observed and seemingly effortless. Bill Gallagher is often addressed as "El-Tee," for lieutenant, and the ensigns are called "Mister." For the most part, the officers call the enlisted men by their first name. This protocol seems to work in military and nonmilitary situations, and this is very important. In the teams, the junior officers and enlisted men live, train, deploy, and fight together. They are teammates first; rank and privilege are secondary issues. All of this is a part of Class 228's training. The First Phase party is a gathering of apprentice warriors. They are a long way from becoming SEALs, but they are already in a class by themselves. They've all been through Hell Week.

By 2200, the beach is almost clear. Some of the partyers head off for the Night & Day Café in Coronado that serves breakfast twenty-four hours a day. BUD/S students are like hunting dogs; they can always eat. John Owens finds Zack Armstrong asleep, propped up against one of the cabanas near the fire. "Hey, pal, the party's about over. Let's go home."

"Over? Already?"

Armstrong rubs his eyes, and Owens pulls him to his feet.

"G'night, Captain Couch."

"G'night, guys."

Leaning on each other, the two of them shuffle off in the direction of the Naval Special Warfare barracks a short walk down the beach.

· · ·

At 0500 on Monday, 13 December, Class 228 officially begins Second Phase with PT on the Second Phase grinder—a blacktop area just outside the dive locker. It is a rough PT. After a run across the base for breakfast, and back, they file into the Second Phase classroom. Their schedule will keep them close to the classroom for the next two weeks. Except for room and personnel inspections, the O-course, timed and conditioning runs, and timed two-mile ocean swims, they will focus on academics. The class takes one morning off for oxygen tolerance tests. In small groups, they are taken down to sixty feet in the recompression chamber, where they breathe pure oxygen. A small percentage of the population has a toxic reaction to oxygen under pressure. The men of Class 228 come through just fine.

The first week is devoted to diving physics. Their proctor, Steve McKendry, is also their instructor—and he is tireless. Classes last most of the day. Each night, they are back in the classroom for study time. McKendry is there, patiently explaining the relationship between temperature, pressure, and volume—Boyle's law and Charles's law. Some of the trainees have difficulty with basic algebra. For others, it's simply a problem of multiplication and long division—with pencil and paper. The diving physics test at the end of the first week is a timed examination, and time runs out for several in the calculator generation. All pass the retest but two; one of them is Airman Harry Pell. He is given a third exam, but he fails this one, too. He's out, and he's not alone. One of the rollbacks from First Phase hydro joins him.

Harry Pell, the former Marine Corps officer, has a hard-won degree in history from the University of Pennsylvania. Between his sophomore and junior years at Penn, he was in a serious automobile crash. The accident left him unable to walk or talk. He had to learn to do both again. He understands the diving physics material, but sometimes he is slow and unable to manage the math and algebra in the allotted time. The Second Phase Review Board recommends that he be dropped from the phase, and the Academic Review Board sends him back to the fleet. Well, almost back to the fleet. They would like to have Pell back, so he is given orders to the Naval Special Warfare Detachment in Bahrain in a physical security billet. There he will be able to stay in shape and work on his diving physics and math skills. It's a twelve-month assignment.

"I'll be back," Pell says with conviction. "This is where I belong."

The loss of Harry Pell, one of the originals from 228, brings the whole class down, especially those that were in his Hell Week boat crew—Shaffer, Armstrong, and Dan Luna. Like most of them during Hell Week, Pell could be up or down. But when he was up, his spirit was highly contagious and he could carry his entire boat crew. He never quit, and he will be missed.

The future of Harry Pell illustrates the fate that awaits any enlisted man who leaves BUD/S, whether they DOR during Indoc or leave training the week before graduation. They are U.S. Navy sailors. Not all are as fortunate as Pell and get a shore assignment. Many are assigned to the fleet and find themselves in a crowded berthing compartment on a carrier in the Indian Ocean or assigned to a destroyer—like the USS *Cole*. A high percentage of these BUD/S attrites are college graduates or men who have left successful civilian careers. They joined the Navy to become a SEAL. Now they find themselves at sea with a highly restrictive lifestyle, long work hours, and few privileges. Some, like John Owens, use this at-sea time to grow and mature, and return to BUD/S better able to succeed. But most simply endure as much as four more years in the Navy, waiting to begin a new life out of uniform.

For the officers, it's different. They will go to a shipboard wardroom or a shore facility with officer's clubs and comfortable quarters. Their pay is reasonable and their life comfortable. If they elect not to stay in the Navy, their time in uniform will become a good bullet on their résumé. This is why the BUD/S instructors, who are all enlisted men, lean heavier on their officer trainees. They know officers who leave BUD/S get treated much differently than enlisted men.

Class 228 finishes the first week of Second Phase on the afternoon of 17 December. That Friday morning, Class 226 graduated from BUD/S. That class was led by two very talented trainees. Lieutenant David Ismay was 226's class leader. Ismay graduated first in his class from Annapolis and is a Rhodes scholar, having taken an advanced degree at Oxford after leaving the Naval Academy. Lieutenant Andrew Ledford, also a Naval Academy graduate, was a captain in the Marine Corps before deciding he wanted to become a Navy SEAL. These two full lieutenants led thirty-three trainees from Class 226 through BUD/S and into the teams.

Class 228's two weeks of classroom work is bisected by the two-week break in training for Christmas leave. The trainees return to BUD/S on 2 January 2000. After the final week in the classroom, they are scheduled for the critical pool competency testing. But not all of them make it to pool comps. In addition to Pell, Seaman Chris Baldwin is forced out of the class. After living with pains in his stomach for several days, he finally turns himself into the BUD/S medical clinic. There he learns that he has a double hernia that will require surgery. He is medically rolled back from Class 228.

Baldwin is put on light duty in the Second Phase dive locker, so he is near his class but not with them. Seaman Chris Baldwin was a solid performer. He will go into surgery the same day Class 228 begins their pool competency testing.

Another loss to the class is Ensign Matt McGraw. Since he joined Class 228 in hydro, he has quietly become one of the class leaders. The enlisted men look to him for guidance, and Bill Gallagher has come to rely on him. McGraw graduated from Ohio State, where he excelled at water polo before attending Officer's Candidate School. He came to Class 228 with stress fractures in his shins that appeared to be healed. He had no problem with the physical evolutions in hydro during First Phase, but then the 228 originals were still healing after Hell Week—PT was light and the runs short. During the first timed run in Second Phase, McGraw turned in one of the fastest times of the class. Then the stress fractures returned. He tried to tough it out, but his injuries are serious; his legs are broken. Still, he tried to limp on, hoping to stay with his new class. Finally, the BUD/S senior medical officers pronounced Ensign McGraw medically unfit to continue training.

This put the Academic Review Board in a bind. BUD/S students are normally not allowed a second medical rollback, and officers are given only one shot at BUD/S training. Unlike enlisted men, they cannot go away and come back a year or two later and try again. McGraw's training record speaks for itself with the board; he is an outstanding trainee and a promising leader, consistently ranked high by the instructor staff and his fellow students.

"Mister McGraw, if we send you away, you will not be allowed to come back to BUD/S," Lieutenant Phil Black tells him at the Academic Review Board. Black is the Second Phase officer and chairs the board. "You know that, don't you?"

"Yes, sir."

"We have a policy against two medical rolls and if we send you back to the fleet, you're gone forever. Doctor Witucki says it may take as long as six months for you to heal. We don't have a lot of options here. In all fairness, we should have given you more time to heal when you were first injured."

"You have to do what you have to do, sir. If I have to leave, I'll resign my commission and come back as an enlisted man. But I will become a Navy SEAL, one way or another."

The board looks for a way to save McGraw and finds one. He will be kept in the community, but sent down the street to the Naval Special Warfare Command. There he will serve as a staff officer until his legs heal, then be reassigned to another BUD/S class in Second Phase. Often the system cannot find a way to keep a man like Matt McGraw, but this time there was a solution.

Four other students, men who joined Class 228 in Second Phase, are lost before the class gets to pool comp week. One man is medically rolled to Class 229 because of an injury to his Achilles tendon, and another is medically dropped from the program. Yet another DORs during the O-course. After two unsuccessful tries at one of the more challenging obstacles, he turns to Instructor McKendry and says, "That's it; I'm done with this." He walks away wanting nothing more to do with training. The fourth member of 228 has a minor run-in with the Amphibious Base Police. There is zero tolerance for trainees who violate regulations; he is quickly separated from the class and from BUD/S.

A relatively high dropout rate for students who roll into a phase from PTRR is not uncommon. While they are in PTRR, it is easy for trainees to lose momentum and get discouraged. PTRR students live in the BUD/S compound and have no class affiliation. They have scheduled evolutions designed to rehabilitate their injuries, but they are not a class. At one time or another, every BUD/S trainee needs his classmates to help him through. Some, like Ensign Eric Oehlerich and Seaman Marcus Luttrell, desperately want to be SEALs and stay focused. They come out of PTRR fired up, ready to pull with their new class. Others are never able to get back on track.

The academic portion of Second Phase concludes at the end of week two. The students must pass exams in diving physics, diving medicine, and diving decompression tables. Only one student gets a perfect score on all three—Seaman Casey Lewis. None of the officers—four Naval Academy men and a Harvard graduate—are able to match this performance. I asked Casey Lewis about this.

"I studied engineering at Oklahoma for two years. I carried a good grade point average there, but I wanted a challenge—a physical challenge. That's why I left college and came here."

"But the three exams," I pointed out. "You never missed a single question."

An easy smile comes over his handsome face. "You just wouldn't believe this high school physics teacher I had. He was incredible. He taught us more than just formulas; he taught us to understand physical relationships—how forces reacted and why. I never had any problem in college with math or physics. And I have no problems here."

On the Friday before pool comp week, the class spends the day at the dive tower. Here the trainees are introduced to free-swimming ascents, or FSAs. They make one FSA from twenty-five feet and another from fifty feet. At the end of First Phase, they swam down to the twenty-five- and fifty-foot levels, tied knots, and returned to the surface. Today they enter a diving bell at each depth, breathe air under pressure, then make the FSA. Breathing air in the bell at twenty-five feet, they will have nearly twice the amount of air in their lungs as they do at the surface—and close to three times the normal amount at fifty feet. As they swim to the surface, they must continuously exhale—blow bubbles—or risk an overexpansion of air in their lungs with potentially fatal results. This training is as dangerous as any they will do at BUD/S; a diving medical officer is on scene and the recompression chamber stationed at the top of the tower is on standby. FSAs are taught so that in the event a SEAL should ever have to abandon his diving rig while on a mission, he can do so and safely get to the surface.

This is a stressful evolution for Class 228. While they rise from the fifty-foot bell to the surface, they must continuously expel air. There is an instructor right there with them, one on one, to ensure they do it properly. If the instructor feels his student is not expelling a sufficient amount of air, he will stop the FSA or jab his student in the stomach to demand a stronger blow. This is the last evolution before the class begins open-circuit training and pool comp week. They all pass FSA training. Only the Otter has problems. Obst is having difficulty clearing his ears due to a persistent sinus infection left over from Hell Week. The medical staff is keeping an eye on him. After FSA training at the end of week two, there are twenty-eight trainees. Only thirteen of them are originals.

Week three is pool competency week. The last time they were in the CTT was during Hell Week for pool games and general surface harassment from the First Phase instructors. Now they are back for diving instruction and underwater harassment. Pool comp week is the Hell Week of Second Phase. With the exception of Hell Week and possibly the first week of First Phase, pool comp week usually has the highest attrition. It's an anxious time for Class 228, just as it is for every class.

The students muster at the dive locker well before 0430 on Monday to prepare their scuba rigs and the required medical and support equipment. Outside the Second Phase dive locker, the twin 80s are charged and gauged to 2,250 pounds per square inch (psi), then arranged in dive pairs—fourteen of them. Next to each set of tanks, the trainees lay out their weight belts and life vests. Lines of swim fins bound upright by face masks stand as sentinels to the prepped dive rigs. After an hour of PT and a run to the chow hall, 228 returns to the classroom for a two-hour presentation on open-circuit scuba—self-contained underwater breathing apparatus. They pay close attention. For many of them, this will be their first experience breathing underwater. For all of them, it's the first time they will use the Jacques Cousteau–style, double-hose regulators.

Class 228 gets a complete briefing on the open-circuit, two-hose scuba. The tanks are two steel cylinders connected by a manifold with a J-valve, manual reserve. They are called twin 80s because eighty cubic feet of air is compressed into each tank when fully charged. The double-hose scuba regulator is something out of the past. In the early 1960s, single-hose regulators replaced the two-hose models because they were simpler, safer, and easier to maintain. Only in BUD/S training do they still teach open-circuit scuba with the old double-hose equipment. There's a good reason for this. Next week the trainees will transition to the Draeger Lar V closed-circuit diving rig. Two hoses are required for closed-circuit operation.

After lunch and a detailed dive briefing by Instructor Michael Peters, the twenty-eight trainees of Class 228 scramble from the classroom to their dive gear. First they are inspected wearing only their life jackets. Following the life jacket check, they get fully jocked-up with twin 80s and a weight belt. Each trainee carries twelve pounds of lead around his waist. With face mask in one hand and fins in the other, they line up to be inspected by their diving supervisor, or dive supe. The instructors check the fit of every diver's straps and weight belt, and ensure that their air supply is fully functional.

"How many fingers should I be able to get in the loop of your quick-release straps!"

"Three fingers, Instructor Calvin."

"Then how come I can only get two fingers in the loop on your chest strap?"

"Uh, I'm not sure, Instructor," the trainee slurs around his mouthpiece. When the students are fully jocked-up with tanks, they always have their scuba mouthpieces in their mouths. "Maybe you just have big fingers?"

"Oh, yeah, wise guy. Well, maybe you just have a little brain." Calvin adjusts the strap and completes his inspection of the student. "Drop."

The hapless student drops and so does his swim buddy. Twin 80s weigh just under sixty pounds when fully charged, slightly less when empty. The weight belt adds another twelve. The two students push them out while Instructor Spencer Calvin moves on to inspect the next swim pair. Infractions are not always punished with push-ups. Sometimes students have to flop down on their backs—on their tanks, really—and do flutter kicks. Once inspected, the trainees board an old school bus for the drive across the Amphibious Base to the CTT.

Second Phase pool evolutions are formatted, well-orchestrated events in which students are expected to follow strict procedures and display specific skills. This begins on the first dive—open-circuit familiarization. The dive has three limited but important objectives: familiarization, buddy breathing, and student gear inspection. After the class has prepared the medical equipment and pool gear, they are again inspected and sent into the pool.

"It was a strange feeling, breathing underwater," recalls Seaman Grant Terpstra. This was his first experience with scuba. "It wasn't so bad at first. Then we had to take off our face masks. Breathing without a mask took some getting used to. Inhaling through the mouthpiece with water in my nose was weird until I got the hang of it. But once I did it a few times, no problem."

"I had a little problem with the double-hose regulator," said Zack Shaffer. "It's harder to draw on than I thought it would be. I did a lot of diving before I came in the Navy, but only with a single-hose rig. For a while, I had trouble clearing water from the mouthpiece. Then I got used to tilting to the left to clear and it was okay."

For the next hour, the swim pairs circle the pool, practicing mask clearing, buddy breathing, clearing their mouthpieces, and getting comfortable with breathing underwater. With twelve pounds of lead strapped to their waist, they half paddle, half crawl around the pool. They also do their first in-water dive supe checks. This is a drill that they will do again and again, under stress and in strict order of precedence. Today there is no harassment from the instructors, although a half dozen of them circle above the submerged swim pairs. Occasionally, they bring two students to the surface for some coaching. Everyone is getting the hang of it. It's an easy day for everyone except one trainee.

Otter Obst is having no problem with the equipment, but he is having problems with his sinuses. When his lingering sinus infection flares up, he cannot clear or equalize the pressure in his ears and sinuses. Obst was able to complete the dive tower evolutions, the fifty-foot free dive in First Phase, and the fifty-foot FSA last week, but today he's having difficulty. Obst is not a whiner; he's in serious pain. Try as he may, he cannot relieve the air trapped in his sinus cavities. When he finally does make it to the fifteen-foot depth in the CTT, the pain overwhelms him and he has to surface.

"I can't clear my ears, Instructor, and my sinuses are killing me."

"Finish the dive or get out of the pool," Obst is told. "And if you get out, you're done."

"I can't go back down," Obst tells them. There's frustration and anger in his voice. "I guess I'm done."

Just like that, Class 228 loses its strongest trainee. The Otter owned the best time on the O-course and the fastest four-mile run time. He always finished in the top two or three pairs for timed swims. Lawrence Obst was one of the few who could do it all and do it well—a complete BUD/S trainee. When examined at BUD/S medical, Obst is found to have a severe squeeze in both ears and his sinus cavities. The senior medical officer immediately takes him off dive status. He needs time to heal. If he can clear up his sinus problems, he will be medically rolled back to the next class. Obst has been a class leader as well as a strong trainee. His classmates, especially the 228 originals, are stunned.

The Otter is gone, but there is little time for reflection. A BUD/S class is like an infantry company assaulting a strongly fortified position. Men get wounded and killed in the assault, but the company has to keep moving; they have no time to bury their dead. Following the post-dive briefing, they form up for the run to evening meal. They will be back after supper to charge the tanks and prepare for the next day's dive. There will be one less set of gear paraded outside the dive locker the next morning.

Tuesday is ditch-and-don day. Technical Sergeant Bruce Barry, USAF, will brief and supervise the ditch-and-don dives. Barry is an exchange instructor from the Air Force's Combat Control Teams. The combat controllers, a component of the Air Force Special Operations Command, are trained to swim or parachute into enemy territory to prepare landing zones for special air operations. After Barry's dive brief, the trainees jock-up for inspection and board the bus for the CTT. Once in the water, they practice taking off all their gear and arranging it on the bottom of the pool. The last item to come off is the face mask. Then they secure all the gear with their weight belt and make an FSA to the surface. All FSAs are controlled by the instructors. When a trainee signals he is ready to go to the surface, his instructor will swim down and tap him twice on the back of the head. The student diver then secures his air, kisses the bottom of the pool, and, while maintaining a steady exhalation, allows the instructor to guide him to the surface. Like the dive tower, pool FSAs are considered hazardous training, and there is a diving medical officer present.

Once on the surface, the trainees get a critique of their ditching procedures. They then swim back down to their gear, reestablish their air supply, and put on their rigs. During this underwater ditch and don, it is essential that the trainees maintain control of their weight belts and move smoothly. Smooth is fast underwater, the trainees are continually reminded. After they are jocked-up, they have to perform a full dive supe check on themselves. Once they have successfully ditched and donned their equipment twice, the swim pairs are released into the shallows to practice buddy breathing until they expend their air.

The afternoon's diving evolution is equipment ditch and don—at night. For this evolution they do the same thing they did in the morning dive, only this time they use blacked-out face masks. Everything is by feel. The only time they can "see" is when they take off their face masks to begin their FSA. The blind ditch and don takes longer, but the trainees are beginning to know and trust their equipment. It's a matter of confidence and familiarity. Seaman Marc Luttrell, the class corpsman, has trouble with the morning evolution. It takes him several tries to properly ditch and don his equipment. Back in the pool that afternoon, he does it perfectly the first time—in the dark.

. . .

"Feet!"

"FEET!"

"Give me a report, Mister Gallagher."

"Twenty-seven assigned, Instructor Surmont. Twenty-seven men present."

"Take your seats, gentlemen," says Petty Officer John Surmont. Surmont is an intense, demanding instructor with a hard edge. He grew up in Kentucky and has a degree in information technology. John Surmont came to BUD/S from SEAL Team Three and has four operational deployments behind him. It's Wednesday morning, 12 January. Today, Class 228 begins their pool comps; he has their full attention.

"This morning we have gear exchange. Gear exchange is nothing more than ditch and don, but in this case, you do it while you buddy-breathe. One man takes the gear off, the other puts it on, understand?"

"HOOYAH!"

"But you have to work together to get the job done. You have to communicate underwater, right?"

"HOOYAH!"

"And hear me on this one, guys, you have to anticipate. Think ahead; don't just react to what happens. Think of yourselves like a linebacker in football, waiting for the play to begin. You have to carefully watch what's going on, access the situation quickly, and react properly. And above all, work together. You will have twenty minutes to complete this evolution. Sounds like a long time, and it is, but you have to think. Remember, smooth is fast."

Surmont walks them through the evolution, beginning with a proper water entry and through the gear-swap procedures. Two trainees—one of them jocked-up in scuba, the other clean—will go to the bottom together. They swap all gear except for their swim trunks and brown T-shirts. When they surface, all equipment has to be in place with no twisted straps. After a critique from the instructor who is observing, they go back down to swap back the gear. At the pool, the members of Class 228 work smoothly through the gear exchange, gaining trust in the equipment and their ability to handle themselves underwater. This morning's dive is the last time they will perform in the pool without physical harassment from the instructors. During pool comp week, they dive morning and afternoon, eating MREs at noon in the dive locker while they charge bottles. They hustle to get their equipment staged, then crowd back into the classroom for the afternoon dive brief.

"Feet!"

"FEET!"

The class has learned to sit on the front of their chairs so there is no scraping when they stand for an instructor.

"Give me a count, Mister Gallagher."

"Twenty-seven men assigned, Instructor Calvin, twenty-six men present. One man DOR."

During the noon break, Seaman Chris Gardener decides that this training was not for him—that, at this point, he will be unable to handle the stress of the pool-harassment evolutions ahead. He quit, requesting only that he be allowed to come back to BUD/S at a later time.

"I was very uncomfortable in the water; I thought I was going to be a danger to myself and to my swim buddy. I plan to take a civilian scuba course and get comfortable in the water. Then I'll be back."

Spencer Calvin surveys the remaining twenty-six men. "Okay, guys, this afternoon we're going to dial it up a notch. It'll be important to stay focused and perform, since this afternoon we're going to challenge you a little. We're going to see if you can handle some adversity and still do your job. That's what being a SEAL is all about. The setup at the pool will be the same as it was this morning, only you will enter the pool one at a time. An instructor will come and get you, and lead you to a lane in the pool." Calvin signals to an instructor in the back of the room and a PowerPoint slide of the pool bottom appears on the screen. "Once in your assigned lane, you are to move between the two weights on the bottom of the pool—back and forth, understand?"

"HOOYAH!"

"If you have fins on, swim along the bottom between the weights. If you don't have fins, and you won't have them for long, crawl between the weights. With twelve pounds on, you won't have any problem staying down. But we want you to crawl—no standing. If you stand up, it tells us that you are panicky and you flunk the dive."

Quartermaster First Class Spencer Calvin is a solid six-footer, weighing close to two hundred pounds. He grew up in Florida and is another BUD/S instructor with a college degree. Calvin came to the Center from SEAL Team Five. The class regards him warily. He has taken over from Terry Patstone as the phase hard-ass. He's one of the haters. Calvin is capable of turning nasty at any time, and they give him their full attention.

"The drill is called pool skills. We want to see if you can think and problem-solve while you're being bounced around a little. This will not be the full-tilt harassment you will experience tomorrow, but it will give you a taste of it. The first thing you will experience will be a pretend surf surge. This is to simulate being tossed about in the surf while on scuba." He gives them a malicious grin. "The size of the surf will depend on the instructor. When Instructor Surmont tries to screw you into the bottom of the pool, you may think you've been hit with a tsunami.

"Expect to have your fins pulled and your face mask ripped off. You will be tumbled about to see if you can handle some disorientation. When the wave passes and you can get your bearings, what do you do? Owens?"

"Petty Officer Owens," the trainee says, scrambling to his feet. "Dive supe check."

"That's right. Always go back to the dive supe check. You will have to execute a good dive supe check to pass this dive and to pass pool competency tomorrow. Let's go over it again. Get over here, Shaffer."

While Calvin has been going through his presentation, Seaman Zack Shaffer has been patiently standing by. He is all jocked-up with twin 80s and weight belt, the regulator in his mouth. He dons his face mask and steps to the podium next to Calvin. Shaffer is perhaps five-eight and a solid 170 pounds—stout for a BUD/S trainee. After high school, he worked as an electrician for two years before joining the Navy. Then he decided he wanted to be a SEAL. He has a brother who just joined the Navy and is slated for Class 332. Calvin grabs the yoke of Shaffer's tanks and jostles him.

"Okay, Shaffer here is being tossed about in the surf. In the process he loses his face mask." Calvin jerks off his mask. "Okay, he finds some quiet water. Now what?"

"DIVE SUPE CHECK!"

"Right. Let's go through it. First thing, release the mouthpiece and extend the hoses over your head—let it free flow." Shaffer removes his mouthpiece and lets Calvin hold it over his head. Calvin jiggles the hoses. "If there's air to the mouthpiece, the regulator will free flow and you'll hear it bubbling above your head. Next trace the hoses from the horns to the mouthpiece."

Shaffer reaches behind his head with both hands and grasps the hoses where they are attached to the regulator—the horns. Then he follows the hoses up to his mouthpiece, grasps the mouthpiece, and pulls it down to his face. As Shaffer goes through the motions, each step of the dive supe check slides onto the screen from the PowerPoint projector. Calvin's presentation is similar to Surmont's briefing that morning, but not entirely. Each instructor composes his own slides.

"Next, bite the bubble and clear the mouthpiece." Shaffer, holding the mouthpiece down, rotates it toward his chin and puts it in his mouth. Then he tilts his head to the left, in the direction of the exhalation hose, and blows. "Now retrace the hoses from the mouthpiece to the regulator horns." Shaffer does this.

"What's next Mister Green?"

"Check air supply and reserve."

"Correct." Shaffer reaches behind his head and turns his air valve fully counterclockwise and back a quarter turn. Then he checks to see that his reserve J-valve is in the up position.

"What next . . . Dougherty?"

Brandon Dougherty grins as the instructor running the PowerPoint laptop prematurely sends the answer to the screen.

"Trace the straps, check for twists in the straps, and that all quick-releases have three-finger loops."

"That's right. Now drop for reading it off the screen. Last step? Lewis?"

While Dougherty cranks out his push-ups, Lewis recites the next step. "Make sure the weight belt is over all tank straps and that the release buckle pulls to the right-hand side." Shaffer leans forward and checks his weight belt and the release buckle with his right hand. Calvin hands him his face mask and tells him to stand by. With his seventy-five-odd pounds of extra gear, Shaffer steps to the side and waits patiently.

"Sometime during the surf hits, you may experience some other difficulties. You may find that you have a kink in one of your hoses. Or that somehow your air got turned off. Imagine that," Calvin adds with a grin. "What do you do? Dive supe check, right?"

"HOOYAH!"

"When the mouthpiece over your head is free flowing, the air is on and your inhalation hose is working. So where is the kink? Probably in your exhalation hose, right? If the regulator is not free-flowing, you have a problem with the inhalation hose or the air is not turned on. Remember, if you can inhale, but can't exhale, you're okay. Just breathe out through your nose, complete your dive supe check, and fix the problem. Got that?"

"HOOYAH!"

"Here's how we fix the problem in the pool. When you trace the hoses with your hands and you find that the hand of an instructor is crimping one of your hoses, tap the hose-crimping hand of the instructor twice. Then trace the hoses from the mouthpiece back to the crimp. Again, tap the hand twice. That will tell the instructor that you are following procedure to clear the crimping. He will release the hose. We clear on that?"

"HOOYAH!"

"If you can breathe and not exhale, continue to breathe while you fix the problem and exhale through your nose. If you can't breathe, hold your breath and calmly—I emphasize calmly—fix the problem. Perhaps you need only to turn your air back on and the problem is solved. If your air is on and you still can't get a breath, what is the problem? What do you do? Karaoguz?"

Adam Karaoguz is on his feet. "Petty Officer Karaoguz. You probably have a crimped inhalation hose. After making sure the air is turned on, trace the hoses from the horns. When you find a hand on the hose, probably the right hose, tap twice. Then trace the hoses from the mouthpiece back to the horns and again tap twice."

"That's it. We see you starting to panic down there and you'll flunk the dive. So just relax and do the job. And don't fight the instructors. Let us do our job, then you do your job. If you have trouble with this evolution, gents, you're definitely going to have some serious problems tomorrow during the final pool competency. Today, I want you to relax, think, and just do it.

"After we finish with the pool skills, it's gut-check time. The last class

didn't get to do this, but we've managed to put it back in the curriculum."
Calvin is suddenly all smiles. "It's one of my personal favorites. We're
going to see if you can tread water for five minutes, fully jocked-up with
your hands out of the water—using only your feet. We'll see how many of
you can suck it up and do it. Okay, let's head for the pool."

At the CTT, the instructors put them through their paces. Often the
simulated surf tumble is more than a gentle surge. Some instructors simply grab the students' tanks and flip them over onto their heads. Others
grab them by the legs and twist full-circle, again and again, like an alli-
gator who has caught a hapless deer drinking at the edge of his glade. By
and large, the students ride out the storm and go about checking their
equipment. A few of the weaker ones are sent back for a second round of
surf tumble. None of them have a serious problem with a crimped hose or
turning his air back on. The harassment is one-on-one. When an instructor is satisfied with a student's performance, he will take him to the surface for a critique, then send him into the shallow end of the pool with
another student to practice buddy breathing. They swim in circles until
they drain their tanks. The Second Phase staff want all the students to
experience the feeling of running out of air, as well as the gentle rush of
air that comes with activating the J-valve reserve. With the bottles
breathed down, the class lines up on the pool deck at the deep end for the
final evolution of the day.

"Proper water entry, people," Calvin yells at them. "Let's do it. It's gut-
check time!"

Class 228 splashes back into the pool. They begin to tread water while
keeping their hands above the surface. With twelve pounds of lead around
their waists and the dual tanks on their backs, they kick furiously to keep
their heads above the surface and their hands visible.

"Five minutes, that's all we ask. Gut it out for five minutes and you're
a winner. Touch the side of the pool or use your hands and you're a loser."

The instructors line the edge of the pool and shout encouragement. Yet
one by one, the students reach for the side of the pool or have to use their

hands to keep from going down. All but one. Seaman John Collins alone is able to kick for five minutes with his hands and wrists above the surface without touching the side of the pool.

Collins was a water polo standout in high school and a serious triathlete. He's only twenty-one, but he has competed in eighteen triathlons, finishing first in his age group in eleven of them. He left the University of Washington after his freshman year to be a Navy SEAL. Collins was rolled back from Class 227 for poor times on the O-course. He is still having problems with the O-course, but today John Collins is able to do what the other twenty-five in 228 cannot do. As a payback for their failure, Class 228 will have to wear their weight belts at all times for a full week—in the classroom, while staging equipment, while doing push-ups, and on the runs to chow. Only Collins will be free of the excess twelve pounds.

After the trainees return to the Naval Special Warfare Center, they set about charging scuba tanks and preparing support equipment for the next day's evolution, the final pool competency dive. Pool comp is the crucible of Second Phase and a major hurdle in BUD/S. The men seem focused on their tasks, but one member of the class is caught taking a break in the compressor room while his classmates work. Worse yet, it's Instructor Calvin who finds him. When this happens, sometimes the individual pays—sometimes the whole class pays. This time it's the whole class.

"You guys just can't deal with prosperity, can you? Drop." While the class pushes out the first set of forty, Instructor Calvin walks among them. In Second Phase, when they drop for push-ups, it's forty at a time. "You did a decent job over in the pool today, and now one of you has blown it. Actually, all of you have blown it, because you aren't pulling as a class. On your feet!"

"FEET!"

"Okay, guys, get jocked-up and fall in a line out here on the grinder. Now!"

There is a flurry of activity as the students race to find their personal dive equipment, get regulators mated to tanks, and put their gear on. In less than ten minutes, the class is on line wearing tanks and weight belts, and carrying their fins and face masks.

"Prepare to make a proper water entry," Calvin tells them.

The students don their fins and face masks. There are twenty-six of them standing in a line. Each has one hand holding his face mask and mouthpiece in place, the other anchoring his weight belt and tank strap. The men are ready to enter the water, but there is no water.

"Gentlemen, the drill is ditch and don. We're all going to do it again. Since we're high and dry, pretend you have just entered the water and that the piece of asphalt in front of you is the bottom of the pool. Standing on the bottom is considered a safety violation, so you better get down on your hands and knees."

After a moment's hesitation, the class melts to the blacktop. Gingerly, the students assume the bottom-crawl position on all fours. They look like a line of aquarium figurines.

"All right, I want you to completely ditch your equipment and prepare for an FSA. That's right, girls, remove your equipment just as you would in the pool and prepare for a free ascent."

Kneeling on asphalt without gear is painful enough, but more so with tanks and weight belt. The swim fins only force them to put more weight forward on their knees. They are in pain, but none wants it to show to Calvin. One by one, they remove their tanks and lift them forward and over their heads.

"Gently! Don't be banging my tanks on the blacktop. Once you have your tanks off, secure your mask and fins with your weight belt and prepare for an FSA. None of us goes to the surface until everyone's ready."

After more struggle, the line of students are kneeling before their diving rigs, mouthpieces in, like a row of Muslims at prayer. Their masks and fins are neatly stowed under their weight belts.

"Okay now, what's the signal to request an FSA?"

Each student holds out a "thumbs-up" signal to one side.

Calvin walks down the line returning the thumbs-up signal to one diver at a time. In turn, each man relinquishes his mouthpiece and makes paddling motions with his hands, and rises to his feet. When a diver reaches the "surface," Calvin drops him for push-ups and moves on to the next man. Soon they are all standing by their dive rigs wearing only swim trunks, booties, T-shirt, and life vest. Their knees are red and abraded from kneeling on the blacktop.

"Now, let's swim back down and get jocked-up."

Minutes later the students are back on their knees, struggling to lift the twin 80s back over their heads and strap them to their backs. Then they don their fins, weight belts, and face masks. They are all in pain, and unable to see clearly as the exertion fogs their face masks. When they are all geared up, they are allowed to "swim" to the surface.

"Some of you guys are getting the hang of handling yourselves underwater, but you still have a ways to go as a class. You officers and petty officers need to show better leadership. You have a lot of work to do to get ready for tomorrow's evolution. Work together as a class, all of you, or you'll pay the price as a class. Am I clear on this?"

"HOOYAH!"

. . .

"Feet!"

"FEET!"

There are twenty-six members of Class 228 in the classroom and almost half as many instructors. It's the big day—the final pool competency evolution.

Instructor Mike Peters mounts the podium and surveys the class. He will give the briefing, as he did for their familiarization dive, and he will be the diving supervisor. Peters is a veteran of SEAL Team Eight. Along the way he picked up the nickname of Batman. He is a serious, intense petty officer, and very professional. Peters knows this is a key evolution for Class 228—for some of them, possibly their last at BUD/S. He has spent several days preparing for this briefing.

"Okay, gents, it's showtime. Today you show us if you can function and follow proper procedure while under pressure. I will be the diving supe,

Lieutenant Black is the diving officer, and Doctor Bell will be the diving medical officer. The entire instructor staff will be standby divers. Okay, let's have a gear check. Medical?"

"Seaman Luttrell, Instructor Batman. All medical gear is up." Luttrell details a list of medical equipment that has been staged for the event.

"Chamber operator notified and on standby?"

"Hooyah, Instructor."

"Very well. Comms?"

Luttrell takes his seat as Petty Officer "Beaver" Cleaver scrambles to his feet. Chad Cleaver joined 228 at the beginning of Second Phase. Cleaver is another medical rollback because of stress fractures in his legs. He's from Costa Mesa, California. After two years in college and a short professional boxing career, he joined the Navy to become a SEAL.

"Comms are up: three Sabers and three extra sets of batteries."

"All tested?"

"Hooyah," Cleaver replies.

"Admin?"

"Petty Officer Karaoguz, Instructor Batman. Three current class rosters are ready with clipboards." Karaoguz has served as the class administrative officer since he took over from Ensign Will Koella at the end of First Phase.

Peters nods his approval. "Equipment?"

"Ensign Oehlerich, Instructor. We have eight extra complete regulators tested and ready to go, plus a bucket of weights for lane markers."

"Toothpaste?" The instructors like a tube of toothpaste at the side of the pool. Toothpaste in an excellent antifogging agent for face masks.

"Hooyah, Instructor Batman."

"Vehicles?"

"Seaman Lewis, Instructor. All the vehicles have been fueled and the trip tickets are current." Peters again nods.

"This is the day, gentlemen. Today you will have to perform under stress. If you can do this, you stay. If you can't, you're history. Each of you must pass this evolution. We'll give you more than one chance, but I don't recommend it. Make it easy on yourself, and us. Pass it the first time and get it over with." After a long look at the group before him, he continues with a detailed briefing of the pool comp evolution.

"Men, it's not that hard. All you have to do is relax, think about what you're doing, and make it happen. When you're on the surface, the instructor will take you to the side of the pool for a critique. If you pass, we'll put you to work to help support the rest of the dive. If you fail, you know the drill. Take a seat along the wall of shame and wait for your next chance." Peters begins to pace the front of the room. "It's like this. You stay with your rig as long as you can. Reestablish your air source—continue with a good dive supe check. When you can no longer get your rig to function, and you've done everything you can to establish your air source, you ditch the rig and go for the surface. This is what you will do in the teams; it's what we want you to do here. Just look at it as a simple series of tasks in a stressful environment." He pauses and regards the remaining twenty-six members of Class 288. "Any questions?" The room is very quiet. "Okay, we're going to watch a video that covers everything we've talked about. Then we're going over to the pool and go to work."

The students and instructors watch a video of a BUD/S student as he is put through a pool comp session. It is exactly as Peters described in his briefing.

"Once again, any questions?" Again, silence. "All right then, let's do it."

"Feet!"

"FEET!"

After the instructors file out, the class falls in on their gear and begins to jock-up for inspection.

· · ·

"CDO, this is the dive supe."

"This is the command duty officer, go ahead."

"This is the dive supe," Peters says into the Motorola Saber transceiver. "We're commencing diving operations."

"Roger, understand you are commencing diving operations."

Mike Peters ensures that the BUD/S chamber is on standby and holsters the Saber. He quickly surveys the pool deck to again make certain that the support and medical equipment are properly staged. He notes that Lieutenant Josh Bell, a diving medical officer, is present. A medical officer is always on-scene when free ascents are a part of the training. Three years ago a student died in this pool after an improper free ascent. Peters turns to Lieutenant Black.

"We're all ready, sir."

Black nods his approval. It's an important day at Second Phase for Class 228. Later that morning, Captain Bowen will stop by to observe the progress of the pool comp evolution.

"Okay," Peters tells the line of waiting students, "first four men enter the water."

They don't have to be reminded to make a proper water entry. Bill Gallagher and Pat Yost, as class leader and LPO, are the first to enter the pool to be tested. Two more students splash into the CTT right behind them, surface, and grip the side of the pool.

"You ready to go, sir?"

"Hooyah, Instructor," Gallagher says around his mouthpiece.

"All right then, I want you to take the second lane over. Stay between the marker weights and let's get this done. Any questions?"

"Negative," Gallagher manages.

"Then, after you, sir."

Gallagher heads for the bottom with the instructor holding his manifold yoke, riding him like a remora. Once between the painted lane stripes, he begins to travel between the two weights, which are about thirty feet apart. Instructor John Surmont immediately pulls off his fins and face mask and delivers them to the side of the pool. Surmont earned a reputation from previous classes as being very demanding in pool comp. If Gallagher had a choice, he would not pick Surmont for his pool comp grader.

Moments later, Surmont swoops down behind 228's class leader and grabs his feet. He tumbles him violently and almost carries him out of the lane. Then he cranks Gallagher's air valve almost off—not quite, but almost. Surmont returns to the surface for a bite of air. By the time Gallagher gets to his knees and begins a dive supe check, the instructor is on him again. This time he grabs his student's exhalation hose and turns his air fully off. Gallagher can neither breathe in nor out. He releases his mouthpiece and begins to trace his hoses from the regulator. He finds Surmont's hand on his left hose and taps it twice. Tracing back from his mouthpiece, he again double-taps the hand on the hose. Then he finds his air valve and cranks it on. Gallagher manages only a few breaths in and out when he finds he again can't exhale. But he can breathe in. Exhaling through his nose, he begins a dive supe check, twice double-tapping the hand crimping his exhalation hose. Then he completes his dive supe check without interruption. He begins crawling along his lane, waiting for the next assault. Bill Gallagher knows John Surmont is above him planning his next attack.

He doesn't have to wait long. On his first pass, Surmont again turns Gallagher's air nearly off and gives him a good tumble. The next time down, he grabs the mouthpiece, allowing Gallagher a full breath before he pulls it from his mouth. Gallagher braces himself on all fours, like a cow being milked, while Surmont fully secures his air and pulls the regulator hoses through the manifold yoke and back up over the air valve. He gives Gallagher a good shove and heads for the surface. Snorkeling above, he watches as Gallagher goes to work.

His dive supe check is short-lived. Reaching back, he finds the horns of his regulator, but the hoses will not budge. Gallagher drops his weight belt, draping it across the back of his knees. Then he methodically pulls the three quick-release straps and brings the twin 80s over his head. With the bottles in front of him, he is able to free the tangled hoses and turn on his air. After a few sweet breaths, he reseats the tanks on his back and begins to strap them on. As he goes for the weight belt, suddenly he can't breathe. He hesitates, but only for a second. He releases the mouthpiece and starts to trace his hoses, finding Surmont's hand clinched on his right hose. Two double-taps later he is breathing normally. Strapping on the weight belt,

Gallagher again starts through his dive supe check. He does not get far. Again, there is a hand on his mouthpiece. Surmont allows him to draw a single deep breath—his last for awhile.

Bill Gallagher waits while John Surmont works. Another shove and it's Gallagher's turn. As before, he can't breathe and he can't find his hoses. Off come the tanks. This time the hoses are rubber-banded around the manifold yoke in a Gordian knot. Gallagher knows he'll not solve this one on the air he has left, but he makes a show of it. Quickly, he steals a glance at the surface. There are several instructors milling above him. He is vaguely aware of a fellow student being tossed about to his left. *That's enough; no way it's gonna come loose! Time to ditch this rig.* Gallagher signals for an FSA and goes back to work. *Just maybe, if I can find a loop in the hose . . .* There it is; the two taps on the back of the head. *I'm outta here!* Gallagher quickly drags his weight belt from the back of his legs and lays it across the tank. He tries to find the tank valve to secure the air, but it is buried under the tangle of rubber. *Outta here!* He kisses the bottom of the pool and begins blowing bubbles. An instant later, Surmont takes a handful of his shirt from the middle of his shoulder blades and guides him to the surface.

"I feel fine!"

"Again!"

"I feel fine!"

Surmont guides him over to the side of the pool. "How do you think you did, Mister Gallagher?"

"Uh, okay, Instructor. I couldn't get the air turned off before the FSA, though."

"I think you did fine, too. But don't look up at me when you have a fouled rig. Do your job; do what you're supposed to, okay?"

"Hooyah."

"Good job, sir. Now get out of the pool."

One of the other instructors hands Gallagher his tanks and he makes his way along the side to the ladder. Surmont looks at his watch and slides down to where Lieutenant Black is sitting on a folding chair with a clipboard.

"Gallagher: eighteen minutes, fifteen seconds. He's a pass."

Without looking up, Black makes a note. John Surmont goes over and gets another student from the queue waiting by the side of the pool near Batman Peters.

Pat Yost is not so successful. Instructor Barry brings him over to the side of the pool for his debriefing.

"Look, you're not having any problems down there, and I can see that you're comfortable in the water. But you're anticipating the sequence of events; you're getting ahead of me. Then you made an improper FSA. I'm going to have to fail you, but you'll do it next time, okay?"

"Hooyah, Instructor."

Yost passes easily on his next attempt. This is not his first pool harassment drill. Yost is a Second Class Navy Diver, so he has a good deal of underwater time. I later asked him how this experience compared with pool comp in Second Class Diver training.

"We underwent pool harassment as a dive pair. You had your swim buddy to help you. The instructors attacked you as a swim pair, and you were able to help each other fix the damage. If they couldn't drive you to the surface, you passed. Here, there is more emphasis on procedure. And you have to go it alone."

"But which would you say is more difficult?" I ask.

Yost grins. "I didn't need a second try to pass pool comp at Second Class School."

Not all the instructors are as understanding as Sergeant Barry, nor all the trainees as proficient as Pat Yost. One unfortunate student is brought up halfway through the trial.

"Didn't you hear anything Instructor Peters said during the briefing? Why are you wasting my time? Piss-poor performance; get out of the pool and against the wall. You failed."

Another is brought up early. "What the hell were you doing down there?

Do you know what a dive supe check is?" The student looks down and says nothing. "Quit feeling sorry for yourself and start thinking. Get the hell out of my pool."

Occasionally, a student is brought up for a teaching point and allowed to go back down and continue. Sometimes there is an equipment problem. Often, one of the hoses pulls loose from the regulator or the mouthpiece, and the regulator has to be changed out. As the day wears on, the class divides into two groups. One group is collecting and sorting equipment, gauging the remaining pressure in tanks, and supporting those yet to be tested. These are the winners; they have passed pool competency and a milestone in their journey to graduate from BUD/S. The other group sits in a line facing a cinder-block wall, waiting to be retested—the wall of shame, the instructors call it, or the wailing wall.

As the retesting begins, the instructors try to focus their students on what they have to do. They will encourage them, but they will not let them slip through. Each has to perform.

"Am I dirty on you, Mister Birch?"

"No, Instructor Troy." The instructors purposely avoid testing the same student a second time. So if a student fails twice, two different instructors will have failed him.

"Do you know what you did wrong last time?" Jason Troy is a new instructor. He came to BUD/S from SDV Team One, where he was a very highly regarded SDV pilot.

"Hooyah," Birch replies.

"Then let's go down there and do it right this time."

"Hooyah, Instructor Troy," Birch says, and they disappear.

Instructor Spencer Calvin picks up another retestee. "What's your name?"

"Seaman Terpstra, Instructor."

"Terpstra, I don't care what you did wrong last time. I want you to relax and get it right this time. So how about let's you and me go down and get this over with, okay?"

"Hooyah, Instructor Calvin."

By the end of the morning it's fifty-fifty. Thirteen have passed pool comp and thirteen have not. The unlucky thirteen will be back at the pool that afternoon for remediation drills, working on the specific areas that caused them to fail their two attempts at pool comp that morning. The next day, they are back at the pool for two more tries. All but four pass pool comp on the second day. There is no third day. While the four failures are sent before the Second Phase Review Board and processed out, the rest of the class prepares for their open-water dive. Class 228 is down to twenty-two men, including twelve of the originals. For these original members who began Indoc together, they are about halfway through their twenty-seven weeks at BUD/S.

The open-circuit portion of Second Phase concludes with a 120-foot bounce dive off Point Loma. It's almost anticlimactic after their struggles in the pool. The water is clear and cold, and there is no harassment. The students are dressed in wet-suit tops and hoods. Four students and an instructor go down the descent line from the boat to a bar at the 120-foot depth. They hang there and watch the jellyfish for a few minutes and begin their ascent. At this depth, due to the pressure, their air bubbles "tinkle" rather than "burble," a distinctly different sound. Otherwise, it is a quick, painless, cold experience—another check mark in Second Phase.

Thirty-six students began Second Phase and now there are twenty-two. Among those who remain, most are solidly meeting every challenge. A few are just hanging on. These few have performance deficiencies they must correct or be dropped from training. Even those performing well, at one time or another, have failed a timed or graded evolution. All but two. On the wall of the Second Phase classroom is a colorful rendering of a UDT frog. The cartoon frog has a white sailor's cap set at a rakish angle and a cigar clamped in his teeth. He carries a submachine gun in one hand and a stick of dynamite in the other. Surrounding the frog is a scattering of class numbers going back to Class 208. Most classes are unrepresented. Of the ones that are, there is at least one name under each class numeral. This is the first-time, every-time wall. Of the hundreds of students who have come through Second Phase, only a dozen or so have passed every test, every swim, every O-course, every graded evolution the first time, every time. After 228's pool comp week, only Ensigns Clint Burke and Eric Oehlerich have zero failures. Yet only Clint Burke has a chance to have his name on the first-time, every-time wall. Good as he is, Oehlerich is not a 228 original; this is his second try at Second Phase.

The balance of Second Phase will be devoted to mastering the Lar V scuba. Instructors and trainees call it by its manufacturer's name, the Draeger. It is a closed-circuit, 100 percent oxygen rig. The Draeger is the current edition of a long line of combat swimmer scubas, tracing its lineage back to crude British and Italian models developed during World War II. The diver breathes pure oxygen and his exhalation gas is sent through a canister that scrubs away the carbon dioxide. Additional oxygen is added to the breathing gas as needed. The theory of the oxygen rebreather has changed little over the past five decades, but the design and safety of these scubas have undergone considerable refinement. The Draeger is a light, compact rig worn on the diver's chest. There are no bubbles; with it, a combat swimmer has up to six hours of underwater time to complete his mission.

The Draeger is a safe rig as long as it is properly maintained and properly prepared for the dive. It is a shallow-water scuba; divers using the Draeger are restricted to a working depth of thirty feet. Below two atmospheres of pressure—pressures found below the thirty-two-foot depth—pure oxygen can become toxic. During the first two days of closed-circuit instruction, the class is introduced to the diving rig that will become their underwater companion in the teams. During classroom and hands-on evolutions, they learn the care and feeding of the Draeger—how to set it up for a dive, in-water procedures, and how to maintain it. In addition to these pre- and post-dive procedures, they learn to recognize signs of hypoxia, an oxygen-deficient condition, in themselves or their dive buddy. They also learn emergency procedures should these symptoms appear or their Draegers become flooded and force them to the surface. The students pay close attention. During the two intense days that precede their first Draeger dive, Class 228 loses two more of their number—two of the originals.

Pat Yost is notified that his father has died and heads home on emergency leave. He is needed there for an extended period of time, and this will cost him his place in Class 228. If Otter Obst was the strongest in 228, Pat Yost was the most dependable. Yost will return to BUD/S, to begin Second Phase with Class 229. He has served as the class enlisted leader with grace and humor; he will be missed. Petty Officer John Owens steps up to take his place as the class leading petty officer. The affable Owens is a solid BUD/S student and well liked by his classmates. He becomes 228's fourth leading petty officer. The class also loses Seaman Grant Terpstra.

Terpstra has problems on the four-mile timed runs. Last week, he missed the thirty-one-minute threshold by only nine seconds. But this week he misses the cutoff by more than a minute, and he is gone. Rollbacks to the next class for performance reasons have become a rare exception at BUD/S. Since Terpstra successfully made it through pool comp, the Academic Review Board does not send him back to the fleet. Terpstra must instead start at the beginning with Class 230 in Indoc. He will again be a white shirt, but will not have to go through Hell Week with Class 230. With Terpstra's departure, Class 228 stands at twenty—ten originals and ten rollbacks.

The loss of Yost and Terpstra illustrates the two dimensions of a successful BUD/S trainee: you have to be lucky and you have to have a complete game—no weaknesses. Yost's loss was unfortunate, yet unavoidable. He was a top trainee, doing everything well, and a superb leader, but there's no way to foresee a death in the family.

"The instructors are good at their jobs," he later told me, "but I was never given the impression that they personally cared all that much about us trainees. Boy, was I wrong. When the news came about my dad, they couldn't do enough. They had me processed out with emergency leave orders in about ten minutes and drove me to the airport. They told me not to worry about training; it'd be here for me when I returned. I was impressed. I hated to leave 228, but I'll get there with 229."

Terpstra is a solid BUD/S trainee, but he was never a consistent runner. Running at BUD/S is a unique challenge. Runs are on the beach in boots and long trousers, often after a recent plunge in the surf. And since BUD/S students run eight to ten miles a day in boots, or more, a runner has to be durable as well as have endurance. Terpstra was a starting wide receiver at Northern Iowa University for three years. He has good foot speed and he's quick, but he lacks endurance on the long runs. Now with Class 230, he will have more time to work on his durability and endurance.

A few days after the loss of Yost and Terpstra, Clint Burke almost becomes a casualty. While surfing on the weekend, he wipes out on a roller and manages to slice his leg with the skeg of his surfboard. It's a nasty gash. With some stitches from the BUD/S medical department and a green light from the Second Phase officer, he's allowed to continue diving.

For the next two weeks, Class 228 dives the Draeger. The first two dives are familiarization evolutions in the pool. Then the students begin boring holes in San Diego Bay. Each time the swims are longer, and each one has a new objective or new combat swimmer technique. Once the trainees master the Draeger during the day, they begin the night swims. They learn to calibrate their kick count, or pace, so they can judge distance on a given course. Each swim pair has an attack board—a pie-plate-sized Plexiglas board with mountings for a compass, a wristwatch, and a depth gauge. The trainees take turns "driving" on a compass heading. Gradually, the class begins to learn the basic tools of the combat swimmer—the ability to swim a good line of bearing and know how far he's traveled. It's underwater navigation, the same as if they were on land with a map and compass.

The third week with the Draeger is, by consensus of the class, the most difficult in Second Phase. Each morning they have a physical evolution— a timed run, a timed surface swim, or the O-course. There is PT most mornings. They dive once in the afternoon and again at night. Because of the lengthy setup and post-dive procedures with the Draeger, as well as the support equipment that has to be staged for each dive, the trainees work halfway through the night. Then they are back in the dive locker well before sunrise. The class is performing well, but they sometimes operate on less than three hours of sleep. Midweek, one of the students lets the dip tank overflow onto the grinder. This minor infraction does not escape the attention of Instructor Spence Calvin. After their weekly four-mile timed run on the beach that day, Calvin makes them do it a second time. In addition to the two dives, and counting the trips to chow, they log about fourteen miles on the run that day. But that's what BUD/S students do. They absorb long days, cold water, periodic harassment, and a lot of running. They do this day after day, and they do it on very little sleep. Few big men with deep muscular chests and large biceps can take this kind of punishment. And that is why there are few beefcakes in BUD/S training.

While week three on the Draeger is something of a gut check, the students are starting to master the basics of a combat swimmer. In addition to the night compass courses and pace work, they conduct underwater hull inspections of patrol craft and a Navy destroyer at night. This is a steep learning curve, especially for those in 228 who, until three weeks ago, had never taken a breath underwater. With a week to go in Second Phase, the trainees are becoming frogmen.

Class 228 begins its final week in Second Phase on 7 February. The final dive problem that week is a night ship attack. As with many of the Draeger dives, the trainees first do it during the daylight, then repeat the same problem again at night. Instructor Steve McKendry gives them their final dive brief. Their proctor will also be the dive supervisor for their last dive. Unlike their hydrographic reconnaissance training, the trainees take no part in the planning or briefing of these dives. The student combat swimmers will be briefed on the mission, then swim the problem as they are briefed. They begin staging their gear late that afternoon, and McKendry briefs them right after evening chow. One last night dive; one last evolution in Second Phase.

No one wants this dive or this day behind him more than Lieutenant (jg) Bill Gallagher. He has struggled with Second Phase. The diving part of it has been easy for him. He was scuba qualified before he came to BUD/S, and he has found the Draeger to be a good rig—comfortable, reliable, light, and safe. He came to Second Phase ready to learn. Like his classmates in 228, he expected more training and less harassment after First Phase. With the exception of Instructor McKendry and the first week or so of academics, they've been worked very hard. As class leader, he gets the hammer when the whole class or any one trainee screws up.

"What bothers me is that they'll beat us for something trivial or for no reason at all. Just when I get to thinking that they're going to treat us as students and really teach us something, we're wet and sandy and getting pounded on the grinder." He smiles shyly and shakes his head. "Maybe that's just the way it is for the whole six months. Maybe I shouldn't expect anything more."

Like most in Class 228, the long days with night dives on four hours of sleep are having their effect on Bill Gallagher. And he's held responsible for the entire class and for all the equipment and preparation for the dives. He led thirty-five trainees into Second Phase and now he's about to take nineteen with him to Third Phase—less if someone doesn't pass tonight's dive. He's lost some good friends from the class. And he's very tired; they're all very tired.

"Which of the Second Phase instructors is the hardest?" I ask.

"Instructor Calvin," he replies without hesitation. "The guy's a sadist. He can turn on you like a rattlesnake, sometimes for the smallest detail. He can be very nasty."

"Which one do you respect the most?"

Again the shy smile. "Instructor Calvin." When I pressed him as to why, he had to pause a moment. "I think it's because I can count on him when I have a problem with the class. I can ask him how we should handle an evolution or how to better organize the class to get the job done. He listens, and he always has good ideas and good feedback. He knows his stuff and he can be very professional—when he's not beating on us."

Right after McKendry's briefing, the trainees jock-up and stand by their Draegers for the bench inspection. Each trainee has predived his rig, and has it laid out in a prescribed manner for inspection. An instructor scrutinizes each rig, checking the fittings and hose connections before the trainees don the scuba. Once they have the Draeger strapped on, they are inspected again. Then they board the bus that will drive them across the Amphibious Base to the waiting boats.

Steve McKendry surveys the dark waters around the San Diego Naval Station piers from the dive supe boat. He's looking for stray surface craft. He notes that his safety boat is patrolling a hundred yards off the piers to protect his divers. Satisfied, he pulls the Saber transceiver from his belt.

"First pair in the water."

On another of the whaler-type support boats, another instructor gives Bill Gallagher and John Owens a final check. "You're good to go," he tells them, and Gallagher and Owens slip over the side.

The bay is about sixty degrees, and the cold knifes through them. It becomes bearable when their bodies warm up the water that seeps into their wet-suit tops and hoods. Owens drove on the afternoon dive; Gallagher will drive tonight. He lines them up on a compass bearing, and they begin swimming on the surface roughly parallel to the shoreline. They have their oxygen turned off and the Draegers rigged for surface swimming. Both have their face masks around their necks and turned back around behind their heads to avoid reflections from pier lights. This surface swimming with Draegers is called turtlebacking. Combat swimmers often turtleback on the surface at night as they approach a harbor and submerge to make their attack. Owens and Gallagher swim like this for close to a thousand yards. As they approach McKendry in the dive supe boat, they execute an emergency dive. This simulates the sudden arrival of a patrol boat or searchlight, and they have to get under quickly. The swim pair drops below the surface, turns on the oxygen to their Draegers, and begins their purge procedures. This replaces the air in their lungs with pure oxygen. Finally they get their face masks in place and are ready to continue. With his surface references gone, Gallagher concentrates on the compass strapped to his attack board. John Owens flies in formation to his right and slightly above him.

The attack plan calls for them to swim another five hundred yards underwater, then make a dogleg turn to the right and swim shoreward between two mooring piers. Gallagher counts his kicks to the five-hundred-yard point and looks up to Owens. He gives Gallagher a thumbs-up; his own kick count confirms the five hundred yards. Gallagher wheels to the right and they head in. Trailing on the surface behind them on a nylon tether is a marking buoy with a Chemlite attached. On a dark night with big ships about, McKendry wants to know where all his chicks are.

Bill Gallagher and John Owens swim between two long mooring piers that are approximately a hundred yards apart. This is confirmed by the rumbling noise off to their left where the USS *Tarawa* (LHA-1) is berthed. Big ships put a lot of noise into the water, even when they're tied up.

The two men continue toward the seawall some 300 yards from the end of the piers. They tag the seawall and then swim a reciprocal compass bearing seaward. Their target ship is on the pier across from the *Tarawa*. Gallagher and Owens kick for 250 yards on their swim count and get ready to make their attack. In order to check their position, Gallagher pauses and Owens does a shallow-water peek. He eases up to within three or four feet of the surface, but is careful to remain underwater. The shallow-water peek was not part of the dive brief. Gallagher hangs below him on the buddy line that connects them. Owens can see the lights on the superstructure of the *Tarawa* and takes a bearing. He estimates that they are between the two piers and that they should be close to the stern of the target ship. He signals Gallagher to adjust the final attack course a little to the right so as to hit their target amidships. They set off, and in less than three minutes are under their target, an old coastal survey ship, long since a derelict. They make their way to the stern, where a line hangs from the surface by the rudder. Owens ties a Chemlite with a tag that reads "Swim Pair #1" to the line. They've made their hit. Had they not found the ship, they would have to begin a box search until they did—more bottom time, more cold water.

Bill Gallagher takes them out on another dogleg course and gets another hit on their extraction point, a channel-marking buoy. Their pickup boat is waiting for them. Owens raises his arm, index finger extended, to indicate their swim pair number. They scramble aboard and secure their Draegers.

"Nice shot, sir," Owens says to Gallagher. "You nailed it going in and coming out."

"Any chance they saw you on the shallow-water peek?"

"Naw," Owens replies, "I was super careful. That's it, sir, the last dive. We're outta here."

For Gallagher, it's not that easy. As the class leader, he will be responsible for closing down Class 228's Second Phase. The trainees will be in the diving locker well past midnight, charging bottles and cleaning the Second Phase spaces. The following day they will have to inventory and return their diving equipment, and get the dive locker ready for Class 229. The Second Phase staff seems to be satisfied that Class 228 is good to go, and allows them to finish their dive locker chores in relative peace.

There is no Monster Mash in Second Phase like in First Phase, just a monster surface swim. They swim from the BUD/S compound south to the pier at Imperial Beach, five and a half miles of open ocean. Since the water is below sixty degrees, they will also get wet-suit bottoms. They are in the water for close to four hours, but the full wet suit makes the swim almost pleasant.

"Good job, sir," Instructor McKendry tells Lieutenant Gallagher on Friday. "You're secure." The trainees are running to the noon meal when it dawns on them that Second Phase is over. Class 228 now moves on to Third Phase—another phase and another challenge in the making of a Navy SEAL. But they did leave their mark on Second Phase—or at least one of them did. In the Second Phase classroom, there's a new entry on the first-time, every-time wall: Ensign Clint Burke, Class 228.

CHAPTER SIX

ACROSS THE LAND

F riday afternoon, 11 February 2000. Class 228 waits in the Third Phase classroom for their proctor. Having Second Phase behind them is an immense relief, but they are still anxious. Two classes have graduated while Class 228 was in training. A third is about to graduate. All lost men in Third Phase. Third Phase is the demolitions and tactics phase. In the past, it was called the land warfare phase. All these terms apply. Third Phase training is divided into two segments—training at the Center and training on San Clemente Island. During the first five weeks of Third Phase, they will be at the Center. This includes four days of training at La Posta for land navigation and four days at Camp Pendleton on the shooting ranges. They will then fly to San Clemente Island for more tactics, more shooting, demolitions, and the field training exercises. Class 228 left Second Phase with twenty trainees. When they arrive in the Third Phase classroom, there is one man waiting for them—a single roll-in. Petty Officer Sergio Lopez is a lanky, handsome Puerto Rican with a heavy Brooklyn accent. He was forced out of Class 227 with broken ribs from a fall on the O-course, but now he's healed and ready for another attempt at Third Phase. Lopez is the last augmentee to Class 228.

Ten weeks from this day, Class 228 will graduate. Who will be here? How many will make it? While the final twenty-one wait for their proctor, they think about this.

"Feet!"

"FEET!"

"Seats, gentleman. Welcome to Third Phase. Lopez, welcome back to Third Phase. I'm Instructor Hall and I'll be your proctor until you graduate. Let's talk about this phase of training." He pauses and surveys his trainees. "Third Phase is hard, gentlemen. You have to pay attention and stay focused. There's a lot to be learned here, a lot more than in First or Second Phase." Eric Hall is just under six feet and speaks with a comfortable southern drawl.

"I'm the leading corpsman here in Third Phase. I went through with Class 122, so I've been around a while. I've had six platoon deployments with SEAL Teams Three and Five. I've been at BUD/S for a little over a year. Let's talk about some of the dos and don'ts here in Third Phase and what we expect of you—what I expect as your proctor.

"I expect you to be on time for every evolution, and I expect you to put out a hundred ten percent all the time. You put out and give it your best shot, I'll back you up. You don't put out, well—you guys don't want to go there. As I said, we have a lot to teach you and we don't have much time to do it. So we don't have a lot of time to hammer you. But, if you screw up, individually or as a class, you *will* get hammered. We don't put up with whiners here and we don't have time for people who feel sorry for themselves. We expect you to conduct yourselves as quiet professionals: confident, not cocky. Show spirit as a class and speak to the cadre in your man's voice. If you have legal problems, family problems, speeding tickets, use your class chain of command first. If they're serious, bring them to me immediately. Medical problems? See your class corpsman first, then come to me.

"Things not to do. Anything to do with illegal or unauthorized drugs, and any alcohol-related incidents, and you're gone. You know this; why do I even need to mention it? Stay out of The Plank, McP's, Danny's, and the Far East Rock. Those are team bars and you're asking for trouble if you go in there. You're going to be too busy to go in bars, anyway. You lie, cheat, or steal and you're done. That's not tolerated here. Again, I shouldn't even have to mention it.

"Things to do. Keep the spaces up and take care of your personal hygiene. Drink lots of water. BUD/S is hard, but we never deny you food or water. Have a good haircut and a good uniform. Take care of your own gear first, then the class gear and the vehicles. Ask questions, pay attention to detail. Safety is a priority; never forget that. And never quit—unless of course, you want to DOR. Class leader?" Gallagher is quickly on his feet, but Hall waves him back to his seat. "I'll want a class roster complete with room numbers and phone numbers. You and your LPO get with me after this and we'll make class assignments for the phase. You draw gear after this, right?"

"HOOYAH!"

"Okay, over the weekend get your personal equipment set up and get it properly stenciled. If you have any questions, see myself or Instructor Wiedmann. Make those blue helmets red. You're now in Third Phase. You'll have the rest of the afternoon to draw equipment, your MREs, and anything else you may need from supply. Next week the pace will be fast and then some." Hall pulls a schedule from his notebook and looks up at Gallagher. "Sir, Monday morning I want the class standing tall at 0500 for a four-mile timed run. You're scheduled for rappelling training right after morning chow. We'll inspect your H-gear then."

"Hooyah, Instructor Hall."

"That's it. You've got ten weeks ahead of you until graduation. Ten hard weeks. Don't blow it now because you do something stupid or you're not taking this training seriously. Work hard and stay focused. Questions?" There are none. "Okay, have a good weekend."

"Feet!"

"FEET!"

. . .

Class 228 has a weekend to celebrate the completion of Second Phase and prepare their field gear for Third Phase. They do both at Sean Morrison's home in nearby El Cajon. Morrison was a medical roll-in from Class 226 who joined 228 right after their Hell Week. He's a tough former Marine Corps sergeant who wants to become a Navy SEAL. While his wife, Kim, barbecues steaks for the hungry new Third Phase trainees, Sean helps his classmates with their H-gear. This Army-issue field gear is new to the sailors in 228, but not to the former marine.

H-gear is simply a canvas utility belt used to carry a light load of personal infantry gear supported by padded nylon suspenders. The trainees have to set up their H-gear in a prescribed manner: four ammunition pouches in front—two on either side of the front buckle-catch—a canteen hung just behind each hip, and a personal first aid kit in the small of the back. The only optional placement of equipment on the H-gear belt is the standard-issue combat knife. Trainees carry their combat knives on their left or right hip, opposite the side they will work their rappelling line.

In addition to the H-gear and their personal field equipment, the trainees also have new uniforms—camouflage utilities. Third Phase trainees used to be distinctive at BUD/S because only they wore camouflage utilities. Now all phases of training wear cammies. All metal surfaces of their personal field equipment are either painted flat black or covered with olive-drab tape to keep them quiet and prevent them from reflecting light. Sean Morrison helps them adjust their H-gear setups so they fit properly and ride comfortably. The class is fortunate to have Morrison's help, and the invitation to his home is a much appreciated break from the barracks. With the loss of Otter Obst, Morrison became the only married man in Class 228.

Third Phase does not start well for Class 228. The four-mile Monday-morning run is laid out on a 4.6-mile course; only five trainees pass. On Monday afternoon, a storm blows in from the Pacific and they have their two-mile swim in very rough water; none pass. None of the Third Phase cadre seem too sympathetic to the adverse conditions. The next day they run the O-course in the rain, so times are slow, and the scheduled conditioning run is in full H-gear with forty-pound rucksacks. With the exception of rappelling training from the sixty-foot tower, and the scheduled runs and swims, they are in the classroom learning radio communications and land navigation. Because of their deficiencies on the timed evolutions, they must get wet and sandy at every classroom break.

"Okay, guys," Gallagher tells his classmates, "enough of this. If you have to go, just pee in your pants; we're not taking any more classroom breaks."

On the positive side, the tactics instructors are excellent. Instructors Jon Wiedmann, Troy Deal, Doug Eichenlaub, and Gary Garbers are very professional and capable instructors. Everyone passes the land navigation test. On Friday morning, they load out for the land navigation practicals at La Posta on Monday. The last evolution on Friday afternoon is a conditioning swim.

Five trainees take an IBS through the surf to serve as a safety boat. The IBS flips in heavy surf and tosses the crew of 228ers into the waves. One of them gets his leg caught under one of the IBS cross tubes. It's Sean Morrison; he washes up on the beach with a badly twisted knee, one that will require orthoscopic surgery. Normally, this being Morrison's second injury and a serious one, he would be dropped from training. But Morrison is a very solid and popular trainee. Instructor Hall speaks up for him at the Third Phase Review Board and takes his case directly to Captain Bowen. Pending Morrison's surgery schedule and the pace of his recovery, he will be held at the Center and rolled into a future class in Third Phase. It's a real blow to Morrison to be set back once again, but the former marine's hopes of becoming a Navy SEAL are still alive. This again leaves twenty men in Class 228—twenty bachelor trainees.

The Naval Special Warfare Group One Mountain Training Facility at La Posta is a rugged military reservation in the Laguna Mountains some eighty miles east of San Diego. It's used by the West Coast SEAL and SDV teams and by BUD/S classes. La Posta is a Spartan facility with limited shooting ranges, old barracks, some highly difficult mountain terrain, and a challenging land navigation course.

At La Posta, the class learns more about patrolling, camouflage, and stealth—first in daylight, then at night. La Posta is at three thousand feet, so the February nights are cold. Sometimes the class is allowed in the barracks with their sleeping bags. Other times they find a lay-up position, or

LUP, in the bush. Each morning they have a killer PT session or a conditioning run. The Third Phase tactics instructors are in excellent physical condition as a group, perhaps the best shape of all the BUD/S phase instructors. They lead PT and the conditioning runs as a team. The days are spent scrambling over the Laguna Mountains. The land navigation practical takes two days. Trainees, armed with map and compass, negotiate different courses that are usually five thousand meters in length, with each leg a thousand meters or more. Some pairs finish quicker than others, but they all finish—and they all pass the navigation practical. Late on Friday afternoon, 25 February, Class 228 is back at the Center. Earlier that morning, Class 227 graduated twenty-six men and sent them to the teams. On Monday, Class 228 checks out their assigned personal weapons from the armory for the week of shooting at Camp Pendleton. Class 228 is now the senior class at BUD/S; their class numerals grace the podium on the grinder.

Camp Pendleton is a 125,000-acre Marine Corps base between San Diego and Los Angeles. The base enjoys seventeen miles of southern California coastline, which makes it one of the most developmentally desirable parcels of land in the United States. The SEAL barracks at Camp Pendleton are warmer, but otherwise differ little from those at La Posta. Camp Pendleton is all about weapons safety and qualification, and proficiency with the M-4 rifle. In the teams, SEALs choose from a variety of rifles, handguns, and submachine guns, but the basic weapon is the M-4. The M-4 is a shortened refinement of the M-16 rifle that has been a U.S. military standard since the early 1960s. It is similar to the CAR-15 in that it has a semicollapsible stock, but the M-4 has a slightly longer barrel. In addition to the care, maintenance, operation, and firing of the M-4, the trainees are drilled continually on safety. Weapons safety is as much a conscious attitude in handling a firearm as it is a set of rules and regulations. Yet each trainee can quote the rules verbatim:

1. Consider all weapons loaded all the time.
2. Never point a weapon at anything you don't want to put a bullet through.

3. Never put your finger on the trigger unless you want to shoot.

4. Know your target and know what's behind it.

Qualification with the M-4 is twofold. First the trainees must shoot a qualifying score on a standard Navy rifle course. This requires precision shooting—marksmanship at two hundred yards. They all qualify, which is not easy with a small rifle like an M-4. Only Ensign Eric Oehlerich shoots an expert score, but several others are very close.

"This was a good day for us," says Petty Officer Adam Karaoguz. "The shooting is great and when we're not shooting, we're in the rifle butts changing targets, and the instructors are two hundred yards away. What was really neat was that the bullets were whizzing by just a few feet over our heads. You could hear the 'snap' as the sonic wave passed. That got our attention!"

Because SEALs rarely engage their opponents at long range, there are rifle proficiency drills that the trainees must pass. These drills, along with their pistol qualifications, are scheduled for San Clemente Island.

Meals at Camp Pendleton, as at La Posta, are MREs, either in the barracks or on the shooting ranges. Each day there is a physical evolution—a hard PT or a conditioning run. Conditioning runs at Pendleton are among the hardest to date. The trainees have to learn to run while carrying weapons and operational equipment. In addition to their H-gear and packs, the class must carry "Stumpy," a short, fat, seventy-pound log with four carrying handles. The trainees take two-minute turns running with Stumpy on these eight-mile runs. Again, the Third Phase cadre make all the tough runs with the class. The physical harassment is less than it was in Second Phase, but still part of the training. Safety infractions or weapons-handling discrepancies are carefully noted by the instructors. These accumulate and have to be worked off. This happens on Wednesday night, when the class is put through a hammer session with water hoses and PT in the mud.

"It's like a bar tab," Bill Gallagher says philosophically. "The chits build up and we have to work them off. Once it's done we move on—no hard feelings. And on the really hard runs and PT sessions, the tactics instructors do them with us. That makes all the difference."

In addition to the range work with the M-4 rifle, each trainee has to pass a weapons assembly exam. This is a bench test during which they must disassemble and reassemble the M-4, the 9mm Sig Sauer pistol, and the Mk-43 machine gun, naming each part as they go. They do this with an instructor standing by with a stopwatch who questions them while they work. "What is the cyclic rate of fire of this weapon? What is the maximum effective range of this weapon? What is the muzzle velocity of this weapon?" Wrong answers or sloppy procedures go on their bar tabs.

On Thursday morning, Class 228 moves on to the SEAL tactical-shooting exercise. This takes place on a range where the trainees run between the shooting stations. Each station is different—a trash can, a vehicle, a window frame. They learn combat shooting techniques, like how to roll on their sides to shoot from under a car or the best way to take a brace on a windowsill. Their targets are metal silhouettes, which "ping" when hit. The trainees race from station to station, double-tapping (shooting twice) each target. The target silhouettes vary in range from fifty to a hundred meters. The trainees' scores are a function of time and the number of hits. As with many combat skills, smooth is fast.

Thursday afternoon begins with famfire, or familiarization firing; no score is kept. The trainees get to shoot the Mossberg Model 500 shotgun and the Heckler & Koch MP-5 submachine gun, both weapons in the SEAL inventory. Thursday is also the day of the class top-gun shoot-off. Each member of the class contributed $10 toward a shooting trophy, a Ka-bar knife with "Class 228 Top Gun" inscribed on the blade. It's a single-elimination tournament with two shooters going head to head on the range. Each has a magazine and ten rounds locked into his M-4 rifle, standing at the ready position. When the senior instructor says "go," the two shooters drop to a kneeling position and shoot at a metal silhouette at twenty-five meters. Then they continue down to a prone position and shift their fire to a silhouette at fifty meters. They can fire as fast and as many rounds as they like; an instructor is standing behind each trainee as a safety observer and scorer. The first shooter to get a "ping" on each target wins; the other is eliminated.

Some fire rapidly, looking for a quick hit; others take their time to sight in and squeeze. Smooth is fast, and the smoothest and fastest is Ensign Eric Oehlerich.

"I guess all that elk hunting in Montana had something to do with it. With elk, a good shot may not last long and you have to take it quickly. And you only get one chance." Oehlerich is quick and accurate—two shots, two pings, every time. He now has a new knife to go with the ski-racing trophies he keeps at the family home back in Whitefish.

The apprentice warriors are beginning to master the techniques of shooting—the art of getting rounds on the target. For now, the targets are numbered, concentric circles on the target ranges. On the combat ranges, they are paper or metal silhouettes. The trainees are too hard-pressed with the pace of BUD/S to think about why it is important to get rounds on the target. That will come later.

Friday morning features another four-mile timed run, and several of the slower 228ers are worried about making the thirty-minute cutoff. The class gathers around their slow runners and they make the run as a class. Casey Lewis and Marc Luttrell are on the bubble because they have yet to make the timed run in Third Phase, but they make this one. Luttrell is still having trouble with stress fractures in his legs. Ensign Jason Birch ties a line between himself and Luttrell, half pulling him on the run. Bill Gallagher and Eric Oehlerich run on either side of Lewis. The whole class runs the four miles under twenty-nine minutes, its best effort to date. Normally, the times on swims and runs are sacred, and the instructor staff religious in their observance. But this time, the Third Phase staff overlooks the individual help on a timed run. The class is working as a team, and that counts for a great deal at BUD/S.

Week four and part of week five at the Center are devoted to the study of demolitions and high explosives. The trainees learn about electric and nonelectric firing assemblies and the types of explosives they will be handling, such as TNT and plastics. On the inert firing range just south of the

Center, the new demolitioneers make up their firing assemblies and set their blasting caps into dummy charges. In the 1950s and early 1960s, forty-pound charges were routinely set off on the Strand during demolition training. In the late '60s and early '70s, the charge limit was brought down to half a pound. Now, due to environmental considerations, all demolitions are conducted on San Clemente.

Physical conditioning continues—weekly four-mile runs, two-mile swims, the O-course, and rucksack humps in the soft sand. On a calm day, all of the trainees swim the two miles under seventy minutes; with that, the class has passed all Third Phase time standards. Just before they begin their load out for San Clemente Island, Lieutenant Rhett Fisher, the Third Phase officer, takes them on a fourteen-mile beach run, the longest run at BUD/S. But this run is in shorts and running shoes. For most of the men in Class 228, it's been a long time since they ran in dry clothes and in something other than boots. It's not a pleasure, but it's almost pleasant. Ahead are the combat runs and ruck humps on San Clemente.

. . .

Late afternoon, 17 March. The McDonnell Douglas C-9, a military version of the commercial MD-80, settles neatly onto the airstrip and takes the taxiway back to a small, two-room terminal. Class 228 has arrived on San Clemente Island—the Rock. They pile their gear and personal weapons into an old white school bus, a twin of the one that took them from the Naval Special Warfare Center to the North Island terminal. It's a two-mile drive to the BUD/S training camp, located on the opposite side of the airfield from the San Clemente terminal.

San Clemente is one of the Channel Islands off the southern California coast. It's a rugged, boulder-strewn strip of land sparsely covered with scrub grass, ice plants, and cactus—lots of prickly pear and golden snake cactus. On a clear day, Catalina Island can be seen to the northeast. San Clemente is young as islands go, some 3 million years old. There are no trees and no groundwater, yet San Clemente was inhabited by Native Americans some six thousand years ago. More recently, it was used by sheep ranchers, fishermen, and smugglers until the Navy took possession in 1934. Since then, the southern portion of San Clemente has been used as a naval gunnery and bombing range. On the northern end of the island, the airstrip serves to train Navy pilots for touch-and-go landings prior to landing on aircraft carriers. Other than a small cadre of civilian workers and sailors, the indigenous population consists of gray foxes, lizards, crows, and a few rare and endangered bird species. The coastal areas and kelp beds host large populations of marine life and California sea lions. The northeastern tip of the island is reserved for Navy SEALs. On this reservation, Naval Special Warfare Group One recently built a training base to support the West Coast SEAL and SDV teams. A short distance up the beach is the BUD/S compound. Right next to these facilities are the weapons and demolition ranges. Most of the coastline consists of rocky outcroppings and cliffs that plunge directly into the sea. The BUD/S compound enjoys a protective cove with one of the island's few sandy beaches.

BUD/S students have been coming to San Clemente Island since the late 1950s for weapons and demolitions training. The training compound had been a blend of tent and prefab wooden huts until the construction of Camp Al Huey in 1989. "Uncle Al" was a Vietnam-era master chief petty officer who dedicated his life to the teams and the training of Navy frogmen and SEALs. Camp Huey is a modern facility that has the feel of a community college—classrooms, a dormitory, a cafeteria. But instead of laboratories and a library, there is a weapons-cleaning building, an armory, an IBS storage barn, and gear-staging facilities. There are no athletic fields, but there is an obstacle course. It's a minicampus for apprentice warriors. San Clemente focuses on weapons, demolitions, and small-unit tactics— the basics of the SEAL trade.

As soon as Class 228 arrives at the compound, it gets a tour of the facilities and quickly settles into its "dorm," which consists of squad sleeping bays. The students arrive with their M-4 rifles, rucksacks, H-gear, a change of clothes, swim gear, and sleeping bags—bare essentials, but everything they will need for training on San Clemente. After the evening meal, the Third Phase cadre welcomes them with a shark-attack video—lots of great whites hitting chunks of meat underwater. Then they jock-up for a night conditioning swim in the cove.

Class 228 quickly learns that life on the island is different from life at the Naval Special Warfare Center. For the first time at BUD/S, they eat, sleep, and live in close proximity to their classrooms and training ranges. The routines and military protocols revolve around SEAL training at their own facility, rather than as a tenant on a Navy base. Each morning, Class 228 forms up in their compound to raise its flag and sing "The Star-Spangled Banner." The men form up again at night to lower the flag and sing "America the Beautiful." Their singing is coarse and off-key, and no threat to the Vienna Boys' Choir, but they get the job done. The spirit is definitely there.

Apart from weekly runs, PT, conditioning swims, and the O-course, the class must do "chow PT." In the morning, they do maximum push-ups and maximum sit-ups in two-minute timed intervals. At noon, they have to run up to Frog Rock, a pinnacle just above the camp. The distance is only a little over two hundred meters, but it's all uphill and the last fifty meters is a steep rocky trail. They have to make the run in less than a minute and thirty seconds. To do this requires an all-out sprint. At night they have to do fifteen chin-ups and fifteen dips. All three chow PTs are done with full H-gear and full canteens of water.

But the teaching to harassment ratio, which made a positive leap from Second Phase to Third Phase, gets even better on the island. This doesn't mean there is no physical penalty for inattention to duty, but as long as the class stays focused on training, the Third Phase instructors focus on teaching. On San Clemente, the trainees use all the weapons, demolitions, and tactics instruction they received at the Center, La Posta, and Camp Pendleton. Here they will experience combat shooting, set off live explosives, and conduct night patrols over unfamiliar terrain—all evolutions that require planning and attention to detail. The days are long on the island, and so are the weeks. The training day begins at 0600 each morning, sometimes earlier, and lasts until 2000, sometimes later—seven days a week.

Class 228 is still vulnerable. Not since Class 223, five classes ago, has a class not lost at least one man while on the island. The reasons why some trainees fail here vary. For some, it's a serious safety violation on the shooting or demo ranges. For others, it's the inability to shoot a qualification score or successfully complete the basic SEAL rifle or pistol proficiency practical. Occasionally, a young man will find that handling live demolitions or close-quarters shooting is just not something he wants to do for a living. Class 228 has four solid weeks—twenty-eight days of training—between them and graduation. Class 228 arrived at San Clemente with twenty men; they want to leave together as a class.

The first two weeks on the island are devoted to tactics and weapons. The weapons range at the BUD/S training camp allows for precision shooting and immediate action drills, or IADs. The precision shooting training with M-4s was completed at Camp Pendleton, where the men shot for qualification. At the San Clemente BUD/S range, they shoot for score with their secondary weapon, the 9mm Sig Sauer P-226 pistol.

"Ready on the right; ready on the left. The firing line is ready. With a magazine and five rounds, lock and load." The first group of shooters rack and tap their magazines into the handles of their pistols. There is a clatter as they release slides to chamber a round and click their weapons on safe. Then they wait facing their targets, weapons at the low ready position.

"Commence fire!" A fraction of a second later, a volley of fire ripples down the line. They've all had classes on marksmanship, but putting rounds down range is really the only way to learn. Instructor Scott Stearns and Chief Warrant Officer Jim Locklear roam the firing line behind the trainees. After each break in the firing, they step up to coach their shooters.

Scott Stearns is a quiet first class petty officer who was raised in Colorado. After two years on an aircraft carrier, he decided to become a SEAL. He came to BUD/S after three platoon deployments with SEAL Team Three. Jim Locklear is the assistant Third Phase officer. Either he or Lieutenant Rhett Fisher is on the island when training is being conducted. This is Locklear's second tour at BUD/S; he was a Third Phase instructor in the early '90s. The class originals remember Locklear from 228's Hell

Week. He's pretty much done it all; he's served with the Underwater Demolition, SEAL, and SDV teams and has six platoon deployments behind him.

"Relax, inhale, exhale, and squeeze on the outgoing breath," they tell their student shooters.

"Sight picture and trigger squeeze; sight picture and trigger squeeze."

"Relax and don't anticipate the shot. If you anticipate, you'll push the rounds off target."

"Front sight focus. You should see your sights clearly; the bull's-eye should be fuzzy."

Shooting is a knack, and most of the class picks it up quickly. Once the trainees have the basics and settle down, they can easily shoot a qualification score. The men with good eyes and steady hands begin to qualify as experts. Only Zack Shaffer and Chad Cleaver are having persistent problems and shooting under qualification. In Shaffer's case, his rounds are going low and to the left. The warrant officer watches him empty a magazine downrange.

"Okay, Shaffer," he begins in a soft Georgia drawl, "here's your problem. You got to squeeze only with your trigger finger. What you're doing, you're squeezing the butt of the weapon with your bottom three fingers, so's you're dropping the nose of the weapon. Hold it firm, not tight, and when you have a good sight picture, squeeze only with your trigger finger."

Shaffer does this and his score comes up. Then Locklear helps him with his breathing, and he nearly qualifies as expert. For Cleaver, it's just a matter of relaxing and not anticipating the shot. Instructor Stearns coaches him in a soothing voice, making small corrections in his grip and breathing rhythm. The Beaver begins to put his rounds on target and qualifies.

Past the basic marksman qualifications, the trainees have to learn to move, shoot, reload, shoot, clear jammed weapons, and continue shooting. There are performance tests for both the M-4 and the P-226. The shooting course for the P-226 emphasizes short-range shooting and speed—manipulation and marksmanship. The trainees, with their instructor shooting coaches just a step behind them, engage silhouette targets at five to seven yards. One drill calls for them to double-tap two separate targets, center of mass, within four seconds. Another has them double-tap a silhouette, change out magazines, and double-tap it a second time within eight seconds. Smooth is fast—manipulation and marksmanship.

Performance tests with the M-4 are much the same, only the ranges are longer and the shooting more precise. From the low ready position, the student shooters must come up to the offhand, or standing, position and make a head shot at twenty-five yards within five seconds. In twelve seconds, they have to make one center-of-mass shot at twenty-five yards, change out magazines and make another center-of-mass shot. From the offhand position, they drop to the prone firing position and make two center-of-mass shots at fifty yards in twelve seconds. Shooting experience in the class varies. A few, like Eric Oehlerich, grew up hunting. The ensign from Montana is clearly the best marksman in the class. At least half of the trainees never fired a weapon until they joined the Navy. As the performance tests progress, the trainees gain confidence and begin putting rounds on target.

One of the most dangerous evolutions on the range are the immediate-action drills—IADs. These drills are to SEALs what parachutes are to combat pilots. However, unlike parachutes, which are a break-glass-in-case-of-emergency item, IADs have to be learned and practiced, and they are serious evolutions. SEALs plan missions to see and not be seen; to be the ambusher, not the ambushee. But they have to be prepared if things don't go as planned. That's why the instructors have IADs. At BUD/S, the trainees learn the basics of IADs. Later on in SEAL Tactical Training, these drills will become more complex. In the platoons, the SEALs will take IAD training to a very sophisticated level.

Class 228 learns two basic IADs—the leapfrog and the center peel. The leapfrog is a simple maneuver in which one element of a squad or a platoon moves while the other shoots. This can be done to assault a target by leapfrogging forward, but it is primarily used to break contact by leapfrogging away. In either case, the trainees are putting live rounds downrange with men in front of them. It is critical that the fire is highly disciplined and that there is clear separation between the firing element and maneuvering element. The center peel is a maneuver to break contact when patrolling in stagger-file order. In open country or with a larger, platoon-sized element, SEALs often patrol in two files—two lines of men moving in parallel with a stagger between the man to the left or right. The point man, who walks ahead and between the two files, encounters and engages the enemy. He empties his magazine and initiates the center peel by running back through the center of the two files. The two men at the head of each file shoot and peel back through the two files, changing magazines on the run. Before they execute these IADs with live fire, they walk through them, then practice them on the run with dry or pretend fire—"BANG, BANG, BANG," they cry, then they move, change magazines, and cry "BANG, BANG, BANG" again. Only then do they perform carefully choreographed, live-fire IADs.

After a week of weapons work with the class still twenty strong, the trainees begin a block of instruction on tactics. But first the tactics instructors break them in with a rucksack run.

"That ruck run has to be absolutely the hardest evolution in BUD/S," Bill Gallagher says after they finish. "It was horrible." I remind him that he said that of Patstone's hydrographic recon without wet suits in San Diego Bay during First Phase. And the same of the back-to-back, four-mile timed runs in Second Phase. "No, really, this was without a doubt the toughest thing we've done—honest!"

The Third Phase tactics crew on San Clemente—Instructors Wiedmann, Garbers, and Eichenlaub—splits the class into three squads and runs them around the north end of the island with forty-pound packs, full H-gear, full canteens, and personal weapons. Each man carries about fifty-five pounds. For eight miles they go up and down hills, through cactus fields, and across rockfaces. Then the squads race around the airfield, another three miles, with each squad having to carry one of its number. The trainees have to work as a team; they distribute the "wounded" man's gear and weapons and take turns carrying him. The three tactics instructors are rucked up like the students and make the run with them. Since it always pays to be a winner, each instructor encourages his squad to be the first in the ruck run. Navy SEALs are proud of the fact that they have never left a man behind in combat. This mind-set begins here, where they learn that they can be totally exhausted and still carry a man out on the run. This is an evolution that emphasizes teamwork, motivation, and spirit. A few in 228 are again developing stress fractures in their legs, so they are the ones who are carried. Distribution of the downed man's gear and the sharing of man-carry duties are essential to sustaining a good squad pace.

Following the ruck run, the trainees hit the classroom and get down to the serious business of basic squad tactics. A key SEAL tactic they learn and will practice again and again is the over-the-beach (OTB) operation. They do this once in daylight, then over and over again at night. First, they paddle to the objective area and anchor the IBSs several hundred yards offshore. Then they send in scout swimmers to recon the beach. Only then is the entire squad brought ashore. Next, they scurry across the sand and crawl into hiding just past the high-water line. SEALs are most vulnerable when coming ashore, so they practice these sea-to-land crossings over and over in full combat gear with weapons. During OTB ops, they wear fins that fit over their boots and partially inflate their life jackets to carry their combat load. Once ashore, they strap the fins to their H-gear for land travel. It's cold, wet, dirty work—and it must be learned well. These future SEALs will do this again and again in advanced training and in their SEAL platoons.

Class 228 also learns basic SEAL skills such as ambushes, hasty ambushes, structure searches, prisoner handling, reconnaissance techniques, and raid planning. For the most part the teaching is crawl, walk, run. The men learn it in the classroom, rehearse it in the field in the daylight, then go out and do it at night in simulated tactical situations. Class 228 leans into the task and works hard. The trainees pass their tactics and land warfare written exams, and then they are ready to move on to a week of demolitions.

The men in Class 228 are still locked into the BUD/S mentality: one evolution at a time—work as a team, get the job done, put out 110 percent, and don't piss off the instructors. They are all but immune to cold water and lack of sleep, and they can almost taste graduation day. But a few of them are beginning to think about the training—or more specifically, about what they are being trained to do. There is no formal discussion about killing or of the time when rounds on target will mean rounds through a man, but a few of the more mature men in 228 are starting to speak of it. Over chow or when they are cleaning gear, they occasionally talk of a time when the job may require the taking of a human life. It's a gut check of a different sort.

SEAL demolitions training includes fixed ordnance like claymore mines and hand grenades. The men also work with illumination and pyrotechnics such as pop flares and 40mm grenade-launched parachute flares. But the heart of demolitions training is the heavy demolitions—the C-4 satchel charges, Mk-75 hose, and bangalore torpedoes. Back at the Center, they learned about electric and nonelectric firing devices, charge initiation, blasting caps, and the safe handling of all these. Now it's time for the real thing. The handling of explosives, like the handling of weapons, is guided by rigorous and precise standard procedures. Supervision by the Third Phase staff is constant and redundant. With the heavy demolitions it's crawl and walk; there is no running. They diagram and plan the demolition shots in the classroom, then head for the range. Class 228 will get four demolition shots—three on the beach and one underwater. On Monday afternoon, 3 April, their third week on the island, the class gathers on a deserted section of beach a half mile from the camp.

"Okay, men, bring it in and listen up," says Instructor Robert Ekoniak (or Instructor Ikon, as the trainees address him). "We have three shots today. The first is a checkerboard shot with haversacks, the second is with Mk-75 hose, and the third is with the bangalores. The procedures for all the shots will be the same: hump the demo down to the beach, lay out the shot, tie in the detonation cord. On all these shots, we'll bring the det cord leads to the landward side of the demo field. Once I've checked the field and the det-cord tie-ins, we'll clear all nonessential personnel up to the road where the vehicles are parked and get a head count, got that?"

"HOOYAH!"

Petty Officer Ekoniak is a boatswain's mate with a degree in economics; he's a veteran of SEAL Team One and a military demolitions expert. "The guy knows so much about explosives," says Eric Oehlerich reverently. "And he really knows how to get it across to the class. He's as good as any instructor I ever had at the Naval Academy."

"The two guys with the firing assemblies," Instructor Ikon tells them, "will then cap in. At that time, I'll want another head count. When the count's right, they will pull the fuse lighters on my signal, and we'll all move to the bunker. I'll want a final muster when everyone's in the bunker, okay?"

"HOOYAH!"

"Let's work smooth, let's work as a team, and let's make it happen. Who's in charge of the first shot?"

"Right here, Instructor Ikon," says Ensign Clint Burke.

"Then let's get to it, sir."

Ekoniak watches as the class unloads Mk-138 haversacks of C-4 explosives from the demo truck and humps them fifty yards down to the rocky shoreline. He and Ensign Burke direct the class as they lay the haversacks in a checkerboard pattern near the water's edge. The class works as a team to tie in the haversacks to the det-cord trunk lines. Det cord looks like clothesline and is an explosive train used to connect and prime separate charges. Preceding classes have placed their charges in this same shallow, rocky cove. Toward the center of the cove, the rocks are smaller due to repeated explosions—little rocks out of big rocks on a grand scale.

Ekoniak is everywhere—directing, teaching, answering questions. "This kind of admin demo is important, guys. When you're in the teams and the admiral wants to blow a hole in the reef or to level a section of beach, this is how you'll do it. The checkerboard can knock down the berm so vehicles can make it from a landing craft across the beach."

Class 228 is hearing more about "when you're in the teams . . ." They didn't hear much of this in the First and Second Phases. They also like Instructor Ikon. He not only knows demolitions, but he treats the trainees with respect and in a professional manner. They don't hesitate to ask questions in setting up the demo field. While Ekoniak moves about to teach and inspect, he keeps his eye on the entire field.

"You ready to cap in, Mister Burke?"

"Yes, Instructor."

"Then get your people up on the beach and get me a good count."

Clint Burke sends the rest of the trainees up the hill and John Owens calls back down, "I got nineteen men, sir!"

"Got 'em all, Instructor."

"Vehicles started, ready to move?"

"Hooyah."

"Then cap in, sir."

Ekoniak hands him a roll of time fuse and Burke goes to work. On one end of the double length of time fuse are two nonelectric blasting caps. On the other end are two spring-loaded, mechanical Mk-60 time-fuse lighters. Burke and his classmates built this firing assembly and carefully clocked the burn time using time fuse from the same reel. This one is set for ten minutes. He carefully tapes the caps to a bend in the det cord and lays out the time fuse.

"Ready to pull, Instructor Ikon."

Ekoniak quickly inspects Burke's work and gets the all clear from Warrant Officer Locklear up on the road. Locklear is serving as the range safety officer, or RSO.

"Do it, sir."

"Fire in the hole!" Burke yells, removes the safety pins, and pulls both fuse lighters. He inspects the fuse lighters to see that they are burning. "I see smoke!"

Burke and his instructor walk up the hill to the vehicles. Ten minutes later, almost to the second, the students and instructors feel the shock wave and blast as five hundred pounds of C-4 goes high order. More little rocks.

They do this twice more, building one field with Mk-75 hose and the other with bangalore torpedoes. The Mk-75 hose is filled with PETN, a high explosive used to dig trenches and blast channels in coral. The bangalore torpedoes are long metal tubes filled with an explosive called

Composition-B. These tubes can be connected end to end to form a long train of explosives. The early frogmen used bangalore torpedoes to blast openings through barbed wire on the landing beaches of Japanese-held islands in the Pacific. Today, beaches that the Marines may have to cross are still protected with barbed wire and antipersonnel mines, so Navy SEALs still remain proficient with bangalore torpedoes.

On Tuesday afternoon, the class prepares its charges for the underwater shot. Seven swim pairs prepare double Mk-138 haversacks for the seven concrete-and-steel beach-landing obstacles that have been positioned in fifteen feet of water. Each haversack contains twenty-five pounds of C-4. Because of the tamping effect of water that will reduce the blast effect, the water shot is conducted on the beach in front of the camp. Seven pairs of swimmers will load demo onto the seven obstacles, and the other six trainees will circle the line of obstacles with a reel of det cord to build a trunk line to connect the charges on the obstacles. After evening chow, the trainees go to the beach and practice dry loading their charges on training obstacles positioned up on the beach.

The next day, the class swims out to their obstacles, towing their demo packs behind them. The men knife the bladders that float the haversacks and follow them as they sink to the bottom. Now they begin loading demo for real. It's high tide, so the obstacles are in close to twenty feet of water. The trainees tie the explosives to their obstacles and cinch the charges in tight. The objective is close, intimate contact between C-4 and concrete. Then they tie into the trunk lines using knots they learned in Indoc and practiced in First Phase. The trainees have weighted themselves so they can work comfortably alongside their charges. Except that the water is colder and no one is shooting at them, it's chapter and verse from a book written by the frogmen of World War II.

The head count on the beach is right. Two swim pairs remain in the water with two instructors. They have the firing assemblies. On the signal from the RSO, the trainees begin to tie their firing assemblies into the trunk line. These are similar to the ones used on the previous day's shots, only they're waterproof DWFAs—dual waterproof firing assemblies. Waterproofing a nonelectric firing assembly is a technical and highly evolved procedure. During World War II, the Navy expended no small amount of time and money to develop a reliable, waterproof firing assembly. None of them worked. The early frogmen solved the problem on the job: waterproof neoprene cement and condoms—two condoms for extra protection from the saltwater. They worked every time. Thirty years ago with Class 45, I made DWFAs like the World War II frogmen. Class 228 does it the same way. And they still work every time.

"Fire in the hole!" yells Eric Oehlerich from the right flank of the field.

"Fire in the hole!" cries Sergio Lopez from the left flank.

The two trainees find the pull rings in the double prophylactics and trigger their fuse lighters. "I see smoke!" Then they and their swim buddies head for the beach. Instructors check their work and quickly follow them to the shore. The obstacle field is dual primed with two fifteen-minute firing delays. The trainees and instructors retreat up to the camp to watch the shot. It goes high order as planned, but forty seconds late.

"Temperature and pressure, gentlemen," Instructor Ekoniak tells his students, "but mostly it's temperature. You'll almost always have a slow burn time from a water shot unless you're in the tropics."

"Does that mean there's no penalty?" asks Lopez. If a shot goes early or late by more than ten seconds, the class owes the instructors a case of beer.

"Heineken, Lopez," Ekoniak replies, "one case, *por favor*. Consider it a lesson learned with time fuse, and better over the projected burn time than under. If the time of a water shot is critical to an operation, put your time-fuse sections in the water when you do the burn tests."

"You want that case tonight, Instructor," says the D-8, Tyler Black, "and maybe some help drinking it?"

Ekoniak chuckles. "You wish. But no beer until after the field training exercise." Then he turns serious. "I'm heading back to the Strand tomorrow morning. I wish I could be here for your field training exercise, but I have to get ready for Class Two-two-nine. It's been a pleasure working the demo field with you, gentlemen. I want you guys to stay focused—stay tight. Work together on your FTX."

With three weeks down and one to go, Class 228 is ready for their field training exercise—almost. On the afternoon of their underwater shot, the trainees have the Combat Run. The Combat Run is the work of Instructor Shane McKenzie. McKenzie is the smallest of the Third Phase staff, but long on spirit and enthusiasm. His specialty is demolitions, but he is equally knowledgeable in tactics and weapons. A veteran of SEAL Team One, McKenzie has been at BUD/S for two and a half years; another six months and he will return to the teams. He divides the class into two squads of ten and briefs them on the course. The squads muster on the pull-up bars by the chow hall in full H-gear. Prior to this, they've staged their rucksacks with forty-pound loads on the beach.

The first evolution is the push-pull. Each squad must do a thousand push-ups and five hundred pull-ups, collectively. The full San Clemente instructor staff is on hand to count the reps. Then the squads race over to the boat barn, pump up two IBSs per squad, and run them down to the beach. Squad One is led by Bill Gallagher and Squad Two by Eric Oehlerich. Once on the beach, they push through the surf and paddle out to the marker buoy a quarter-mile offshore. On the way back in, they have to dump boat; the last time they did this was back in First Phase during Hell Week. When they hit the beach, Squad Two holds a two-minute lead. From the beach, each squad takes two mounted truck tires that have been rigged with nylon towing straps. Each squad must drag two of these tires to the rifle range, which is half a mile away and all uphill. The straps are short, which accommodate only two or three men at a time; the squads have to use teamwork and trade off on the drag straps as they pull the tires up the long hill to the range.

There are two events at the rifle range—grenade toss and shooting competition. Each squad member takes a hand grenade from a bucket and tosses it at a box target bound with concentric circles for proximity scoring. Accuracy and proper procedure count. The grenades, color-coded by squad, are practice grenades with safety pins, release spoons, and three-second delays. On the rifle range, the trainees' personal weapons are laid out by squad. The silhouette targets are at twenty-five meters. Oehlerich's squad is still in the lead, but Gallagher and his men are closing. Once the squad is on line on the rifle range, they have ten seconds to lock, load, drop to a prone firing position, and fire five rounds. Only center-of-mass rounds score. From the range, Instructor McKenzie declares one of the men from each squad "down," and the other squad members have to carry him back to camp and down to the beach. Along the way, they are attacked by Instructor Ikon. He has placed small radio-controlled charges that detonate along their route back to the camp. When these charges go off, the squads have to take cover and, using the newly learned IAD techniques, leapfrog away from the "contact." Once in camp, they run with their downed man to the water. There they pull their fins over their boots and grab their rucks for the combat swim portion of the Combat Run. As they've been taught during OTB training, they inflate bladders in their rucks and tow them behind themselves through the surf. As a squad, they have to swim the same course as they took with the boats—quarter of a mile out, around the marker buoy, and a quarter mile back. When Squad Two comes through the surf, Squad One is right behind them. Several instructors are on the beach tossing artillery simulators. The squads must leapfrog across the beach as if they were under mortar fire. The finish line is a hundred-yard sprint from the beach up to the camp. It's a close contest; the winners will be the trainees who can pull and stow their fins, ruck up, and get moving first. Squad Two manages to scurry off the beach first. Squad One gives chase, but can't quite run Oehlerich and his men down.

The Combat Run is a three-hour evolution that puts a premium on teamwork, spirit, and grit, which makes them all winners. But only one team will win the race, and the stakes are high. For the winners, Camp Al Huey bragging rights; for the losers, evening chow cleanup. BUD/S trainees are never dainty eaters, but at chow that evening, I noted that Squad Two was a little more sloppy than usual. After evening chow, each squad cleans and stows the equipment used during the Combat Run, and cleans all personal gear and weapons. Then the men turn in for a rare eight hours of sleep. At 0800 the next morning, they're back in the classroom.

"All right, gentlemen, this is what you've been waiting for: the FTX. BUD/S is a long pull, and you've had a long eight weeks here at Third Phase. This is where we put it all together—put it all in one sock. Everything you have learned throughout training you will use in one form or another during the next week. It's going to be a lot like Hell Week— long hours, not a lot of sleep. You've got to stay focused for just a bit longer. You will definitely have to work as a team."

Instructor David Johnson just arrived on the island to work the FTX. He's a sharp-featured, seasoned BUD/S instructor with a ruddy complexion, sky-blue eyes, and a Philadelphia accent. He's a veteran of SEAL Teams Two and Four, with four platoon deployments under his belt.

"Myself and the rest of the staff are here to help you. We will present you with the problems; you solve them. Use us as a resource. Got a question? Got a problem? Bring it on. The only stupid question is the one you don't ask. We can't hurt you anymore, and we have just a few short weeks to get you ready for the teams. And only one week of serious training out here. Any questions to this point?" Silence. "When there are, and I guarantee there will be, come to me or any of the instructors, anytime, day or night. If we're in the rack asleep, get us up. We're here for you. This is your last chance to learn and lock down some very important information before you leave BUD/S."

Johnson hands Lieutenant Gallagher two folders. "These are your missions for tonight, sir. Keep one for your squad and give the other one to the second squad. Work quickly and carefully. This is a night reconnaissance and we want your Warning Orders ready at ten hundred this morning, so that doesn't give you a lot of time."

"Hooyah, Instructor."

Johnson leaves them and the class splits up into two 10-man squads— one squad in each of the two classrooms. Bill Gallagher will be in charge of Squad One for the FTX and Eric Oehlerich will have Squad Two. Oehlerich is emerging as a strong leader who can get things done. He's the smallest of the five officers in the class, but does everything well. Basic

SEAL skills like shooting and fieldcraft seem to come naturally to him. It's almost like he's done it all before. The two squads go to work on their Warning Orders, which have to be ready in a little more than an hour.

"Time hack . . . stand by . . . five, four, three, two, one . . . Mark. Time is now ten-twelve Tango, April fifth. I'm Ensign Birch and I'll be giving the Warning Order for our mission tonight." The Warning Order is a short brief given by the patrol leader to alert his men on the kind of mission they will be conducting. He will let them know what operational gear to prepare and to assign duties to help prepare for the mission. Jason Birch reads the mission statement verbatim from the flash training message, then gives a quick update of the enemy situation.

"The basic mission concept is this: We insert by helicopter, patrol in on foot, do the recon, collect intelligence, foot patrol out, and extract by helo. Everyone will have their basic combat load, full H-gear, full canteens, and full cammie face paint, just as I've outlined it here on the Warning Order board, plus the following special equipment as noted. Seaman Black will bring the sketch kits and camera. Assignments: I'll be the patrol leader, Mister Oehlerich is the APL, Lopez the radioman, and Armstrong will be my point man. The rest of you will fill out the squad file as indicated on the board. Our time log is as follows: the Patrol Leader's Order will go down at sixteen hundred, inspection at seventeen hundred, and rehearsal at seventeen-thirty. At eighteen thirty we board the helo to begin the operation. Any questions, guys?" There are none. "Our actions at the objective will require two recon stops. Once we find a suitable ORP [operational readiness position] near the objective, Armstrong, Lopez, and I will recon the target using a cloverleaf pattern to cover the two stops, make sketches, and take pictures. Then we'll rally at the ORP and proceed to the extraction point. Your special briefing assignments are on the board. Keep me advised if you have any problems in completing them prior to the Patrol Leader's Order at sixteen hundred. This completes the Warning Order for Squad Two." In the adjacent classroom, Ensign John Green finishes his Warning Order with Squad One.

"Questions, comments?" Birch asks.

Again there are none—from the trainees. "Just a couple of points, Mister Birch," says Instructor Scott Stearns. "Since you have plenty of men in your squad, why not assign two recon parties, one to do each recon stop while you control both from the ORP? Sure, there will be some command and control issues to consider, but you might shorten your time on target with two elements working the problem. Just a suggestion, sir; think about it." He adds a few more comments about the Warning Order, then says, "I'll be available all day if you have any questions."

Stearns is what is called the lane grader for Squad Two's first FTX problem. He will be with the squad during its briefings and all mission preparations, and he will accompany it on the mission. He will critique the squad at various stages of the problem, just as he did the Warning Order. He'll also conduct the final mission critique. He's there as a resource and as a safety observer, but in all other respects, the trainees are to ignore him; he's just a shadow.

The trainees of both squads begin to plan their mission and work on their assigned portions of the mission preparation. They also have to stage their personal gear and weapons. They're on a timeline and have to be ready to go at 1600, just five hours away. Collectively, they work on portions of the Patrol Leader's Order, but Jason Birch will do most of the briefing. Their mission is the reconnaissance of a communications site. It's a sneak-and-peek operation—gather intelligence, without making contact or being seen. John Green and his squad are to recon a SAM missile site.

Ensigns Birch and Green lead their squads into the field that night. I have my choice and decide to fall in behind Jason Birch's squad. The last time I walked in the field at night in a squad of men with their faces blackened was in the lower Mekong Delta in 1971. Neither mission goes as planned. The helos, which are pickup trucks, dump the two squads near their infiltration points, but not exactly. The squads have to adjust their route to the target. There is a low overcast, making for a very dark night. Squad members have to patrol within touching distance of each other. Both squads miss their targets and have to patrol back to find them. There are rocks, ravines, and cactus to contend with. Once on target, they creep close to their objectives, and the squad leaders send out their sketch teams to survey the enemy sites. They are back in the classrooms by 0230 for debriefings and critiques. The lane graders tell them what they did right and what they did wrong. Then the patrol leaders type up their reports for submission the following morning.

The next night, Squad Two attacks the target that Squad One reconned using the intelligence Squad One gathered the previous night. Squad One attacks Squad Two's target from the night before. They attack with blank ammunition, fire, and maneuver using the leapfrog technique they learned only a few days ago. Ensigns Oehlerich and Burke lead these squad attacks. The second day of the FTX is much like the first; the trainees plan most of the day, patrol most of the night, and get about three hours of sleep. They're learning. There are a lot of mistakes, start to finish, but not so many as the night before.

Class 228 has completed two of the FTX problems and has two more to go. The first were squad actions—recons and blank-fire assaults. The final problems are platoon-size, live-fire exercises. The trainees will have two days to plan and rehearse for these last two missions. These are the big ones.

"You guys are learning, but you've got to pay attention to detail," Warrant Officer Locklear tells the class officers and John Owens the following day. They are in full greens and H-gear and soaked to the skin. The classroom-to-surf distance on San Clemente is about the same as it is at the BUD/S compound. Periodically, Locklear gets the class leaders off alone for an informal teaching session. Earlier that morning, during the live-fire rehearsal for tonight's mission, the class forgot to bring radios and ear protection. And one man was unaccounted for. Locklear lectures them in his easy southern drawl.

"Sometimes we have to send you down to the surf to wash off the stupidity," he tells them. "Am I right in assuming that you'll not be forgetting any gear tonight?"

"HOOYAH!"

"I expect you people to think and to be students of the game. You're the class leaders; I expect you to set the example for the others. You can't be making these silly mistakes and forgetting gear—losing track of a man. Today it's a trip to the surf. Tomorrow it could be a man's life. All right, 'nuff said; let's move on. LPO?"

"Hooyah, sir," Owens replies.

"It's your job to have a good head count at all times that the men are working on their assignments. Know where every man is at all times, okay?"

"Hooyah."

"Accuracy. I know you're gonna have other members of your platoon brief portions of the operation, but the patrol leader has to make sure their briefings are accurate. I caught one of you guys posting data on high and low tides that was wrong. The level of the tide will determine how much beach you'll have to cross on insertion—how much danger area. Right?"

"HOOYAH!"

"Contingencies. Y'all gonna need to have well thought out contingency plans on insertion, extraction, infiltration to the target, and exfiltration from the target. And you gotta brief these contingencies to the troops so they understand 'em. And finally, you have to spend more time with the actions at the objective. The AAO is the whole enchilada. Your boys have to know what to do and what to expect at the target. You've got whiteboards, sand tables, and flip charts to get the job done. A picture is worth a thousand words. You guys seem to love that PowerPoint stuff, but all it can do is project words. Draw pictures; the troops can carry that image in their heads, but they won't remember a list of what-comes-next steps. Y'all have your Patrol Order this afternoon, right?"

"HOOYAH!"

"Well then, you'd better get to work. An' I wanna see some kick-ass drawings in your briefings."

"HOOYAH!"

"Fair enough. See y'all at the Patrol Order."

. . .

"Security is set, all doors and windows closed, blinds drawn. This will be your Patrol Order for our direct action mission tonight. At this time we'll update our time hack . . . five, four, three, two, one . . . Mark. Time is fifteen thirty-seven on Saturday, April eighth. I'm Ensign Oehlerich, and I'll be the patrol leader for tonight's operation. We're on for a live-fire, demolition ambush and intelligence collection mission, and we have to submit a post-op report no later than zero nine hundred tomorrow morning. This will be a full platoon-sized operation. You've had your Warning Order this morning; any discrepancies—problems? Everyone good to go? Fine. I'll now read the mission tasking." Oehlerich reads from the training message that tasks them with intercepting and neutralizing a van carrying a load of dissident nuclear scientists.

"Concept of operations." He turns to the whiteboard and an elaborate sketch of the northern tip of San Clemente Island with the airfield running through the middle of the drawing. "We'll insert in two Zodiacs and paddle to here, anchoring the Zodiacs two hundred yards off this beach just south of the western end of the airfield. We'll swim in to this point and insert across the beach to an ORP here. From there we'll infil by foot patrol along the base of this cliff, skirting the western edge of the airfield, and cross this flat area to our objective. At the objective, we'll deploy along this berm and set the ambush. When we're finished, we'll exfil from the objective along the coast back to a rally point here, then back to the insertion point." He follows their route in and out on the drawing with a pointer. "From there we'll exfil over the beach to the Zodiacs."

Oehlerich hits the PowerPoint and brings down the rules of engagement, which he reads from the screen. Seaman John Collins briefs the trainees on the environmental and hydrographic conditions, as well as the terrain features. For hazards they have sea lions, which have been known to nip at a fin or an ankle, and the occasional shark, "the man in the gray suit." Leopard sharks are sometimes seen around San Clemente, but they are curious and relatively harmless as sharks go. Adam Karaoguz briefs the class on the enemy situation and specifics about the reaction force that may be in the area. Zack Armstrong, who again has the key job as walking point, takes the platoon through the infiltration route to the target. Oehlerich trusts Armstrong. Both of them grew up in the mountains, hunting and hiking, and both know how to move at night and in the bush.

"Actions at the objective. Once we reach a position close to the target," Oehlerich says as he taps a point on the whiteboard drawing, "we'll form an ORP and set security. Myself and Armstrong will conduct a patrol leader's recon of the target. When we get back to the ORP from the PL recon, I'll pass along any additional information as necessary. Then we'll patrol in stagger-file formation to the objective area and deploy along this berm near the road. Everyone remember your place along the berm from the rehearsal? Good. Once we're in place, I'll give the command 'demo team out.' I want that word passed up and down the line; everyone has to know that we have men leaving the line and going downrange. Dougherty and Lopez will move forward and set out the claymores so they have good coverage in the kill zone." Claymore mines are small packs of C-4 explosives backing a sheet of ball-bearing-like steel pellets—simple and lethal. "When they come back into the line, they'll give me the firing leads to the claymores. While they're out setting up the claymores, each of you will lay out three full magazines. Then we wait for the target vehicle to approach the kill site."

The live-fire FTX problems have a good deal of realism along with a heavy dose of administrative time-outs and strict range-safety procedures. The "target" is a derelict van towed into the ambush site. It's seen previous duty as an ambush target, and is riddled with holes. Inside the van, are cardboard silhouette targets from the shooting range taped to the seats.

"After the target is in place, I'll lock and load with a full magazine. No one loads until the demo team is back and I have a good count, okay? When you hear me chamber a round, everybody locks and loads. Make sure you're well down on the berm. After we're ready to shoot, the RSO will give me the clackers [claymore triggers], and I'll connect them to the firing leads. Then I'll crank off the claymores. When the shot goes, that's your signal to come up on line and start firing. Keep up a sustained rate of fire until I yell 'cease-fire.' We'll then clear and safe all weapons, and you'll hear me call 'search team out.' Lewis, Shaffer, and Armstrong will go forward and search the vehicle to look for any intelligence materials. The rest of us will stay on the berm, on line, covering them. As soon as they return to the line, I'll give the word and we'll fall back to the ORP. Karaoguz will be on the far left side of the line, and he will lead the platoon file out. Move quickly in a hasty patrol; we're going to want to clear the target area quickly. Mister Burke will be the back door. Everyone taps him on the way out, and he gets the head count coming off target. Once back at the ORP, we'll get a second head count and begin the exfil. Now, we've rehearsed this a half dozen times and we had a good live-fire rehearsal this afternoon. Let's go over it again on the sand table."

The class gathers around a sand table mock-up of the target area, and Oehlerich again takes the men through the actions at the objective using little toy soldiers. When he's finished and there are no more questions, Zack Armstrong briefs them on their exfiltration route and the extraction back over the beach. Petty Officer John Owens is the radioman, or RTO. He covers call signs, frequencies, prowords, and other details of the communications plan. Seaman Marc Luttrell briefs them on the medical contingencies and Dan Luna covers the escape and evasion plan. Oehlerich again claims the podium for his final comments.

"Okay, guys, we've rehearsed it and everyone knows their jobs. Let's be alert, have good hand and arm signals, and let's have good noise discipline." He checks his watch. "From here we go to chow, then back to the barracks to jock-up and cammie-up. I'll hold the patrol leader's inspection at eighteen hundred. We'll hold the final rehearsal and walk-through at eighteen thirty. At nineteen thirty we board the bus for the trip to West Beach, where we'll launch in Zodiacs. Questions? Then this concludes my Patrol Leader's Order."

Warrant Officer Locklear and Instructor Johnson punch through a quick critique of the briefings. They're both complimentary and critical. The class takes notes on how the presentation or the mechanics of the mission could have been done a little better or a little differently. Just after midnight, a van full of paper-silhouette nuclear scientists suffer multiple claymore and rifle hits by Class 228.

· · ·

Two nights later, the moon is higher in the sky at dusk and a little fuller. The tide is high as a gentle surf crashes on the beach just down from Camp Huey. A pair of dark figures tumble from a breaker and scurry across the sand to the cover of the beach grass just over the berm. They're dressed in full combat gear, faces black. They carry their swim fins looped over their wrists and their rifles at the ready. Moments later, another pair follows them. They quickly form a small perimeter and wait, watching and listening. Then a single pair rises and begins a careful, cloverleaf reconnaissance of the area, looping out and back to clear their assigned sectors. They're back in less than ten minutes and re-form the perimeter. Bill Gallagher is wearing a waterproof Saber 3000 radio with earpiece and boom microphone.

"APL, this is the PL, over."

Out on the anchored Zodiacs, Ensign John Green, Gallagher's assistant patrol leader for the final FTX problem, waits with the rest of the platoon.

"Go ahead, Patrol Leader, over," Green replies over his Saber.

"We're secure; let's do it."

"APL, roger, out."

The other sixteen trainees, fins strapped over their boots, quietly slip over the side of the Zodiacs and begin to swim to the beach. Gallagher guides them ashore and across the beach with a red-lensed penlight. The platoon melts into the scarce beach vegetation, weapons at the ready. From there the men move fifty meters away from the beach to their first ORP. They set up a circular perimeter with Gallagher, Green, Cleaver, and Owens in the center. While they get their bearings for the first leg of the patrol, the rest of the platoon ties their fins to the back of their H-gear in preparation for land travel. The head count comes around and everyone is ready to move. Beaver Cleaver is on point. He leads them off the beach and up along the coastal cliffs toward their target. From the shadows off to one side, the Third Phase staff quietly watch their students insert across the beach and begin their foot patrol to the objective.

As did Oehlerich on the previous FTX mission, Gallagher sets another ORP near the target. The platoon goes into a security perimeter while Gallagher and Cleaver creep forward to observe the target. They are just off the road that leads to the enemy base. It's a radar and communications site that consists of two small wooden buildings, two radar dishes, two 6X6 trucks, and a water buffalo—not the four-legged kind, but a trailered water tank. Since they're pushing the long end of their time on target, Gallagher decides to call his men up rather than return to the ORP for them.

"APL, this is the PL, over."

"Go ahead, PL."

"We're in place. Bring the platoon forward in two files, your squad on the right side of the road and Squad One on the left. How copy, over?"

"Understand Squad Two up the right side of the road, Squad One on the left, over."

"PL, good copy, over."

"We're moving. APL, out."

Soon there are two files of dark shapes picking their way along the dirt road that leads to the enemy site. As briefed during Gallagher's Patrol Leader's Order, the two files turn ninety degrees left and right as they come on line at Gallagher and Cleaver's position. They assume a prone firing position. The platoon enjoys the cover of a slight rise about thirty meters from the radar dishes and vehicles. Gallagher taps his transmit key.

"APL, prepare to assault."

"APL, roger, out."

Gallagher and Green are positioned on a rise directly across the road from each other. They each pass the signal to prepare to assault. Down the line, left and right, the members of the platoon pull loaded magazines from their ammo pouches and lay them out at the ready. Only two trainees, Matt Jenkins and Seaman Warren Connor, are not on line. They take a position about ten meters behind the line of shooters to serve as rear security. They're also the grenadiers. Instead of magazines, they lay out illumination rounds. Slung beneath the barrels of their M-4s are M-203 grenade launchers. On either side of the two grenadiers, several instructors meld in behind the line of students on the skirmish line. With them is Captain Bowen, who has come out to watch 228's final FTX. There is no talking. Instructor Johnson looks up and down the line; there's enough moonlight for him to see the thumbs-up from his staff safety observers. This is a range, and the range is clear. He walks over and taps Gallagher on the foot.

Bill Gallagher is waiting for this. He locks a full mag into his M-4 and taps his bolt release tab. The bolt rattles home, chambering a 5.56mm tracer round. A mechanical tap-and-clatter ripples down the line of trainees as Class 228 goes hot. Johnson receives another up-check from his safety observers and he again taps Gallagher on the foot. For a nanosecond, a flash of red connects the closest structure to the muzzle of Gallagher's M-4 as the tracer round makes contact. Dozens more follow as the platoon engages the target. Some of the men come up to a kneeling firing position as they change out magazines—three magazines, twenty rounds per mag, over a thousand rounds, all well-aimed, single shots. Full automatic is only for the movies; the drill is accurate, sustained fire. It's over in about forty seconds.

"Cease-fire! Cease-fire!" Gallagher yells. "Clear and make safe all weapons!"

The operation "goes admin" as the instructor/safety observers quickly check that all weapons are clear and safe. Every thirty seconds or so there is a whoosh and a pop as Jenkins and Connor keep the target lit with their 40mm illumination rockets.

"You're clear, Mister Gallagher," says Instructor Johnson. "Continue with the problem."

"Squad One maneuver!" Gallagher calls loudly. No need for sound discipline now. "Squad Two is base!" The two squads echo the commands so everyone gets the word. Ensign Green's Squad Two will remain in place as the base element; Lieutenant Gallagher's Squad One, as the maneuver element, will assault the target.

"Ones up!"

"ONES UP!"

"Ones forward!"

"ONES FORWARD!"

Bill Gallagher and four men from Squad One move forward. Off to their right, Green's squad covers them from the flank. To Gallagher's left are the remaining members of Squad One.

Bang, bang! Bang, bang! This is night fire and maneuver without the live fire or blank fire. There is no time to stop and fit blank-firing adapters to their weapons.

"Ones down!"

"ONES DOWN!" Gallagher and his men drop to a prone firing position.

"Twos up!" Clint Burke, Gallagher's assistant squad leader, gets his element on their feet.

"TWOS UP!"

"Twos forward!"

"TWOS FORWARD!" Burke and his men move up on the run. If this were a live-fire exercise, they would be changing magazines.

Bang, bang! Bang, bang! Gallagher and Green "fire" while Burke and his element advance. As Squad One leapfrogs forward, Squad Two shifts its fire to the right, still on target but away from the advancing maneuvers of Squad One. While this is pretend fire, it is serious business. Crawl, walk, run. Within a year, these same trainees will cover their SEAL platoon mates with live fire and move downrange while other SEALs behind them are hot.

Gallagher yells, "On line!"

Squad One replies, "ON LINE!"

"Forward!"

"FORWARD!"

Squad One moves into the target area, line abreast with weapons shouldered, while Squad Two simulates shifting their fire off target. In the eerie glow of the parachute flares from the illumination rounds, Squad One moves into the target. Gallagher is like a sheepdog moving behind the skirmish line.

"Hold!"

"HOLD!"

"Clint, you and Owens clear that dish!" The two men close on the mobile radar platform while the rest of the squad holds.

"I got long!" yells Owens as he points his M-4 past the radar site watching for a threat behind the target. Burke quickly searches the area around the radar.

"Clear!" Burke reports.

"Clear long!" echoes Owens. They drop to one knee and await further direction from their patrol leader.

"On line!"

"ON LINE!"

"Forward!"

"FORWARD!" The skirmish line continues through the target area.

"Hold!"

"HOLD!"

"Cleaver! Luna! Clear that vehicle!"

Luna yells, "I got long!"

Squad One moves through and clears the remaining radar dish, vehicles, and structures. Once through the objective area, Gallagher orders the platoon to set security. Ensign Green leads Squad Two up on the run, and they establish a loose perimeter around the target.

"Search teams out! Demo teams out!"

Two 2-man teams begin a search of the structures and radar installations for documents and other intelligence. They find some files and computer disks stashed in one of the small plywood huts. The two demo teams lay their charges out on the ground rather than on the radar dishes; these targets have to remain intact for Classes 229 and 230.

"Demo team one ready!" yells Seaman Tyler Black.

"Demo team two ready!" yells Petty Officer John Collins.

"Understood," Gallagher answers. "Stand by!" He's waiting for his search teams to report back in.

"Four minutes, thirty seconds, sir," reports Brendan Dougherty. It's his job to keep the elapsed time on target. He reports in every thirty seconds. The enemy reaction force in this FTX problem has a response time of ten minutes, so safety considerations aside, they have to get off target as soon as possible.

As soon as both search teams report in clear to Gallagher, the patrol leader says, "Demo team one, pull!"

Black responds, "Fire in the hole . . . I see smoke!"

"Demo two, pull!"

Collins reports, "Fire in the hole . . . I see smoke!"

"Five minutes, Mister Gallagher."

"Got it, Dougherty. Collapse security! Bring it in! Cleaver, where are you?"

"Right here, sir."

"Take us out of here, hasty patrol; Mister Green has the back door—let's go, guys, move it!"

John Green is waiting on the perimeter. Cleaver runs past him and gives a quick high five on his way out of the target area. As the rest of the platoon collapses in on the target and forms a single column, the men pass Green and slap his hand. Gallagher is the last man off target.

"Got 'em all?"

"You're twenty; last man!"

The two officers fall in at a trot away from the objective. Two hundred meters off target, Cleaver pauses and the platoon goes into a hasty perimeter. With administrative time subtracted, their time on target was just over five minutes—good, but not great.

"Okay," Gallagher says in a low voice, "standard patrol formation, quick and quiet. Let's boogie."

Cleaver takes a bearing on the initial leg of his exfil route and heads into the night. Gallagher and the rest of Class 228 file in behind him. Soon after they begin walking, two explosions erupt from the target, now well behind them.

Midway through their exfil, instructors with blank-firing automatic weapons ambush them. The platoon leapfrogs away from them to break contact—*Bang, bang* and move; *bang, bang* and move. They're back in an ORP near the beach just after midnight and begin their extraction by squads—back across the beach and out to the anchored Zodiacs. At 0240, the platoon is back in the classroom in their seats, faces streaked and black. There is a small pool forming under each chair as seawater drips from the men's clothing. Lieutenant Gallagher conducts his patrol leader's post-op briefing on the whiteboard. When he finishes, Instructor Johnson joins him.

"Mister Gallagher," Instructor Johnson says when Gallagher concludes the post-op, "how do you think you did?"

"I think we did okay, Instructor. We could have been a little quicker getting off target, and, well, our leapfrog maneuver to break contact on the exfil wasn't terribly smooth. We had to rush on the setup to make our timeline, but I think it went all right; my guys did a good job."

"I think you all did a good job, Mister Gallagher. So do the rest of the staff. Now, we threw you a few curves, but nothing really too bad—just enough so you know what it will be like. You have to understand that a special operation seldom goes according to plan; often you have to improvise, think on your feet, make adjustments, react as new situations arise. We have a lot of administrative constraints here in BUD/S. It's basic training; there's a lot of artificiality." Johnson pauses and regards them thoughtfully. "But we want you to see the process, understand the basics of mission planning and taking that plan into the field. Now you're ready for the more complex training you'll get at STT and in your platoons. And always, always remember the three requirements of a direct action mission: the element of surprise, violence of action, and fire superiority. Warrant Officer?"

"Y'all did well; I'm proud of you," Locklear adds. "You have anything for them, Captain?"

"Not right now," Ed Bowen replies. "I know you still have work to do. But I like what I see; you're a good class. We'll talk more next week when you get back to the Strand."

The men of Class 228 have finished their last formal training evolution. After a quick cleaning of their weapons and themselves, they get about five hours of sleep. The next day is a workday. They clean the camp, police the ranges, and prepare personal and training gear for the trip back to Coronado. They work hard, grin at each other a lot, and nobody is sent to the surf zone. Training is over. The last night on the island, they have a keg party and do skits for the instructors. The class officers man the charcoal grill and cook steaks and fresh sea bass. Spearfishing is good around San Clemente, and the Third Phase instructors take advantage of this. Well into the evening, Instructor Johnson again takes control of the class.

"Okay, fall in, two ranks facing me. C'mon, c'mon; we don't have all night." The partyers quickly revert to their role as BUD/S trainees and line up. "You guys have been at this for what, six months now? You're starting to learn something about this business. So I want each of you to come up with one single word or trait you think is necessary to get through training. You first, Mister Gallagher."

"Perseverance."

"Very good, sir. Fall out." Gallagher drops away from the first rank.

"Commitment."

"Good one, Owens. Fall out."

"Courage."

"Good. Fall out, Shaffer."

"Determination."

"Okay, Lopez."

"Humility."

"Excellent, Mister Birch—very important. Fall out, sir."

"Tenacity."

"Excellent, Armstrong. Fall out."

"Stamina."

The list grows as each member of the class makes his contribution. "Who's your admin officer?" Johnson asks. Karaoguz raises his hand. "I want each of you to give your word to Karaoguz, and I want him to type them into a list. This is your list, your words. Make a copy, put it in your wallet. Later on in your advanced training and in the teams, when your classmates are no longer around, you'll still have their words with you. Pull 'em out—read them—live by them. BUD/S is over, but training is not. We train our whole lives. Then someday, just maybe, you get to do it for real. Then the success of your mission and the lives of your teammates will depend on just how well you trained. Understand what I'm saying here?"

"HOOYAH!"

"Okay, guys, party on."

The next day the scheduled airlift is canceled and Class 228 endures the ten-hour ride back to the Amphibious Base in the open bay of a utility craft. But they're happy travelers. After Indoc and the brutal attrition of First Phase and Second Phase, Class 228 has achieved a rare distinction. They return from San Clemente with the same twenty men who left the Strand four weeks ago.

. . .

Graduation week. Once a dream, now a reality. It's an easy week with administrative chores like dental X rays, jump school briefings, wet-suit measurements, and course critiques. Captain Ed Bowen meets with the trainees and presses them for a candid assessment of their training. Class 228 was the first class to begin its training during Bowen's tenure as commanding officer of the Naval Special Warfare Center. He will read the men's critiques closely.

The trainees are out almost every night eating hamburgers, having a beer or two. They've made it and they know it. The last graded physical evolution is the SEAL physical readiness test, or PRT. It consists of maximum push-ups, sit-ups, and dead-hang pull-ups in a two-minute interval. Following the exercises, the men immediately complete a three-mile timed run and a half-mile timed open-ocean swim. There is no punishment for those who finish last, but they're still BUD/S trainees; they fight to be first.

Their individual scores will improve when they get to the teams and their bodies recover from the rigors of BUD/S, but they don't do badly. The top scorers in each event:

Seaman Warren Conner	230 push-ups
Lieutenant (jg) Bill Gallagher	158 sit-ups
Ensign Jason Birch	37 pull-ups
Seaman Larry Romero	15-minute, 33-second three-mile run
Petty Officer John Collins	12-minute half-mile swim

For the best overall score out of a possible five hundred, Petty Officer John Owens is the iron man of Class 228 with a top score of 460. Ensign Eric Oehlerich is a close second at 458.

There are two more physical evolutions between Class 228 and graduation, Hooyah PT and the Balboa Park Run. Both evolutions are designed to be fun and to build class spirit prior to graduation. Hooyah PT for Class 228 is a swim trunks, T-shirts, and boots evolution, but it's not an easy one. They run the O-course, run seven miles in the soft sand, then run the O-course again. Ensign Jason Birch, who finished last in the Monster Mash at the end of First Phase, wins the Hooyah PT. Most classes are bused over to Balboa Park in San Diego for their final run. Due to time constraints and scheduling, 228 is driven ten miles south on the Strand Highway to Imperial Beach, and they run back to the Center along the Strand bicycle path. It's an easy trek; most run at a conversational pace, but Seaman Larry Romero is well ahead of everyone else.

On Thursday, the members of Class 228 complete their BUD/S check-out, collect their new orders, and rehearse for graduation. At long last, the flags and the rows of folding chairs and the raised speaker's platform will be for them. On Thursday afternoon, Class 228 meets for a few hours with one of SEAL Team Two's most famous alumni, Lieutenant Tom Norris, USN (Ret). Tom was my classmate in BUD/S Class 45. He won the Medal of Honor for making his way into North Vietnam to rescue two downed

American pilots. The operation was the basis for the 1988 Hollywood movie *Bat 21* staring Gene Hackman and Danny Glover. Several weeks after this daring rescue, Petty Officer Mike Thornton of SEAL Team One won the Medal of Honor for saving the life of a badly wounded Tom Norris, after the two of them found themselves in a shoot-out with a North Vietnamese battalion. Following two combat tours, Tom Norris enjoyed a colorful and storied career with the Federal Bureau of Investigation.

"When's the last time you went to a BUD/S graduation?" I asked him a few months ago.

"When we graduated from BUD/S back in 1969," he told me.

"Then you better come out here and help me graduate Class Two twenty-eight. You just gotta meet these guys. They're terrific."

It was good to see my old friend Tom with this new generation of BUD/S graduates. They fell right in with each other—talking about the teams, swapping stories about training. I couldn't really tell who was enjoying themselves more, Tom or Class 228.

. . .

21 April 2000. A threatening line of storms hangs off the southern California coast, but a slight offshore breeze comes up midmorning and holds them offshore. The BUD/S compound is turned out as it is for every graduating class. The BUD/S grinder is ringed by state flags, and there is a tent in one corner for punch, cookies, and the graduation cake. At a table in the opposite corner are two instructors selling BUD/S T-shirts and SEAL memorabilia. A raised dais served by three steps rests on the west side of the grinder before the backdrop of a huge American flag. There are close to five hundred guests packed into the rows of folding chairs. This is Class 228's last day at BUD/S. Two Medal of Honor recipients are on hand to honor the class. This is my second graduation address: I also spoke at Class 182's graduation.

"Vice Admiral Stockdale, Lieutenant Norris, Captain Bowen, Naval Special Warfare Center staff, distinguished guests, members of the Naval Special Warfare community, and members of Class Two twenty-eight. And especially the friends and families of Class Two twenty-eight, for without your support, these fine young men may not have made it through this difficult and demanding training. This is very much your day too.

"Class Two twenty-eight . . . hoo-yah! You made it. Congratulations on a job well done. I can't tell you how proud I am of you, and what a distinct honor and privilege it is for me to serve as your graduation speaker.

"Today I have three duties. One is to speak to the accomplishments of Class Two twenty-eight. The second is to offer a few words of wisdom as you move on to advanced training and into the teams. The third, as is the prerogative of an old warrior, is to tell a story or two about how it was in my day. In regard to this latter duty, I'll try to be mercifully brief.

"The numbers and the statistics say nothing about the spirit, teamwork, and dedication of the men seated here before me, nor of the obstacles they've overcome to make it to this stage in their journey to become Navy SEALS. But the numbers do speak to just how selective this training is, and the rigor of the selection process.

"One hundred and fourteen men had official Navy orders to Class Two twenty-eight." As I talk about the attrition in the ranks of 228, I can see a number of old SEALs nodding appreciatively. "At one time or another, one hundred and thirty-seven young men were listed on a roster with Class Two twenty-eight behind their name. The twenty men seated here today are the ones who made it.

"What happened to all those others? Why aren't they here today? A few of them arrived at BUD/S and quickly found that this training and this way of life were simply not for them. A few tried their best, but simply did not have the physical tools to get through this training—not many, but a few. Others were injured and are still at BUD/S. They hope to be seated up front in this place of honor at some future BUD/S graduation. But most of those who left Class Two twenty-eight had good intentions and strong bodies, but they lacked a key ingredient; they lacked the heart of a warrior. That's what BUD/S is all about—heart. These twenty men have shown that they have the heart to become a warrior.

"Words of wisdom. Advice. I have nothing original to offer, so I'm just going to recall a few words of wisdom and advice that came from your BUD/S instructors and mentors. They're worth hearing again.

"Remember back to the end of your two-week Indoctrination Course when your Indoc proctor, Instructor Reno, told you that in the teams you'll be closer to your teammates and platoon mates than you ever were to your high school or college friends. But he told you to never, ever, neglect your family. In the teams you will live and fight alongside your teammates, but never forget your family; they come first. If you remember Instructor Reno's words about the importance of family and follow them, then you will honor Instructor Reno.

"In First Phase, during one of your core values presentations, Chief Schultz talked about right and wrong. He told you that in the teams and when you're out in town on liberty, you'll have times when you'll question whether something is right or wrong—a good idea or a bad idea. The chief said that if it's a close personal debate between right and wrong, it's probably wrong. I wish some chief petty officer had said that to me when I was a young officer in the teams. It would have saved me a few headaches and some personal embarrassment. This is good advice. Trust me on this one, guys, you will often be challenged by the hard right and the easy wrong. If you think twice and do the right thing, then you will honor Chief Schultz.

"Let's next recall that Friday on the beach at the demo pits when Ensign Joe Burns said those magic words: 'You're secured from Hell Week.' Remember how good you felt at that moment? You'd finished Hell Week." I pause and look at Class 228 and all twenty are grinning, even those who completed a previous Hell Week. "But think back to what else Ensign Burns said. He told you that Hell Week was just a speed bump at BUD/S. I saw the look on your faces when Joe said that. Five days of pain, cold water, and no sleep! And the man just called it a speed bump! As you leave here and take up the challenges of advanced training and platoon duty, remember this perspective. There are some tough days ahead for each of you, and some very demanding duty as a SEAL operator. Think of these challenges as speed bumps on your journey to become a warrior. If you work hard and meet these challenges well, you will honor Joe Burns.

"In Second Phase, your proctor was Instructor Steve McKendry. During his proctor briefing, he talked about alcohol. Instructor McKendry said that he didn't drink because it affected his performance as a Navy SEAL—his personal goals as a warrior. Steve McKendry didn't tell you not to drink, but he did tell you not to let alcohol get between you and your goal to become a SEAL. No words of mine can possibly put a proper value on this advice. If you use alcohol, do so responsibly. And if you never let alcohol come between you and your goal to become a warrior, then you will honor Instructor Steve McKendry.

"And finally, I want to remind you of what Instructor David Johnson said after your final field training exercise on San Clemente Island. He complimented you on your performance in the field, but he also told you that you'd just scratched the surface of your professional careers, that you'd always be in training—always learning your trade. He said that it would never get easier, but that it would get better—that you would get better. Think about this as you train and work to elevate your professional skills. Do this as you continue your journey to become a warrior, and you will honor Instructor Johnson.

"You've had some excellent mentors during your stay here at BUD/S. As you move on and take up new duties and challenges, take their words of wisdom with you. You will honor them in the teams.

"And finally, a few words about what it was like when I was a BUD/S trainee—the old days, back when Moby Dick was a minnow. We go through this training as a class, but we leave training as individual BUD/S graduates. Since you began this training you've been told that reputation is everything. It's a small community; everybody knows everyone else. As you move on to the teams, the reputation you earned as a BUD/S trainee will follow you. It was the same way when I graduated with Class Forty-five. Like Bill Gallagher, I was a junior grade lieutenant from the fleet and my class's leader. We began with seventy-some trainees, and thirteen of us graduated. Like Bill, at times I felt like Colonel Travis at the Alamo as the class got smaller and smaller.

"Some of you in Class Two twenty-eight are leaving here with a great reputation. You came here and ate this program up. Sure, you had a few anxious moments along the way, but barring serious injury, you always knew you'd make it. Others of you have struggled with this training. For one or two of you, you weren't sure you'd be sitting here today until you got on that boat leaving San Clemente Island for the long ride back. It was just the same in Class Forty-five.

"There were any number of gritty performances I saw while observing Class Two twenty-eight. If I had to single one of them out, it was Ensign Clint Burke during the last few days of Hell Week. Clint is big for a BUD/S trainee, and he never stood taller than in Two twenty-eight's Hell Week. Whatever boat he was under almost always won, because Clint carried his share of the boat and then some. We had a guy like that in Class Forty-five. His name was Al Horner. Al was six-four, almost as tall as Clint, and he was a horse—best swimmer in the class and a solid BUD/S trainee. But under the boat he was awesome. I led the little guys in my boat crew and Al led the big guys in the other boat. I don't think we won a single race during Hell Week." Al had flown in with his wife and I asked him to stand. The group gave him a nice round of applause for what he'd accomplished three decades earlier.

"Al was one of the best in-Class Forty-five and he took that fine reputation with him to Underwater Demolition Team Twenty-one. He served the teams and his Navy with distinction. Clint, I know the staff here at BUD/S, as well as your classmates, think you did a terrific job in BUD/S. We know you're going to be a success in the teams.

"Not all of you in Two twenty-eight performed as well as Clint Burke. It's a tall order, no pun intended. And I know many of you struggled just to be here today. Some of you may still be wondering if you belong in this business. It's been a long, hard pull, and you may still have doubts about yourself. There's more tough duty ahead. Well, it was the same for us back in Class Forty-five. I remember one of my classmates particularly well; I didn't think he was going to make it. He was last on most of the swims and on most of the runs. When we finished Hell Week, he looked like Don Knotts on a bad day. I know my instructors spoke openly about his suitability to be in the teams. There was serious talk about dropping him from training. However, he's also here today. I am speaking, of course, about my friend Tom Norris.

"It is with a deep measure of reluctance and humility that I talk about the shortcomings of a man like Tom Norris. But there's a valuable lesson here. That medal, the Medal of Honor, that Tom and Admiral Jim Stockdale are wearing today represents the highest honor our nation can bestow on a warrior. We are honored to have them with us on this special day. But hear me on this one, guys, because it's very important; what you do in the teams is more important than what you did at BUD/S. If you have earned a good reputation here at BUD/S, keep up the good work. What the sign over the entrance to the grinder says will be true as long as you're in the teams: 'The only easy day was yesterday.' For those of you who struggled and sweated and barely made it to graduation, as did Tom Norris in Class Forty-five: I want you to keep struggling, keep sweating. Once your new teammates and platoon mates find that you're ready to work hard— to listen and learn—they won't care what you did at BUD/S. Trust me on this. Work hard, stay focused, do the little things. You can have a great career in this business, even a courageous one. And if you still have doubts about that, then I want you to have a talk with Tom Norris after this ceremony.

"In closing, I want to ask you a favor. We SEALs get our share of recognition for what we do. In the teams, there are a number of non-SEALs who work very hard to make us look good—to make you look good. I'm talking about the technicians in the armory and the dive locker, the supply folks, and the administrative personnel. They deserve our respect and appreciation. So at least once a day, I want you to compliment one of them, or give them a good word. They do so much for us and seldom get credit for it. And there's another group of warriors we SEALs are privileged to serve with, men who seldom get the recognition they deserve. I'm talking about the combatant crewmen in our Special Boat Units. Many of you will fight alongside them. These men are professionals in their own right, and if you don't think running across a state-five sea on a moonless night at forty knots doesn't take the right stuff, then you have a good deal more to learn. The combatant crewmen in the Special Boat Units are our brother warriors; treat them with respect.

"Class Two twenty-eight, once again, congratulations. Speaking for Tom Norris and Al Horner from Class Forty-five, and all the other old guys here today, let me say that we admire you and we wish you luck in the teams. God knows, we envy you. On behalf of a nation that is sometimes slow to value or even understand your sacrifice, thank you. You have chosen the difficult, dangerous, and often underappreciated path of a warrior in America. The words of the Canadian national anthem say it well: thank you for standing on guard for all of us. Thank you for being there so the rest of us can enjoy America's blessings and freedoms. On behalf of myself, thank you for allowing me to share just a small part of your journey.

"Friends and family of Class Two twenty-eight, thank you again for your sacrifice. Only with your continued support and understanding will they be able to reach their full potential as warriors and Navy SEALs."

As I look into the faces of Class 228, and past them to the old guys—to my generation of SEALs—I again realize just how much all this meant to me back when I was a young warrior, and continues to mean to me now that I'm an old one. And how proud I am of these marvelous young men who want to be Navy SEALs.

There is a big lump in my throat, but I manage to say, "This concludes my remarks."

. . .

Captain Bowen presents each man in Class 228 with his graduation certificate. Tom Norris and I are there to shake each of their hands. Then it's time for the Honorman Award. The Honorman is chosen by the BUD/S staff and is based on physical, academic, and leadership achievement. There are several in the class who could receive this award. Bill Gallagher led his class well. Adam Karaoguz and John Owens were superb petty officers. Clint Burke was a rock. It is not an easy choice for the staff, and it's the only individual award in the BUD/S graduating class. The Class 228 Honorman Award goes to Ensign Eric Oehlerich. I believe it was a good choice. I would be proud to have any of these men in my platoon, but if pressed to choose the man I would most like to have beside me in a firefight, it would be Eric Oehlerich. As the Honorman from Class 45, I was proud to shake his hand and offer my congratulations.

"Thanks, guys," Oehlerich says to his classmates from the podium after receiving his award. "They gave it to me, but it's for all of us. Hooyah!"

It is customary for each class to present a memento to the Center, usually some form of ornate plaque with a class picture, the names of the graduating class, and an inscription or motto. More often than not, the inscription is a few macho words or a tough-guy motivational phrase. Not in the case of Class 228. Bill Gallagher steps to the podium.

"Captain Bowen, we'd like you to have this memento from Class Two twenty-eight. In addition to a picture and our names, it's inscribed with a poem. I'd like to read it, if I may." Only Bill Gallagher doesn't read it; he delivers it verbatim—from memory and from the heart.

> Out of the night that covers me,
>   Black as the pit from pole to pole,
> I thank whatever Gods may be
>   for my unconquerable soul.
>
> In the fell clutch of circumstance
>   I have not winced nor cried aloud.
> Under the bludgeonings of chance
>   My head is bloody, but unbowed.
>
> Beyond this place of wrath and tears
>   Looms but the Horror of the shade,
> And yet the menace of the years
>   Finds and shall find me unafraid.

It matters not how strait the gate,
How charged with punishments the scroll,
I am the master of my fate:
I am the Captain of my soul.

"Sir, I request permission to ring out Class Two twenty-eight."

"Permission granted," Bowen replies, returning his salute.

Gallagher leaps from the platform and races around the gathering to the corner of the grinder. Three clangs on the BUD/S bell and it's over for 228. How fitting that Lieutenant Bill Gallagher, who so capably led Class 228 from the beginning, should have the last word from the podium before he rings out his class. From across the grinder, a new class leader calls the ranks of new trainees to attention.

"Two . . . Two . . . Eight!"

"HOOYAH, TWO-TWO-EIGHT!"

"Two . . . Three . . . One!" Gallagher replies.

"GOOD LUCK, TWO-THREE-ONE—HIT THE SURF!"

Class 231, currently in Indoc, is a big one—some 230 strong. They break ranks and head for the Pacific. They quickly return, cold, wet, and sandy, just in time for Chaplain Freiberg's benediction and to watch the SEAL honor guard retire the colors.

CHAPTER SEVEN

BEYOND THE BASICS

Basic Underwater Demolition/SEAL training is over for the men of Class 228. It took them six months—seven including the Christmas break and holidays—and a great deal of sweat and pain to get through BUD/S. Half of the men in that class had been there a lot longer. The day after 228's graduation, a pair of new Third Phase trainees were on the BUD/S grinder to change the big gold numbers on the PT platform. They now read 229. Class 228 is history, but who were those guys? Why did those 20 men make it to this graduation and the other 137 fail? What made 10 of the original 114 who went straight through so unique? I thought a great deal about this as I left BUD/S with Class 228. Certainly, these men embody the Navy's core values of honor, courage, and commitment. But so did many of the men who failed and dropped out. Perhaps the key attribute is some rare, ill-defined personal quality that can only be rendered by a long trial of pain and cold water. Perhaps this is a quality found only in the heart of a warrior. And it's still not over. The odds are that two or three of the BUD/S graduates in Class 228 will never achieve deployment status as a Navy SEAL. They will find the higher standards of advanced training too difficult. Or perhaps, once they get their SEAL pin, they will

will to excel. And still others are surprised that it
e life of a warrior is one of sacrifice and contin-

Class 228 when I met their parents. Uniformly,
who had high expectations of their children;
goals and subscribe to a strong work ethic. I sensed there
was a commitment to personal and family values in their homes. It was difficult to tell who was more proud, the parents or the graduates, but few of
the parents were surprised that their son made it through BUD/S. They
expected it and were simply delighted to attend the graduation and share
in their son's accomplishment.

I personally have come to believe the single trait that will get a man
through BUD/S is the will to win. The desire to win is different from refusing to lose, or not quitting. A man can get through BUD/S by refusing to quit,
if he can meet the performance standards, but he will not be a leader—a "go-
to" guy in his SEAL platoon. BUD/S cultivates this will to win, but to one
degree or another, top trainees bring it with them when they walk through
the door of the Naval Special Warfare Center. Some realize this only after
they leave BUD/S.

Seaman Ken Greaves first came to BUD/S in 1975 and classed up with
Class 85. He wasn't sure if he wanted to be in the Navy or go to college.
His girlfriend wanted him to leave the service. He got through Hell Week,
but didn't have the desire to finish BUD/S. He DORed. The thought that
he was a quitter stalked him for years—even decades. There was also the
knowledge that somehow he belonged with this group of warriors. Not
many get a second chance, but Ken Greaves did—and he didn't waste it.
With his Naval Reserve affiliation and an extremely rare age waiver, he was
able to return to BUD/S. He graduated with Class 197 in March 1995—
twenty years after his first attempt. Ken Greaves was two months shy of
his thirty-ninth birthday. He was also the class Honorman. After a tour at
SEAL Team Three, Petty Officer Ken Greaves returned to the reserves and
his civilian job—mission accomplished.

Ensign David Nicholas joined up with Class 40 in January 1967. During First Phase, he was medically dropped due to a strained Achilles tendon. But Dave confided to a classmate that the injury was just an excuse. He wanted to DOR; BUD/S was just too painful. After a year in the fleet, he knew this was not right, and that he had unfinished business at BUD/S. Fortunately, or so it seemed, there was a war on. Dave was able to get back into BUD/S and graduated in August 1968 with Class 46. He was assigned to Underwater Demolition Team Eleven, but he immediately volunteered for SEALs. His request finally granted, he joined SEAL Team One early in 1969 and began SEAL cadre training in preparation for deployment to Vietnam. On 17 October 1969, David Nicholas was killed on his first combat operation.

Today, BUD/S graduates don't automatically become SEALs, nor are they immediately ready for duty—far from it. Following BUD/S, they are ready to begin the serious skill building that will make them qualified SEALs and then "deployable" SEALs—SEALs who are certified mission capable for specific maritime special operations. Up to this point in their careers, they have toiled in the protective cocoon of BUD/S. For the most part, they were told what to do and they did it. BUD/S was a blend of testing and teaching, and the teaching was highly structured, force-fed basic knowledge. This will change. For the next six months, they will learn individual combat and operational skills to qualify for their coveted SEAL pin—commonly called the Trident or the Bird. And, for the most part, they will be in a teaching environment. Following their Trident qualification, they will be assigned to a SEAL platoon and begin the eighteen-month platoon work-up and training cycle. In the platoons, they will have to integrate their individual skills and personalities to the mission requirements and disposition of their units. SEALs are organized into teams, but the work of Navy SEALs is done by platoons. As a platoon, they conduct a range of maritime special operations. Within the platoon team, there are individuals with assigned specialties—air operations, special weapons, communications, ordnance, combat swimmer operations. Each man has a role to play, even the new guys. SEAL platoons are a lot like a professional sports team in that each platoon has a unique chemistry, its own distinct character and personality.

The teams already know about the men in Class 228 and how they performed at BUD/S. Naval Special Warfare is a very small community. Every team has an alumnus or two who are BUD/S instructors. Team commanding officers, command master chiefs, platoon chiefs, and platoon officers have all asked about these new BUD/S graduates. Who are the strong ones? Who are the smart ones? Which officers and petty officers show the most promise as future platoon leaders?

For seven months, Gallagher and company had a collective goal: graduate from BUD/S. The men from 228 will stay in touch and occasionally they may train together in small groups, but never again as a class. A few may even be platoon mates. Probably the next gathering of Class 228 will be at some future UDT/SEAL reunion. For now, each of them has the individual goal of qualifying as a SEAL: earning his Trident. The earliest a man can qualify for his Trident is six months after he reports to his team. During this six-month probationary period, there is a series of schools and team qualifications each must meet before they can wear the Trident. Much of what they have to do will keep them away from their new team—their new home.

One member of Class 228 has a somewhat different path to follow—corpsman striker Marc Luttrell. Luttrell will have to meet the same Trident requirements as his classmates, but he will begin this process after the Eighteen-Delta course. Eighteen-Delta is a twelve-month, intensive medical training course designed for Army Special Forces medics. Eighteen-Delta students get extensive training in combat medicine as well as hands-on training at civilian hospitals. They work in emergency rooms and even deliver babies. SEALs often operate in isolation, far from other friendly forces and without access to medical help or even a timely evacuation. Luttrell and others like him may be responsible for keeping their teammates alive and moving under the most extreme circumstances. The SEAL teams send their corpsmen to this course, but break it up into two six-month blocks. Corpsmen graduating from BUD/S, prior to a team assignment, will take their initial six months of Eighteen-Delta training right after the three-week Army airborne training, or jump school. On graduation from Eighteen-Delta, they will be sent to a team and begin their six-month Trident qualification process.

For the five officers of Class 228, the four-week Junior Officers Training Course starts on the Monday following their BUD/S graduation. The JOTC is one of the advanced courses that is taught at the Naval Special Warfare Center. Over a four-week period, the officers will spend seven hours a day in the classroom studying combat leadership, mission planning, and administrative skills they will need as they prepare for a platoon officer's responsibilities. The program also serves newly commissioned warrant officers and officers in the Special Boat Squadrons and Units.

JOTC approaches leadership through case studies and group discussions. These case studies range from platoon members in a bar fight to a legal order from a superior that could recklessly endanger a platoon officer's men. These are not hypothetical situations; they are drawn from the experience of previous SEAL platoons and deployed Navy Special Warfare (NSW) detachments. The leadership labs also deal with the warrior-monk syndrome. Occasionally, a young officer will think that all SEALs are simply pure warriors—celibate and temperate. The reality is that young SEALs are spirited young men who occasionally need a steady hand from their officers and senior petty officers.

One of the more compelling parts of the JOTC curriculum is the two days devoted to lessons learned—SEAL combat engagements that did or did not succeed, and why. When possible, SEALs and former SEALs come to the Center to address the class. Lieutenant Moki Martin, USN (Ret.), comes in to talk about Vietnam. He was on the failed operation to rescue escaped American POWs in North Vietnam, an operation that cost the life of Lieutenant Spence Dry, the last SEAL killed in the Vietnam War. Captain Bob Gormley, USN (Ret.), who commanded SEALs during the invasion of Grenada, talks about the four SEALs who lost their lives there. And Warrant Officer Randy Beausoleil, whom the 228 officers remember from Hell Week, talks about Panama. Randy conducted successful limpet attacks on two Panamanian gunboats and put them on the bottom. This was one of those rare textbook operations where, in Beausoleil's words, "it went according to plan, exactly as we rehearsed it." When these SEALs talk about inadequate intelligence, tactical mistakes in the field, or the benefit of good rehearsals, it means something. And when they talk about fighting alongside wounded SEALs and carrying dead comrades from the field, it means even more.

The JOTC students also get an overview of the special operations community from presentations on the Army and Air Force special operations components. They have classes on rules of engagement, laws of war, and career options within the NSW community. There are dry but important lectures on security management issues, naval correspondence, enlisted evaluation reports, and the Uniform Code of Military Justice. These officers will have to command, manage, counsel, and lead their SEALs. This is where they sharpen their basic leadership skill set.

The last two weeks of JOTC are built around mission tasking, mission analysis, and mission planning. The new officers build on and refine what they learned in BUD/S about Warning Orders and Patrol Leader's Orders. As platoon officers, they will be expected to manage the administrative and personnel requirements of their platoon, as well as lead in combat. Computer skills are all but essential in platoon administration and SEAL mission planning. Any SEAL officer who cannot type and does not have good basic computer skills will most certainly struggle in his platoon.

While in JOTC, the new graduates from 228 meet their senior SEAL officer, Rear Admiral Eric Olson, Commander, Naval Special Warfare Command. He warmly welcomes the new men to the community, but is unambiguous about what he expects of them.

"As officers, you will hold different jobs than the enlisted force. Your position is not about rank and power; it is about responsibility and accountability. Use your authority to lead, manage, champion, and nurture the force. As naval commandos, you serve as the maritime arm of the nation's special operations forces and the special operations arm of the Navy–Marine Corps team. This gives you a dual identity and a dual purpose that will pervade all that you do. It means you must be doubly knowledgeable, responsive, and loyal. And it gives you war-fighting responsibilities that can be answered by no one else."

The admiral gives them his guidelines for a SEAL officer:

- You are not expected to know everything yet, but you are expected to work and lead at the upper levels of your knowledge, skill, and authority.
- Be a teammate. What's good for the team has priority over what's good for you.
- Demonstrate professionalism in all that you do. Be sharp, look sharp.
- Learn the capabilities and limitations of your people and equipment. Acknowledge that the prime measure of your performance is their performance.
- Realize that your people are sharp, motivated, aware, and skilled. Teach, coach, guide, and mentor your force, but don't claim experience you don't have.
- Never sacrifice what you know is right for what is convenient.
- Communicate up, down, and across the force to build maximum situational awareness for leaders at every level.
- Live the life of a leader—one of values, character, courage, and discipline. Use your off-duty time constructively, doing things that make you or others better in some way.
- Realize that what you do and what you tolerate in your presence demonstrate your standards far more than what you say.
- Empower your subordinate leaders to work to the full level of their authority. Cause them to take responsibility for their leadership decisions. Train them, trust them, and hold them to standard.
- Understand that this is not a popularity contest. You don't have to be liked to be effective, but you have to be respected.

- Above all, remember that you serve as a member of a most demanding branch of a most honorable profession. Treat every day in Naval Special Warfare as an opportunity and a privilege.

In closing, the admiral updates the recent BUD/S graduates on new operational concepts and force organization. Then he reminds them of the five core tenets of the naval commando:

1. We commit to the team and its mission.
2. We persevere.
3. We prize victory.
4. We excel in ambiguous environments.
5. We keep one foot in the water.

Admiral Olson tries to meet with his junior officers, or JOs, on a quarterly basis to talk about the community and current events that affect Navy SEALs. This is good management practice on the admiral's part, but it's more than that. At the end of their five- or six-year service obligation, Navy SEAL officers may or may not elect to stay in uniform. Team officers are highly sought after by industry and graduate business schools. Eric Olson wants the best of these young men to stay in the Navy, but the life he offers them comes with long hours, long periods away from home, and barely adequate pay. The qualities that make for a good SEAL leader also make them prized by business. Young ex–SEAL platoon officers often find themselves working half the hours for twice the pay, and they get to be with their families at night. But they pay a price for these opportunities in the business world and the potential for affluence: They are no longer warriors, and they will never again lead other warriors in harm's way. As one former platoon officer put it, "The money's there but not the rush. God help me, but I do miss it."

While the officers of Class 228 are at the Center completing their JOTC requirement, the fifteen enlisted members of the class are at jump school at Fort Benning, Georgia. For most of the sailors, this is their first taste of an Army school and Army life. Because of the nature of joint-service requirements and standardized air operations, this is a basic but important school. In the Army, it is also a basic school for their new airborne troopers. The short runs and conditioning periods associated with basic airborne training are baby food for the new BUD/S graduates, but they have to conform and do as they are told. They have been warned about showing off or harassing the Army instructors, or Black Hats, but clearly the apprentice SEALs are a breed apart from the Army paratrooper. They know this, as do the Black Hats.

"The guy dropped me for twenty-five push-ups," one of them scoffs. "Imagine, going down for a lousy twenty-five push-ups."

John Owens and his men make their five static-line parachute jumps and collect their silver Army Jump Wings. Then they scatter—four of them to the East Coast teams in Little Creek, Virginia, ten of them back to Coronado and the West Coast teams. Shortly after the enlisted component of Class 228 leaves Fort Benning, their officers check in for their three weeks of Army airborne training.

For all their hard work and suffering, the men of Class 228 finally arrive at their team with the distinguished title of "new guy." Even when they qualify for their Tridents and are looked on by the rest of the Navy as qualified Navy SEALs, they will remain new guys until they complete their first deployment. Ahead of them now is perhaps the most intensive and important block of instruction they will have in their young careers: SEAL Tactical Training, or STT. In STT, they continue their professional development, and more importantly, they are more deeply immersed in the culture of the teams:

> Never fail the mission.
> You fight as you train.
> Never leave a Teammate.
> Read and learn the history of the Teams—you're not going to get it from some movie.
> Show enthusiasm and passion for all physical and mental endeavors.

288 • DICK COUCH

Set the highest example.

Remember, no one ever did anything absolutely right. Perfection's impossible, but striving for perfection is not. You have the power to do that.

This is not a movie or a video game. This is not adventure training.

There is no second place in a gunfight. Winners kill, losers get killed. Fight to win; train to fight.

Learn it the right way and you'll do it right for the rest of your life. Learn it wrong and you'll do it wrong and spend the rest of your life trying to get it right.

You cannot just aim; you must hit.

A warrior is hard from the inside out.

Your teammates, your team officers, and your team chiefs may not believe everything you say or everything they hear, but they will believe everything you do.

Keep that determination to excel—develop your reputation now.

Lose the BUD/S mentality; you're in the teams now. Take full responsibility and accountability for your conduct and performance.

These are the words of the two men in charge of STT. On the East Coast it is Master Chief Bob Tanenholz; on the West Coast, Chief Warrant Officer Mike Loo. These are hard men, committed to the training of Navy SEALs. It's their job to take new BUD/S graduates, among others, and get them ready for platoon duty. They have between them the equivalent of eighteen platoon deployments and close to sixty years of SEAL team experience. STT is the prep school for the teams. Currently, STT on the West Coast is a fourteen-week course; it is slightly shorter on the East Coast. West Coast training takes place in the San Diego area and at Camp Billy Machan, the NSW desert warfare training facility just north of the Mexican border near the Chocolate Mountains—a three-hour drive east of San Diego. The East Coast teams train their STT students at Camp Pickett and Camp A. P. Hill in Virginia, and in the Little Creek area.

In the past, each SEAL team conducted its own advanced training. It was called SEAL cadre training. I went through SEAL cadre training with SEAL Team Two in 1969 on the East Coast and again when I arrived at SEAL Team One on Coronado in 1970. SEALs just back from Vietnam taught us new guys the finer points of small-unit tactics and jungle fighting—and little else. This system of team veterans breaking in the new men carried through to the mid-1990s, when the Naval Special Warfare Groups assumed this training responsibility. Today, STT is conducted by Group Two for the East Coast SEALs and by Group One on the West Coast. This group-sponsored approach allows for a measure of standardization and a more efficient use of training resources. It also frees the individual teams to concentrate on training their platoons for operational deployment. Currently, there are plans for further consolidation of the STT process, placing this advanced training under the direction of the Naval Special Warfare Center.

SEAL Tactical Training is high-risk, high-speed training. It is the most labor- and logistics-intensive course in Naval Special Warfare. Ten to 20 percent of the class are Trident holders returning to the teams from a staff tour or an educational assignment—veterans who need to polish their professional skills before returning to the platoons. For the first time, the new guys from Class 228 will train alongside Navy SEALs. Training is conducted six or seven days a week, up to fourteen hours a day. STT classes average between forty and fifty students and experience one to three failures each class. An STT student must meet certain proficiency and testing standards, or he will never become a Navy SEAL. For those in 228 who doubted their BUD/S instructors when they were told that training is never over, they quickly lose that notion in STT.

STT takes Second and Third Phase BUD/S skills to the next level and then some. The first week is an intensive course in combat first aid and battlefield casualty management. It's an emergency medical technician course, including how to administer IVs and morphine. They learn in the classroom and practice under simulated combat conditions, dragging victims across difficult terrain and treating them while others in the squad return fire. If Third Phase training started these men thinking about what happens when they're shooting, this is where they learn what happens when they're being shot at. Following first aid is a week of field communications. There are nine radios in addition to the intersquad, Saber-type sets in the SEAL inventory. Many have sophisticated encryption and satellite capability. The STT students operate and communicate with each of them, and learn to deploy the standard and field-expedient antennae. Frequencies, ranges, and specific uses of each radio are on their communications test as well as the STT final exam.

The course also includes a week of land navigation and a week of air operations. The new guys from Class 228 make their first water jumps; after completing the five scheduled jumps, they qualify for their gold Navy–Marine Corps jump wings. Each training segment is more sophisticated than the last; each adds to their tactical repertoire.

During weapons training, the STT students spend a great deal of time with their team-issue M-4 rifles. Immediate action drills are more sophisticated and intricate than in BUD/S. The squad fire-and-movement drills are done with live fire and at night. It's still crawl, walk, run—but the running is much faster. One of the most popular evolutions is the combat stress course. It's a timed shooting course that puts a premium on smooth and fast shooting. Shooters begin in full H-gear and run from station to station firing various weapons—shoulder-fired AT-4 rockets, M-79 and M-203 grenade launchers, M-14 and AK-47 rifles, as well as their personal M-4s. There's a grenade toss, a fireman's carry, and a ruck run. They finish by having to shoot a silhouette with a pistol while wearing a gas mask. The score is a combination of elapsed time on the course and accuracy. There is a minimum qualification score, but the real issue is who is the best, the most proficient? Who in the class is earning a reputation as a man who can run and shoot?

The demolitions and tactics taught at STT build on BUD/S Third Phase. The new guys learn more advance patrolling and assault techniques. The range demolitions involve improvised explosives, I-beam and timber cutting, and shaped charges—precision demolition in which explosives are used in a surgical as well as a destructive manner.

The new guys are introduced to outboard motors, piloting, and navigation. They spend days and then nights offshore learning to drive Zodiac boats from over the horizon to a designated point on the shore. For most, it is also their first exposure to global positioning system (GPS) equipment and precision navigation. This skill set will be very important in their future platoon work-ups. Deployed SEAL platoons and squads routinely parachute from combat aircraft with Zodiac-type boats far out to sea. They then rig their boats in the water and come ashore, ready to deploy combat swimmers or cross the beach for a direct action mission.

The longest and most comprehensive portion of STT is the combat-swimmer course. Many of the STT instructors have trained with French frogmen and German *Kampfschwimmers,* and bring a broad range of experience to the business of underwater-swimmer attack, harbor penetration, and harbor reconnaissance. The students wear wet suits as needed under cammie battle dress, and modified H-gear with their Draeger Lar V scubas. And as they would on a real-world swimmer attack, they carry side arms on their H-gear. Much of the training involves ship attacks. For this, the STT combat swimmers carry practice limpet mines on their backs. Depending on the objective, they could also carry rifles or demolitions. At the beginning of the course, they swim lap after lap with their combat load to establish their pace and time-distance parameters. Then they begin a series of underwater attacks and reconnaissance exercises that culminate in a six-thousand-meter two-ship attack at night. Most training dives last up to four hours. Two dives per day, plus an almost equal amount of time with gear preparation and administration, make for some very long days. But as the new STT students now know, training is never over. The only similarity between the STT combat-swimmer course and Second Phase in BUD/S is the near-religious practice of diver safety.

The most positive aspect of STT for the new guys from Class 228 is the attitude of the instructors. For the first time, they're treated as team guys. Training is still hard and, in many ways, more difficult than BUD/S. The

STT instructors can still come down on their students and they do, but it's usually because of an unsafe condition or to emphasize a critical aspect of training. In BUD/S, part of the instructor's job was to see if the trainees had the right stuff to be in the teams. In STT, the instructor's only job is to prepare their students for a seamless integration into a SEAL platoon.

STT is a period in which the new BUD/S graduates begin to absorb the warrior culture of the teams. Over a beer after training or while taking a break on the shooting ranges, the talk runs to platoon deployment and platoon operations, and about combat—about killing. The new men are sponges, wanting to learn all they can about this mystical thing called combat. Occasionally, one of the veteran STT instructors will bring it up.

"I want you guys to become technically proficient, because you fight as you train," one of the cadre tells them. "When the time comes, you'll react instinctively and there'll be no time to think. But I want you to think about it—now, and when you get to your platoons. Killing a man, even some scumbag terrorist who needs to die, is very serious business."

SEALs constantly talk about jumping, diving, and shooting. I listened to animated discussions about tactics, demolitions, and weapons. But the business of killing is addressed only obliquely. When the subject does come up, it's always in a measured, serious manner—never cavalierly or with any sense of bravado. It was much the same in my day during SEAL cadre training. I clearly recall one of my cadre instructors at SEAL Team One, a petty officer named Talmadge Bohannon, teaching us how to set a good ambush. "Let's call this what it is, gentlemen," Bo told us. "An ambush, pure and simple, is premeditated murder. If done properly, there is very little risk to you, and the poor bastards in your kill zone will never know what hit them." I never forgot Bohannon's words or what they meant, especially when I was sitting on the bank of a canal in the Mekong Delta with a Stoner rifle draped across my lap.

STT classes are made up of graduates from several BUD/S classes. One former member of Class 228 knows something about killing, perhaps more than his STT instructors. Seaman Miguel Yanez, who left 228 on Monday evening of Hell Week with a separated shoulder, graduated with Class 230.

Before he joined the Navy and came to BUD/S, he was a police officer working narcotics in Houston. His law-enforcement career lasted only a few years, but they were active ones: Yanny, as his classmates call him, shot and killed three people in the line of duty. His former BUD/S and current STT classmates, some of them qualified SEALs, seek him out. In one way or another, they ask the same thing: What is like to kill someone? I asked Yanny the same question.

"I felt a little nauseous right afterward, but have no regrets. I did what I had to do, and I reacted just as I'd been trained to. Training is everything; you fight as you train. Only it's hard to duplicate the confusion in a combat situation. I got knocked down and had to shoot someone while I was flat on my back."

STT is also a period of evaluation. Which of these new guys are quick, smart, smooth, and quiet? Which ones are not? Who listens and who doesn't? They all have stamina, but which of them can ruck up the heaviest load and carry it the farthest? Who are the sled dogs—the ones who will run until they drop and never complain? All of them are good in the water, but which ones hit the target ship on time, every time? Who has the strongest will to win? As in BUD/S, the new guys break out by ability; there's separation between the good ones and the really good ones. In a small community where reputation is everything, the team platoon chiefs and platoon officers are trying to find the really good ones. They want them for their platoons. When the new guys from Class 228 report back to their respective SEAL teams, their reputation precedes them.

None in Class 228 were assigned to the SDV teams. Had they been, they would have reported directly from Army Airborne School to Basic SDV School in Panama City, Florida, for their initial training in piloting the underwater SEAL delivery vehicles. Then from SDV School or their assigned SDV team, they are assigned to the next STT course.

With STT behind them, the new men must now qualify at their team to earn their Tridents. Each team does this in its own way. For a perspective on Trident qualification and platoon predeployment training, I went to SEAL Team Three.

. . .

"Everybody here? Good. Mister Cremmins, you want to close that door? Thank you, sir."

Eight men fresh from STT and newly assigned to SEAL Team Three are seated in a small classroom in the Team Three building. SEAL Team Three is located south of the Naval Special Warfare Center next to the obstacle course. SEAL Teams have area specialization and Team Three is assigned responsibilities in Southwest Asia—the Middle East. Team Three SEALs are conspicuous among the West Coast SEALs in that they wear desert camouflage, or "Gulf War" utilities, rather than the green, woodland-patterned cammies. Master Chief Mark Kauber is the command master chief for SEAL Team Three—the team's senior enlisted man. He's a Puget Sound native, having grown up in Everett, Washington. Kauber is a short, solid man with a round, handsome face softened by an Asian influence; he's half Filipino. He has a generous smile that is both disarming and genuine.

"I've met all of you individually, but as a group, I want to again welcome you to SEAL Team Three. As far as I'm concerned, it's the best team on the coast. We've got a good reputation, and it's a well-earned reputation. My purpose in meeting with you this morning is to let you know what we expect of you here at Team Three and to get you in the proper mind-set for your Trident Board that convenes tomorrow. Congratulations again on successfully completing STT. Mike Loo tells me that you all did a great job."

The eight new guys are from the last STT class but different BUD/S classes. Two of them have reached their six-month probationary time with Team Three. On the successful completion of their Trident Boards, they will be awarded their Tridents. The other six will still have to wait out their six-month probation before they get their Birds, even after they pass the boards. During their non-STT time, new guys are sometimes sent to special schools as they become available. Or they are assigned to work in various departments in the team—airops, subops, the armory. Occasionally, they may be assigned to a newly forming platoon before they get their Tridents. Sometimes a new guy is sent off to a language school, either the

Defense Language School at Monterey or to a Berlitz course. At Team Three, the language is Arabic, and the school can last six months to a year—that's six months to a year additional time until the new guy can earn his Trident and get to an operating platoon.

"Every team is different," the command master chief continues, "but let's talk about what we expect here at Team Three. First of all, I want you to understand that this is the very best job in the military. Consider it a privilege to be here. You've come a long way and gone through hell to get to this point. But it's not over, not by a long shot. Stay focused, ask questions, keep working. Keep a wheel book with you and write things down. Myself and every operator in this team want you to succeed. But it's up to you.

"What we don't have time for are pissy attitudes, whiners, liars, or excuses—things like that. Until a man has been here for at least five years, we consider him a guest. If your priorities are beer, women, or lots of time off to strut your stuff around town, then this is not the place for you. This is a team. The 'I got mine' or 'me-first' attitude does not sit well with me. You show me that you didn't come here to work hard and become a warrior, and I'll see that you get a set of orders back to the fleet. It's happened before. On the other hand, we bend over backward to help the guys who are hard chargers. I'm talking about the guys with great attitudes who volunteer for the hard jobs without bitching or whining. If you're this kind of guy, you'll be rewarded, and you'll go far in this community. Know your priorities; be ready to work hard and to operate hard.

"Alcohol. If you drink, do so responsibly. A DUI is a quick way to lose your Trident and leave the teams. Use the buddy system to look out for each other, and if you're out drinking, have a designated driver. It's not hard. You'd be surprised how many guys here don't drink. We keep a fund on the quarterdeck for cab fare. If you find yourself with too much to drink and no way home, call a cab. They'll bring you here and you'll be okay. Drugs—it's a no-brainer. Fool around with any illegal, nonprescription drugs and you're history. We give urinalysis frequently and with no notice. This is a dangerous business and there's no place for drugs, okay?

"The bottom line is that I expect you to be responsible for your own actions. Don't lie; don't hide anything. Little problems are easier to solve than big problems. If you have any problem, take it to your platoon LPO or your platoon chief. I have an open-door policy here, but I expect you to use the chain of command first. If you end up having to see me, you're either in a heap of trouble or you've done something great. I hope it's for something great. I'm not a headhunter, but I want you to know how it is as long as I'm command master chief of this team."

Kauber doesn't appear to have any hard edges, but he softens as he continues to address the new men. "Our job keeps us away from home a great deal. If you have a wife or girlfriend, make sure she understands the importance of your job and why you're gone so much. How does she feel about these long separations? Does she support you? These things are important. Our team cares about family members and will happily help them out—drive them to the doctor, help them if a problem comes up while you're gone. We have a pool of money at the team available for this. We keep this low-key so they don't feel uncomfortable in asking for help. Those who support us in what we do are important. Don't neglect them.

"Now, let's talk about your Trident Board tomorrow. For you enlisted guys, the oral Chief's Board is your only board. You officers will still have the Officer's Board after you've completed the Chief's Board. At the Chief's Board, each chief, senior chief, and master chief will ask you about a basic SEAL skill that you have learned or should know at this point in your training. These questions will be about communications, diving, air operations, land nav, medical—things that you know. There are no trick questions, so don't make it hard on yourself or try to read something into it. Just relax and answer the questions. We'll have a few questions that relate to your attitude and mind-set as a new member of this team. Bring your wheel book with you so you can take notes on anything you miss and can get back to us with the answer. Depending on you, the Chief's Board will take no longer than a half hour to forty-five minutes. Once we are finished, we will excuse you for a few minutes, talk among ourselves, and call you back in for the results. If you did well, we will make a recommendation to the commanding officer that you are ready for your Trident. If you did not do well, you'll work on your weak points, and we will reschedule you for another oral board in a few days. The key is to relax, listen carefully, think about the question, and tell us what you know."

The officers will have a second board conducted by Team Three's commanding officer, executive officer, operations officer, and command master chief. Each officer is given a special operations mission tasking. Much like they did on San Clemente Island during their FTX and at JOTC, they will study the problem and prepare a Courses of Action Brief—how they plan to tackle the mission. Then the officer will stand before the Officers's Board and present his brief, just as a deployed platoon officer would present his alternative courses of action to a task group commander. Navy task group commanders are admirals or senior captains. The Team Three CO wants to see the briefing skills of his new officers as well as their professional knowledge. Then the Board will choose a mission-specific course of action, or ask the new officer which alternative he would recommend. The officer will then work up a detailed plan for executing the mission and present that plan to the Board. But first, all have to pass the Chief's Board.

. . .

"Ensign John Cremmins was a pretty strong BUD/S trainee," Master Chief Kauber tells his fellow chiefs in the CPOs lounge at SEAL Team Three—the goat locker. "He did very well in STT. He's a Naval Academy ensign, and he looks like a promising young officer. You guys ready?" There is a volley of murmurs and grunts around the room. Kauber steps to the door and pokes his head into the hall. "Mister Cremmins, you can come in now."

John Cremmins graduated from Annapolis with the Class of 1998—a class ahead of the Naval Academy ensigns in Class 228. Ensign Cremmins grew up in New York City and seems almost a little too smooth for a team officer—self-assured and even a little cocky. He looks younger than his twenty-three years, but he's smart and tough, and he has a good reputation. Cremmins is dressed in starched desert cammies and brushed sand boots. He has a close haircut and a fresh shave. Arrayed around him are thirteen chief petty officers. Among them are three master chiefs and a sprinkling of senior chiefs—over three hundred years of SEAL Team experience.

"Mister Cremmins?"

"Yes, Chief?"

"Sir?"

"Excuse me. Yes, Senior Chief?"

"Mister Cremmins, you and your swim buddy are making an attack on an enemy ship. You've been in the water for two hours; both of you are on Draegers. You are under the keel and getting ready to attach your limpets to the bottom of the ship. Suddenly there is a tension on your buddy line— it's tending down. This causes you to check your swim buddy. You shine a penlight in his face mask and you see that he is unconscious. What do you do next?"

"Real world, Senior Chief, or training?"

"Real world, Mister Cremmins."

· · ·

While John Cremmins sweats out his Trident Board, Lieutenant Gus Kaminski and Chief Petty Officer Joe Quinn are sitting in a two-room office in the platoon spaces at Team Three. This is the home of Foxtrot Platoon. They are dressed in canvas UDT shorts, blue T-shirts, and running shoes. Together, they review projected platoon training schedules. Kaminski is a sturdy officer, just under six feet, with an easy smile. He is from West Virginia and a graduate of the Naval Academy. Since coming from BUD/S to Team Three, he has deployed once to Southwest Asia as a liaison officer with an amphibious ready group and once as Foxtrot Platoon's assistant officer in charge, or AOIC. Joe Quinn is a quiet, affable man from Bainbridge Island, Washington. He has five platoon deployments, all in Southwest Asia and all with SEAL Team Three. During that time, he managed to complete his bachelor's degree in workforce education and development with a 4.0 GPA. Joe Quinn enjoys a very solid reputation at SEAL Team Three. Kaminski, who is twenty-eight years old, is Foxtrot Platoon's OIC. Quinn is thirty-seven and the Foxtrot platoon chief. Fully manned, there are seventeen men and a lot of moving parts in a SEAL platoon, but to a significant degree, Gus Kaminski and Joe Quinn *are* Foxtrot Platoon.

SEAL platoons live in cycles. They go through an eighteen-month training cycle or work-up, deploy overseas for six months, and stand down for approximately six months. When a platoon comes back from deployment, there are changes. One or two men will leave the platoon because they are leaving the Navy, either through retirement after a career or after a single hitch. Perhaps two or three of them will rotate from the platoon to the Team Three training cell or get orders from the team. They could be going to language school, to BUD/S for instructor duty, or to another team. The platoon OIC, a senior lieutenant, will definitely leave the platoon. The chief could stay for another deployment, but he will usually leave to make room for another platoon chief. More often than not, the AOIC will move up to OIC. Sometimes a platoon first class petty officer, if he is advanced to chief petty officer, will make the next deployment as the platoon chief. Sometimes the platoon chief is a new chief returning from BUD/S or he may come from the team training cell, as did Joe Quinn. Platoon chief petty officers are perhaps the single most important leadership position in the teams. They are selected and assigned with a great deal of care.

Foxtrot's current training-deployment cycle began with Kaminski and Quinn. They will be on deployment in the Middle East for only six months, but they will spend at least half of the remaining eighteen months of platoon work-up away from home at military schools or remote training sites. Some platoons have a number of holdovers from the previous deployments, and some build to platoon strength from a small nucleus of platoon veterans. For Kaminski and Quinn, it was the latter. There was a great deal of attrition from the last deployment, so they will have an unusual number of new men on this deployment. By necessity, the new platoon OIC and his chief had to draft new men, and they decided to draft for youth. Kaminski and Quinn used all their resources and contacts to find the STT students and new team guys with the best reputations. For one or two key roles, they will look for specific veterans, making their case with the Team

Three operations officer or command master chief to get this man or that one. The food fights over who gets what in the way of platoon assignments is ferocious. Again, reputation is everything. So is chemistry. Kaminski and Quinn are like a pro basketball franchise—drafting new talent, looking for the right veterans to glue the team together.

Lieutenant Gus Kaminski is typical in that his OIC tour is the apex of a young SEAL officer's operational career—for some officers, their entire career. This is his platoon; he's the boss—the platoon commander. It took him eighteen months to get through BUD/S and get his Trident. He's had four years in the teams on deployment or in training. Now, after more than five years of learning and apprenticeship, he has his own platoon. It will be close to seven years from the day he classed up with Class 198 (he graduated with Class 200) that he will lead a combat-ready platoon on deployment. Not all officers in the teams get this far. There are cuts along the way, and the competition for platoon OIC jobs is intense. It's a matter of experience, deployment requirements, and—above all—reputation. After this tour, Gus Kaminski will decide whether he will stay in the Navy. This means he will have some form of nonoperational tour, such as team operations officer or BUD/S phase officer. He could be assigned overseas to a special operations staff attached to one of the theater commanders. Perhaps the Navy will send him to graduate school. Unlike his enlisted classmates from Class 200, his future operational time will be limited. There are great opportunities ahead for him—perhaps an exchange tour with a foreign special operations component, like the Australian SAS. He could command a SEAL team or a Naval Special Warfare Unit overseas. Later on, he might command a Naval Special Warfare group. But the fact remains that the bulk of his SEAL operational time is behind him, not ahead. When he returns from his OIC deployment, he may never again give a Patrol Order or lead men in harm's way.

There's a saying in the teams: The enlisted men operate too much and the officers don't get to operate enough. The teams lose good men every year—officers because they want more and enlisted men because they've had enough. Joe Quinn has been in the Navy for seventeen years; he'll be one year shy of a twenty-year retirement check when he returns from this deployment. Quinn is typical of his generation of chief petty officers. In the early 1970s, he saw these people called frogmen on TV as they attached floatation collars to Apollo space capsules. He told his father, "That's me." Now, three decades later, he is at the zenith of his career as a Navy SEAL. Quinn has paid his dues. He's made five deployments during his twelve years in the deployment cycle, and has spent perhaps seven of those twelve away from home. It may be rare for a chief to have had six platoon deployments with the same team, but six or more deployments in twenty years is not uncommon among SEAL team chiefs.

If Joe Quinn elects to stay in the Navy, he could return to the training cell at Team Three, helping other platoons to prepare for deployment. He could go to BUD/S or STT, or serve as a staff officer at one of the two Naval Special Warfare groups or the Naval Special Warfare Command. He will be most welcome wherever he goes; he's smart, talented, and experienced. With staff experience to match his broad operational background, he could reach the top rung of his trade, a command master chief like Mark Kauber. But the SEAL teams keep their senior enlisted men busy. They travel a great deal, even the training cadres and staff officers. Joe Quinn has three young boys at home. If he wants to see more of them as they grow up, he may have to leave the Navy. And all that talent and experience will be lost. Quinn has options. Corporate America pays headhunters quite well to find men with Joe Quinn's experience and leadership ability.

But for now, for the next two years, the future of Gus Kaminski and Joe Quinn is Foxtrot Platoon. They are at the top of their game—the best of their breed. Given the selection process that brought each of them to this point in their career, they are very special, perhaps one in a hundred. If good platoon chemistry is important, then good OIC–platoon chief chemistry is essential. Together with the Team Three training cell, these two SEALs will train and lead the platoon through the deployment cycle. Everything that was taught at BUD/S, STT, and in the many specialized schools will be accelerated in the platoon work-up. With the help of veterans, the new guys' learning curve will explode. In platoon training, individual skills such as parachuting, diving, shooting, and demolitions will be integrated into multidisciplined operational scenarios. Old SEALs like myself marvel at this training and preparation. In June 1970, I arrived at SEAL Team One in Coronado. I deployed to Vietnam as the platoon OIC of Whiskey Platoon in October, and we were back home by 1 May 1971. My platoon chief, Pat McKnight, came to Whiskey Platoon right out of BUD/S. Lucky for all of us, my LPO, Walt Gustavel, was going back with us on his sixth combat deployment.

The culture of this eighteen-month training cycle is as unique as it is long and difficult. There are special individual and platoon schools to attend. Their training will include search and seizure of ships and oil platforms at sea; long-range, low-light-level photography; working with close air support dropping live ordnance; advanced underwater ship/harbor attack training; extended, long-range patrolling and navigation in desert and mountain terrains. The list goes on. Toward the end of the work-up, the training gets more intense, more high-speed. During platoon IADs, the break-contact drills may consist of running and shooting over miles of open terrain at night, calling in live air strikes from helicopter gunships.

More than half of what makes a Navy SEAL special is his commute to the job site. It's a tough commute—through the air, under the sea, or across the land. As he begins the serious business of platoon training, more time is taken with the job-related skills—how to fight and actions at the objective.

This is especially true for SEAL combat shooting skills. The platoons attend several civilian and military shooting schools that emphasize close-quarter shooting in urban settings. These are scenario-driven exercises with live rounds that require good headwork, good teamwork, and fire discipline. They do this as squads and as a platoon—full tilt, with live fire. Live rounds teach the SEALs how to shoot together safely in close quarters. Simunitions teach them how to kill as a team. Simunitions are a relatively new development that allow opposed, close-quarter shooting. One school that features Simunitions is the Close Quarter Defense School operated by Duane Dieter. Dieter is a highly experienced martial artist and shooting specialist on contract with Naval Special Warfare. The platoons know how to shoot. Duane Dieter teaches them how to fight and win. The SEAL's MP-5 submachine guns and pistols are modified to shoot 9mm paint-loaded rounds—Simunitions. These are not paint balls from paint-ball guns, but rounds from the SEALs' personal weapons—automatic or semi-automatic fire with the same cyclic rates and short-range trajectory as the real thing. The platoon SEALs, wearing head and eye protection, are able to attack adversarial role players who physically resist and shoot back. This is full-tilt fighting; losers get shot. These scenarios are built around hostage takings, terrorist activity, and irregular-force opposition. The platoons learn to be gunfighters as well as shooters. In a gunfight, it pays to be a winner.

A new guy in Foxtrot Platoon could find himself doing everything from a lead-line-and-slate hydrographic recon on a beach in Oman to rappelling by fast rope onto an Iraqi freighter in the Straight of Hormuz to look for contraband. If you're a Navy SEAL, this is what you train for and what you live for.

No SEAL platoon is allowed to deploy into an operational theater until it is thoroughly trained and tested. A critical goal of the eighteen-month platoon work-up is the operational readiness evaluation, or ORE. The OREs are conducted by the Naval Special Warfare groups—Group One on the West Coast and Two on the East Coast. The team commanding officers train platoons for deployment; the group commanders certify them as fully combat ready—C-1 status. The group ORE cells conduct the platoon OREs, and they are by no means a formality or a free ride. It is not uncommon for a platoon to flunk a portion of the ORE or an entire ORE full-mission profile. A second failure usually results in a change of platoon leadership. Since the group commanders personally sign off that a platoon is combat ready, they usually observe key portions of the operational readiness evaluation. For Gus Kaminski and Joe Quinn, Foxtrot Platoon's ORE is both a test and a validation. As they work their platoon into fighting shape, it's a chance to show their stuff under operational conditions. But if the platoon performs poorly or comes up short, they will be held accountable, personally and professionally. Their reputations are on the line.

The ORE cells at the groups are headed by an experienced officer and a small cadre of very capable chief petty officers. A few months before the date of a platoon's deployment, the ORE cell begins to feed the platoon information on a range of targets. By this time, the platoon is trained and conducting sustainment training to remain current and sharpen their combat and teamwork skills. The platoon knows within a range of mission profiles what they will be asked to do, and approximately when. But what and when are not nearly so important as where. The group's ORE cells go to great lengths to find challenging and unfamiliar terrain over which to evaluate their platoons. Where possible, the OREs use live ordnance. When it happens, it's quick. A platoon is recalled from wherever they happen to be training and placed in isolation, just as they would be on a real mission tasking. Once in isolation and under strict security protocol, they are tasked with the planning and execution of a special operation mission. They will see and talk to no one not connected with the operation until the mission is complete. Much like Bill Gallagher and Eric Oehlerich did on San Clemente Island during their final FTX problems, the platoon commander assigns tasks to members of the platoon, and they begin the planning process. But on a platoon ORE, the targets are far more difficult and the expectation of mission execution is several orders of magnitude greater. The platoon will study and evaluate target folders; they will have to draft a number of mission support requests. The platoon will almost certainly ask for additional intelligence and supplemental rules of engagement. A great deal of expense, effort, and ingenuity goes into reducing the artificiality of the ORE mission taskings and targeting. Moreover, the ORE cell will arrange for some surprises along the way and provide for spirited opposition.

ORE mission scenarios are designed to parallel real-world contingencies, and for that reason they are classified as secret or even top secret. They also reflect real-world targeting in theater. For Team Three and Foxtrot Platoon, the Middle East is their area of operation. SEAL Team One's AO is Southeast Asia. Their OREs often involve jungle warfare. Team Five's area is Korea and the North Pacific. They specialize in cold-water operations and winter warfare. On the East Coast, SEAL Team Two's AO is Europe; Team Eight's, Africa. SEAL Team Four's AO is Central and South America. At Team Four, they need all the Spanish-speaking SEALs they can find, like Sergio Lopez from Class 228 and Miguel Yanez from Class 230.

A typical ORE, like the one that Foxtrot Platoon might be asked to do, could be an over-the-horizon, over-the-beach operation. In this ORE, the platoon, in two squads, parachutes at night into the sea from a C-130. Leaving the aircraft with them are two Zodiacs, each carefully rigged with its own parachute and the squad's equipment. Once in the water, the squads rig their Zodiacs and mount the outboard motors that parachuted with the boats. Then they make a thirty-mile, over-the-horizon transit to the shore. Once they're close to shore, they will conduct an over-the-beach operation, just like they did in Third Phase at BUD/S, with scout swimmers going in first. Once ashore, they patrol inland. Their mission may be a platoon objective or two squad targets. It could be a standoff target such as an infrared photoreconnaissance, disabling an aircraft at long range with a .50-caliber sniper rifle, or illuminating a building with a portable laser for a precision air strike. They may have a direct action mission, such as a demolitions raid. Perhaps their mission will be to storm a building to rescue a hostage. After their actions at the objective, they will have to execute their exfiltration and extraction plans. Along the way, they may lay up for a period of time to establish a satellite communications link and send an encrypted burst transmission with critical intelligence. At any time, the ORE lane graders may change the game, or insert obstacles in the exercise play. Opposition forces may compel the squads to fall back on one of their alternate courses of action. After the mission, Foxtrot Platoon will return to isolation for post-mission briefings and to produce its after-action reports and messages. This is as close as it gets to the real thing. The next time Foxtrot Platoon goes into isolation, it could be an operational mission tasking somewhere in the Persian Gulf.

Each ORE follows the same basic mission-planning and mission-execution format that the platoon SEALs first learned in BUD/S. The art of special operations requires planning and execution that draw on skills and teamwork that take years to develop. A combat-ready platoon not only conducts the mission as a team, but they plan it as a team. Because of the quality and experience of the individual SEALs, and their recent platoon training, they are able to do this quickly and with minimum rehearsal time. This is critical on a time-sensitive operation, and could spell the difference between mission success and mission failure. A combat-ready, C-1 SEAL platoon has a broad range of capabilities, so it is very flexible. If the job can't be done one way, the SEALs will find another.

As this book goes to press, Lieutenant Gus Kaminski, Chief Joe Quinn, and Foxtrot Platoon are on deployment somewhere in Southwest Asia. They will operate from the Naval Special Warfare Unit in Bahrain, but they could be just about anywhere in the Middle East.

EPILOGUE: A LOOK AHEAD

In the spring of 1994, I sat in on a briefing conducted by Rear Admiral Ray Smith, then the commander of the Naval Special Warfare Command. This briefing was for Richard Danzig, then undersecretary of the navy. Mr. Danzig later served as secretary of the navy in the Clinton administration. A host of staff officers and a few young operational SEALs crowded into the command briefing with the undersecretary. On hand was one of the SEALs wounded in Somalia in the engagement superbly documented in Mark Bowden's fine book *Blackhawk Down*. After some nice action-video footage of young men with blackened faces doing an assortment of SEAL-like things, Admiral Smith brought up a slide showing the overseas deployed posture of Naval Special Warfare forces. There were more than five hundred personnel, most of them SEALs, scattered across the globe in some thirty foreign nations or aboard deployed units of the fleet. It was an impressive briefing. At the conclusion, the admiral asked if his guest had any questions. Undersecretary Danzig, who has seen more than a few snazzy briefings, cut to the heart of the matter.

"You seem to have a good sense of yourselves," Danzig began. "That was all very impressive. Tell me, Admiral, what is your annual budget?"

"Right at five hundred million dollars," Admiral Smith replied. Naval Special Warfare then received 10 percent of the Special Operations Command's $5 billion annual budget.

"So," Danzig continued, "it costs about a million dollars a year to keep one trained, operational SEAL on the job in a deployed status."

After a moment's hesitation, Admiral Smith replied. "Yes, sir. That's about right."

This figure of $1 million per year for one Navy SEAL is both deceiving and instructional. That number accounts for the training, administrative support, and logistic infrastructure that support the SEAL teams, the SDV teams, and the Special Boat Units—the tail as well as the tooth. Nonetheless, the training and support costs required to bring and keep a fixed number of SEAL and SDV platoons at a high state of operational readiness are ongoing. SEALs are not short-lead-time, off-the-shelf items like artillery shells. If we want Navy SEALs who are good to go in time of crisis, they have to be trained well ahead of time. But this figure of $1 million per SEAL, deployed and ready to go, calls to mind an interesting analogy. Cruise missiles cost about $1 million dollars each.

A Navy SEAL and a cruise missile are at the opposite ends of the military response spectrum. Conventional cruise missiles are superb weapons. They can deliver a thousand pounds of high explosives accurately and impersonally. They are surrogates for all precision-guided weapons. If you happen to be a national security adviser with a personal or political aversion to American casualties, a cruise missile is a very handy military option. It is also a very impartial weapon. If the technology fails and the missile becomes lost, it may destroy something other than its intended target. When a cruise missile does find its target, whether it's a building, a bridge, or an embassy, people die—often civilians who just happened to be in the area when the warhead arrived. A weapon that can damage the enemy with no risk to your own troops is a valuable tool—and a seductive one. It allows us to kill others without the risk of casualties. In the past, Americans have fought their wars on principle, in the cause of freedom or to oppose tyranny. If it was worth killing for, it was worth dying for. Now technology has given us an option to the dying, at least on our side of the kill ledger. We no longer have to send in the Marines. We can send in the cruise missiles. We did this in Yugoslavia when televised Serb atrocities became more than we could bear. But cruise missiles and high-altitude bombing killed fourteen civilians for every Serb in uniform.

Navy SEALs, unlike cruise missiles, practice their trade up close and personal. For them, long range is within reach of a sniper rifle or close enough to illuminate a target with a laser beam to make a precision-guided weapon more precise. The defense against cruise missiles can be as simple and as low tech as several meters of reinforced concrete. Intelligence estimates suggest that dictators like Mu'ammar Gadhafi and Saddam Hussein may be doing just that to protect their weapons of mass destruction. Sometimes, to gather intelligence or to destroy a potential threat, someone has to go in and do the job on the ground—or in the water. That can usually only be done by risking American lives in very dangerous ventures. Skill, training, and courage can only reduce these risks, not eliminate them.

It's an interesting question. Given the availability of cruise missiles and smart bombs, and our public and political aversion to young Americans returning home in body bags, does our nation really have a need for warriors? Has their time passed? Is war simply work for technicians? Most of the military recruiting commercials suggest that our military wants young people to sign up for computer classes and technical job training. Little is said about fighting. Do we need to continue to develop, refine, and nurture a warrior culture like the Navy SEALS? This seems to be a question of our national interest and the nightly news. A regional conflict, like the Gulf War, is an ongoing possibility. The Middle East, with its unique blend of religious fundamentalism, despotism, and petroleum-driven wealth, could quickly draw us into another regional war. So could Korea or Taiwan. The same possibilities exist along the Pakistani-Indian-Chinese border and in the former Soviet republics, but these situations may be beyond the reach of our expeditionary warfare capabilities or the commitment of our allies. The nightly news is another source of involvement. Thanks to modern telecommunications, we now enjoy barbaric activity in distant parts of the globe real-time and in living color. If the footage is really good, it's made available twenty-four hours a day on CNN or C-Span. Both oil and atrocity are capable of pulling us into a foreign military adventure.

If the Gulf War is to serve as a prototype for future major regional conflicts, we need to be very careful. It is unlikely we will find so inept a foe the next time around. Navy SEALS played a minor but important role in the Gulf War. They boarded and inspected Iraqi ships on the high seas.

They captured oil platforms that served as Iraqi military outposts. SEALs rescued downed pilots and stood ready for POW rescue operations. Their diversionary attack on the Kuwaiti beaches to simulate an amphibious landing froze elements of two Iraqi divisions, contributing to the success of the main allied thrust across the northern desert. A dozen SEALs neutralizing a division-size force, if only for a few precious hours, validates this use of special operations in a major regional conflict scenario. And if you're an attack pilot flying air strikes on Kuwait, or Kosovo, it's comforting to know that there are some very committed men who will come for you if you bail out over enemy territory.

It is reasonable to assume that ethnic and religious differences, authoritarian regimes, and poverty will continue to create suffering and instability in the new millennium. Humanitarian considerations alone may force us to intervene, and these situations are seldom candidates for cruise missiles. Often they are nasty little pieces of business, where the value of human life is quite different from our own. Each situation is different; each calls for a different application of force and different rules of engagement. These ROEs, often driven by bureaucrats in Washington or allied military protocol, can be complex and unwieldy. Today, there are a lot of young American military peacekeepers riding around in Humvees with ROEs the size of telephone directories, and these rules still don't cover all the bases.

In the spring of 1995, Commander Kim Erskine, then the commander of the Naval Special Warfare Unit Two in Stuttgart, Germany, accompanied a platoon of his SEALs into the U.S. Embassy in Monrovia, Liberia. Civil unrest had threatened the U.S. legation there; American lives were in jeopardy. The Navy SEALs were the first to arrive to augment the embassy Marine contingent and provide security for an evacuation. The text of their ROEs, when reduced to usable form, said they could open fire if fired upon, or a threat of hostile fire was imminent. Shortly after the SEALs arrived and established a defensive perimeter at the embassy, a Liberian youth with a rocket launcher approached the compound. He then aimed his rocket at several SEALs who were guarding the main entrance. A SEAL sniper had the youth in the crosshairs. By the guidelines of the ROEs, he could shoot him; it was a legal kill. But the SEAL held his fire. After some sign language and broken-English communication, the youth was persuaded to leave the area. He simply wandered off into town with his rocket launcher.

"What did you do about your SEAL sniper?" I asked Kim.

"Gave him a medal," Kim replied, referring to the commendation his SEAL received for exercising good judgment.

"What would you have done if he had shot the young Liberian?"

Kim smiled sadly. "Give him a medal. Making that shot could have saved a few lives—our lives."

This incident illustrates the complexity of sending "our boys" over there. Even though they have been volunteers since the end of the draft in 1973, and they willingly chose this profession, they are still our boys—and girls. Had the Liberian fired and killed the SEALs within the bursting radius of his rocket, the headlines would have read: "Navymen Killed in Monrovia; Congress to Investigate Role of U.S. Troops in Africa." Had the SEAL fired, we would have gotten this: "Navy SEAL Kills African Youth; Congress to Investigate Role of U.S. Troops in Africa." And think about the young SEAL sniper, the man in the arena. Had the rocketeer fired, the death of his comrades would have been on his conscience. Had he followed the ROEs to the letter, he would have taken the boy's life. If the action precipitated a riot, perhaps many more lives would have been lost. The rules don't cover all the contingencies, nor are they of much comfort to the soldier whose action may have been legal but, in hindsight, ill-advised. Some situations defy a set of regulations. In Somalia, Muslim women came at the young Rangers with automatic weapons swaddled with their infants. In such cases, the ROEs quickly deteriorate; a moment's hesitation can cost you your life. It becomes kill them all and let God sort them out. The difference between the rules of engagement and a war crime may be a twenty-three-year-old's split-second decision: Do I shoot, or don't I?

Increasingly, our military is being used overseas as an instrument of national policy. If our conventional forces are to be a global police force, then our special operations elements become global SWAT teams. This is happening as funds for operational training are being reduced in favor of platforms and hardware. Our deployed forces on the ground are being asked to do more with less preparation. All this is taking place in a climate where fewer members in Congress are veterans, and each commander in chief is a little more distant from the forces he commands. Without getting into a discussion about Vietnam and the current political elite shaped by that conflict, I believe it is safe to say this: The number of policy makers today who understand the culture of the military is less than it was several decades ago. And that number is shrinking. I believe this applies as well to the media and those who report on military affairs.

There is a widening gulf between the general military culture and the civilian culture of the nation it serves. And I'm not just speaking about a generation who may have sidestepped military service during an unpopular war. Many of my contemporaries who served in Vietnam do not want their sons and daughters in uniform. They want them in business. If this cultural gulf applies to the military in general, what about the military special operator; what about the Navy SEAL? How does the true warrior view giving so much to a nation that regards his sacrifice and professionalism so impersonally? How does he feel about serving people who at best may support a strong military, but not for their sons or daughters? And how does he view a government that increasingly sees him simply as an instrument of foreign policy—simply as the guarantor of globalization and our ongoing prosperity at home?

While following Class 228, I asked many BUD/S trainees why they wanted to do this. It was a simple question: "Why do you want to be a Navy SEAL?" I seldom heard a BUD/S trainee express his desire to become a SEAL in patriotic terms. One exception was Seaman Chris MacLeod's declaration that he wanted to "stand with the best and fight for my country" before he was forced to leave Class 228. Adam Karaoguz said he always wanted to serve his country, and that he thought he could best do that as a Navy SEAL. Most said they welcomed the challenge or that they wanted to be part of an elite force. Others candidly admitted they were taken with the excitement and adventure of parachuting and scuba diving.

A few admitted they just wanted to be someone special. I suspect that these men do in fact have a very real pride in serving their country, but that was not why they volunteered for BUD/S. To one degree or another, they are simply talented, determined, motivated young men who were looking for a yardstick by which to measure themselves. So the question remains, do our armed forces need the conspicuous support of a grateful nation? Will they continue to serve, and fight, for a token remembrance on Veterans Day? And why?

In his fine book *The Soul of Battle*, Victor Davis Hanson talks about the terrible and magnificent force that is a democratic army in pursuit of evil. Mr. Hanson cites several historical examples, the most recent of which is General George S. Patton's Third Army in the closing days of World War II. The success of the U.S. Third Army, apart from Patton's tactical genius, was the general's ability to motivate his men to fight. He did this by vilifying the enemy. German soldiers, not just Nazi Germany, represented the dark forces of tyranny; they were immoral and must be vanquished at all costs. Patton told his soldiers they were the agents of decency and light— that they were saviors. This was a contest between good and evil, and the fate of Western civilization was in the balance. Did it work? The German army was a professional, seasoned force with the advantages of fighting a defensive campaign with a shrinking perimeter on home ground. Logistics and lines of communication favored the defenders. Patton's army of clerks, car salesmen, farmers, and factory workers routed the Wehrmacht and poured into the German heartland like a horde of locusts. It was much the same in the Gulf War. Saddam was portrayed as an evil man, though his demonization may have been more for Congress and some of our allies than for the troops.

The Navy SEAL today is a much different animal than he was just a few decades ago. He has always been a volunteer, so little changed with the abolition of the draft. But there has been an evolution since the first SEALs were culled from the UDTs in the early 1960s. In those early days, they were hard men whose character was forged in the jungles of Vietnam. BUD/S training separated the men from the boys, and the men went to

Vietnam. Often they learned on the job. Knowledge and jungle-fighting skills were passed from platoon to platoon. SEALs became warriors by necessity, not so much by some well-conceived training program. They became excellent jungle fighters and did little else. The platoon officers were transient, usually leaving the teams or leaving the Navy after one or two combat deployments. But many of the enlisted men stayed—tour after tour. It was these dedicated enlisted men who laid the foundations of the modern SEAL warrior culture. They are the soul of the Navy SEAL teams.

The teams have always been a refuge for tough men, but in times past, they were often rugged, hard-drinking guys—as comfortable in a bar fight as a firefight. These weren't men who necessarily appeared macho or well buffed from hours in the weight room, but the sort who could handle trouble. They were men who could get the job done, even if they sometimes had to operate outside the regulations. They weren't so much warriors as they were street fighters.

Today's SEALs have brought forward that hard-core, get-it-done tradition, and built around it a true warrior culture. Modern SEALs are not only afforded better training, but they understand that continuous training is a warrior's work—a lifetime's work. And with each generation, they seem to get better, more professional—and a little less driven by ideological and patriotic considerations. If a new guy is an apprentice after thirty months of training and becomes a journeyman at three years when he returns from his first deployment, who then are the veterans? When are you a "made man" or a soldier in this SEAL-warrior Mafia? In the officer corps, they are SEALs like Gus Kaminski, heading out on their third deployment with some experience and a great deal of responsibility. The enlisted petty officers embarking on their second or third deployment are the backbone of the Navy SEAL platoons. They have experienced most of what will be asked of them on an overseas peacetime deployment. A few of them have seen combat. They know what to do, and the younger SEALs look to them for leadership. Their experience has earned them respect within the platoon and the team. A first class petty officer with a solid reputation on his fourth platoon deployment is what the Navy SEAL teams are all about. And who are the masters of this trade? A good candidate would be Joe Quinn. But even with his reputation, eighteen years of service, and six platoon deployments, there are SEALs he looks to for guidance and expertise. They are the senior and master chief petty officers and the warrant officers, men like Master Chief Bob Tanenholz and Chief Warrant Officer Mike Loo. These men embody the corporate knowledge and culture of the SEAL warrior craft.

Bob Kerrey won the Medal of Honor in Vietnam in 1969. He was reluctant to accept the award because he felt that it was unfair that he be singled out when the other SEALs in his platoon had performed so well. His men and his BUD/S enlisted instructors persuaded him to accept the honor, not just for himself but for all of them. Bob entered BUD/S with Class 42 in December 1967. The action for which he was decorated took place fifteen months after he began BUD/S training. At fifteen months from the first day of Indoc, Ensign Clint Burke at Team Three and Ensign Jason Birch at Team Four recently received their Tridents. They have just begun their eighteen-month platoon work-up. They won't leave for deployment, or be considered "apprentice warriors," for another year and a half. And Bob Kerrey was lucky. Some BUD/S graduates assigned to the UDT and SEAL teams during the Vietnam era were being shot at within months of their BUD/S graduation. My friend Teddy Roosevelt IV, great-grandson of the president, was in the Rung Sat Special Zone dodging bullets just four months after he graduated with Class 36.

I often speak to civilian organizations about the trials of Class 228 and the culture of the Navy SEAL teams. I am frequently asked about women serving in the SEAL teams. Women currently serve in all branches of the armed forces, including combat support and combat aviation. But Congress has upheld a ban on women serving in direct ground combat roles. I have heard senior SEAL leaders cite this as the reason there are no women in the teams, but that begs the question. Should they be? If Congress relaxes this restriction, should women be allowed to attend BUD/S? There is no politically correct answer to this question, but let me try. In my view, it is a question of priorities: gender equality or combat effectiveness—which god do you serve? I cannot imagine a culture in the military being so severely or adversely impacted by the inclusion of women as the Navy SEAL teams. Are there women who have the upper-body strength to handle the physical requirements? Possibly. Could they handle the cold water and the pain? Probably. Are there women who have the burning will to win? Absolutely. But I believe the inclusion of a woman or women in the platoon deployment cycle will make a hard and danger-ous business more difficult and more dangerous. This is a cultural thing, not a gender one. The gain in gender equality would come at a tremen-dous cost in operational effectiveness, and ultimately, in human lives. SEALs live and work together for long periods of time under some very basic and demanding conditions. I feel the inclusion of women would adversely alter the chemistry that is so vital to the teamwork of a combat-effective SEAL platoon.

Perhaps the most dramatic change in the development of the modern Navy SEAL is the inner strength to fight and win—to be a complete war-rior. Aside from technical specialties—like long-range shooting, strategic reconnaissance, and underwater swimmer attack—much of what SEALs do is to train for that single moment when they will fight—kill or be killed. In his Close Quarter Defense School training, Duane Dieter tells the pla-toon SEALs, "The truth of combat is; to fight is to risk death." Therefore, SEALs have to master a skill set that will enable them to dominate their space and their opposition. This demands total focus from a warrior—mind, body, and spirit. At any time, a deployed SEAL can quickly be put at risk in a dangerous, unfamiliar land. He will not have the luxury of learning to hate his enemy as did the soldiers in Patton's army, nor a lengthy period to prepare for battle like the coalition forces in the Gulf War. On very short notice, his nation can send him into harm's way. Here the warrior-SEAL may have to take another human life. Or exercise the judgment not to.

The development of this modern warrior within the Naval Special Warfare community is an ongoing process. At first glance, this lengthy and often brutal regime of training may appear too long and too difficult. There is a reason for this. The young men who come to BUD/S have had from eighteen to twenty-eight years of the good life in the United States. They come from the malls, not the steel mills; from a culture where "tough" is a look or an attitude, not a way of life. These young men are not samurai. A great deal of change has to take place in them before they become warriors. It takes years—a lifetime. And warriorship is as much a tempering of the spirit as a physical rendering. Even if toughness were measured in terms of a bar-fighting brawler or some Hollywood-generated macho facsimile, that conduct has no place in military society or in the company of true warriors. In fact, a warrior who has depth—one with sensitivity, compassion, and a strong spiritual sense of self—has a decided advantage. He enters the arena from a firm moral grounding—a worthy platform from which to project his power. The business of a warrior is not intimidation or posturing; it is combat and it is to risk death. For a SEAL warrior, this requires judgment and training. He may have to hurt, maim, or kill in the practice of his trade. When it comes to a fight, he must fight and win. Anything less will risk the mission and perhaps cost him his life.

In his excellent history of the UDT and SEAL teams, *Brave Men—Dark Waters,* Orr Kelly concludes that the Naval Special Warfare community and the modern-day SEALs are still looking for their niche—trying to find their role in the post–Cold War U.S. military. Yet Mr. Kelly suggests that if the SEALs ever find that specific role, it will cost them dearly in terms of innovation and versatility. I would submit that they have found their niche: the self-generation and maintenance of a small, highly capable warrior culture. They are talented generalists with a specific set of maritime special operations skills. This makes them highly flexible and very adaptive war fighters. Their mission could be almost anything, anywhere, with very little time to plan or rehearse. Then all those years of training and team building become a smart investment for the nation. These warriors can come from under the sea, from the air, or across the land. And when they get there, they can fight and win.

POSTSCRIPT: CLASS 228

AND THE WAR ON TERRORISM

The special operations camp in Afghanistan was close to the airport near Kandahar. Late afternoon on 15 February, 2002, barely five months after the attacks of September 11, a SEAL officer, a junior-grade lieutenant, dragged himself into the Naval Special Warfare compound at the camp. "Compound" is a loose term for the two old buildings surrounded by concertina wire that was home to the SEALs in southern Afghanistan. He was the third officer assigned to a SEAL strike platoon aboard one of the aircraft carriers in the Indian Ocean. He had been cut away from his platoon to help provide security for some of the explosive ordnance disposal teams. As the coalition forces swept south, a great deal of ordnance and weapons were abandoned by the retreating Taliban forces. SEALs and Army Special Forces worked side by side with EOD teams to destroy this material. The officer had been in the field for the better part of a week and looked it. Carrying only his rucksack and rifle, he was looking for a bunk and badly in need of a shower.

"Sir, does the lieutenant need some directions or maybe some help with his gear?"

"Thanks, pal, but I can handle my own gear. What I need is a . . . well, I'll be damned. They must let just about anyone into this war."

The enlisted SEAL, who was having a laugh at the officer's expense, had also just come in from the field and looked as scruffy as the new arrival. They grinned, then fiercely embraced each other. They were both from Class 228.

"What I could really use is a cold beer. Got any of that here?"

"We don't have any here, but the Germans do. They're special operations guys so they're pretty good about sharing. Since I had to carry you through training, sir, I suppose I can find you a beer."

"You, carry me! That'll be the day."

One has to be in the field for a week, humping a combat load, sweating all day, freezing all night, to really appreciate the meaning of a cold pilsner. Soon the two men were on a berm near the camp, enjoying a beer and watching the Afghan sun sink into the hills northwest of Kandahar. They talked about their platoons, what they had seen—what they had done. They talked about the other guys in Class 228. Because of luck, timing, and platoon deployment requirements, they were the only men in 228 who had made it to the combat zone to date, and for that, they toasted their good fortune. The others were still in various stages of platoon predeployment workup. Some would get there in the next few months. Some would deploy into other theaters where SEALs were needed. But mostly they talked about the war—their war. This is why they struggled through BUD/S and became Navy SEALs. These two brothers from Class 228 have come a long way in a short time, and they are just beginning their careers as Navy SEALs. One can only guess where the course of this conflict may take them. But tonight, they're content to sit in the dirt in a strange place a long way from home, share fellowship as warriors, and talk about their war.

. . .

The world has changed since Class 228 graduated from Basic Underwater Demolition/SEAL training some thirty-three months ago. The events of September 11 shocked us all, but for the military services in general and the Navy SEALs in particular, the odds of going into combat increased dramatically.

Yet, in many respects, nothing changed. Those SEALs deployed in and around the Middle East at the time of the 9/11 attack did what they were trained to do. Operations in Afghanistan were a validation of their forward-deployed posture. SEALs and other Naval Special Warfare assets in predeployment workup continued to prepare for deployment, albeit with a greater sense of purpose. Class 243 just graduated from BUD/S and is preparing to enter advanced training. The twenty men from Class 228 have all qualified as Navy SEALs. About half of them are now deployed, scattered around the world at various Naval Special Warfare Units or aboard U.S. Navy warships. Others are in platoons preparing for operational deployment. A few of them have returned from deployment and are attending advanced military schools and professional development courses to prepare them for their second deployment.

This is the life they have chosen, a life of continuous training and overseas operational duty. I stay in touch with the men of Class 228 by e-mail. To a man, they are proud to be in the teams; all are anxious to have a go at al Qaeda and those who would try to bring about a repeat of 9/11. They are like professional basketball players on the bench, waiting to get into the game or, in a few cases, back into the game—wanting their number to be called.

In the fall of 1999, when the men of Class 228 began their quest to become Navy SEALs, BUD/S was a serious business. Most of the men in Class 228 arrived at the Naval Special Warfare Center with the simple goal of getting through BUD/S—taking that first step toward becoming a SEAL and joining the teams. The notion of becoming a Navy SEAL and serving in the teams was exciting, more of an adventure than duty to country. When I spoke with them during training about what brought them to this place—and what kept them going when their bodies said "stop"— most talked about a desire to excel or to challenge themselves or to serve with an elite force. Few of them ever mentioned patriotism as the reason they came to BUD/S and endured all those hardships. All that changed with 9/11.

Events following the attacks in New York and Washington, D.C., have elevated special operations to the premier force in the fight against terrorism. Men entering BUD/S today can be certain of operational deployment in this war. For many, it will be a combat deployment. And while the training of Navy SEALs has not changed—they always train as if war is imminent—the fact that their teammates and fellow warriors may at any moment come face-to-face with the enemy cannot be ignored or forgotten.

The attacks have also changed the ground rules for journalists and writers like myself. There is now greater emphasis on protecting the SEAL identities, tactics, and mission profiles. And rightly so. We are at war, and the identities and methods of those in the fight must be respected and discussion of them restricted. I am currently at work on a new SEAL book, scheduled for release by Crown Books in the spring of 2004. It follows the path of a BUD/S graduate as he earns his SEAL qualification and prepares for operational deployment with his SEAL platoon. As with *The Warrior Elite,* I am following a group of men through their advanced SEAL training—the training BUD/S graduates must successfully complete before they are awarded their Naval Special Warfare insignia, the Trident. But I will never show you their faces or use their real names. I'm also observing SEAL platoons and SEAL teams preparing for operational deployment. However, there are certain training venues that I will not be allowed to see and certain aspects of this advanced SEAL training I will not show the reader. These restrictions are in keeping with a nation at war and a nation that cares about the safety of its warriors.

About Class 228—the men in this book. Since their BUD/S graduation, the men in Class 228 have gone through the normal progression of BUD/S graduates as they make their way into the teams. All attended Army Airborne School for military parachute qualification and all attended SEAL Tactical Training (now SEAL Qualification Training), both prerequisites to earning their SEAL Tridents. The five class officers attended the Junior Officers Training Course at the Naval Special Warfare Center. Most of the officers have also attended the schools that qualify them as range safety officers and diving supervisors, courses that allow them to better manage the safety of their platoon's training. All in the class have attended SERE (Survival, Evasion, Resistance, Escape) School. Three have attended Military Free Fall (HALO) School and two have qualified as SEAL snipers. One in Class 228 has completed Army Ranger School, but others may attend as they rotate back from their first deployment, as scheduling and platoon training allow.

The enlisted men from Class 228 have attended schools and training that directly relate to their particular duties and special assignments within their platoons. These include the Naval Special Warfare Communications Course, parachute riggers school, a CRRC (combat rubber raiding craft—a military Zodiac) operations/maintenance course, and close air support (CAS) training. Officers and enlisted men from 228 have received specialized training in terrorism conducted at the Air Force Special Operations Command at Hurlburt Field, Florida. Many of them have attended the Navy's tactical Arabic language course, as well as other language courses. The three-month Arabic course is taught by contract civilian linguists who have native Arabic skills. In this course, SEALs learn to conduct basic field interrogations and to handle prisoners. Those who came to BUD/S with native language skills or basic language training are assigned to platoons where those skills are best used.

Two of the officers from Class 228 are now serving as platoon assistant officer in charge, or AOIC, while the other three are third officers. Third officers in a SEAL platoon are officers training to move up to the AOIC position. These officers will help with the platoon-officer duties and carry a weapon in one of the platoon's two squads. The platoon AOIC will be one of the two squad leaders in the platoon. He also serves in place of the platoon commander, or OIC, when the platoon commander is away from the platoon. On the following platoon deployment, he will become the platoon commander.

The enlisted men from 228 are all filling assigned roles within their platoons. Their duties include air operations, diving, communications, ordnance, CRRC maintenance, and intelligence. They carry a variety of weapons depending on the mission and their role in their squad or fire team. Some are "60" gunners and carry the Mk-43 machine gun. Others are "SAW" gunners, armed with the lighter squad assault weapon or the Mk-46—a 5.56mm machine gun. Those armed with an M-4 rifle usually have an M-203 40mm grenade launcher attached. When duties call for close-quarter urban battle or ship-boarding operations, most favor the Heckler & Koch MP-5 submachine gun. The standard issue secondary weapon in the teams is a Sig Sauer 9mm pistol. In the field, each man will carry a variety of grenades, signal devices, radios, and mission-specific equipment. They are all junior members of a SEAL platoon, perhaps the most lethal special-operations unit in the world. These new SEALS are still learning their craft and will look to the veterans for leadership and guidance, but they are full-fledged members of this combat team. They will be expected to move, communicate, and fight, and to do what is expected of a combat-capable Navy SEAL. They are, at last, members of the warrior elite.

The men from Class 228, indeed all operational Navy SEALs, are either on, returning from, or preparing for one thing—operational deployment. The only break from the platoon training-deployment cycle is instructor duty, which has its share of fourteen-hour days and travel away from home, or perhaps a total-immersion language school. Not all SEALs deploy in support of the U.S. Central Command with responsibilities in Afghanistan, but all those I talk with want to be there, or in another hot spot around the world, such as the Philippine Islands. If their duties take them to a theater where they are less likely to see action, they are very disappointed. Yet they know they must be ready; their combat skills could be needed almost anywhere, at almost any time. These warriors want to get into the fight and they want to contribute; they want to make a difference. The War on Terrorism is a global struggle, but the Central Command, with its focus on the Middle East, is where much of the action has taken place. Tomorrow it could be somewhere else. For this reason, Naval Special Warfare maintains a robust forward-deployed posture and rapid-response capability within its force structure.

One senior Navy SEAL was quickly drawn into the middle of this war. Following the 9/11 attacks, Captain Robert Harward was ordered to Afghanistan. He temporarily left his duties as Commander, Naval Special Warfare Group One, in Coronado and deployed as Commander, Joint Special Operations Task Force–South during Operation Enduring

Freedom. In this capacity, his duties included far more than just operational control of Navy SEALS. As the joint Special Operations Forces (SOF) commander, he commanded all U.S. and coalition special operations forces in southern Afghanistan. Commanding special operations in Afghanistan was a role Bob Harward seemed destined to fill and one for which he was uniquely qualified.

This 23-year veteran has extensive operational, staff, and command experience in special operations. He has a master's degree in National Security Affairs and Strategic Studies. He was the Honorman from BUD/S Class 128. And he knows the territory. Bob Harward graduated from high school in Tehran. Prior to enlisting in the Navy, he spent a summer hitchhiking across Afghanistan. He speaks Farsi.

As a deployed special-operations commander and "end user" of Navy SEALS in time of war, Bob told me about the warriors he led for six months in Afghanistan. His comments offer a compelling picture of what these elite warriors did in Afghanistan and why they were so effective in this rigorous, non-maritime environment:

> Within weeks of the attacks in New York and Washington, D.C., the Chairman of the Joint Chiefs of Staff asked Naval Special Warfare to conduct combat operations in Afghanistan. Our goal was to eradicate the Taliban and al Qaeda forces operating in the country. This call to action, in most aspects, was little different from the myriad of conflicts where SEALs have been called upon to quickly go in harm's way. We have gone before to places such as Vietnam, Grenada, Panama, Desert Storm, Haiti, Somalia, and Bosnia.
>
> What was unique about this first stage in the War on Terrorism was the role SEALs would play. Not only would they fight throughout the country, from the desert plains of the southwest to the rugged mountains of the northeast, but they would also exercise command and control of a combined and joint war-fighting organization. The focus of their combat operations would be Special

Reconnaissance and Direct Action missions. I was privileged to command this task force in southern Afghanistan, and the bulk of my staff were Navy SEALs. This Naval Special Warfare-centric organization would direct Army and Air Force Special Operations Forces as well as marines and the premier SOF forces from seven nations.

The tactical capability Navy SEALs demonstrated in the inhospitable conditions of Afghanistan validated the arduous training and physical hardships SEAL trainees endure in BUD/S and the intense training SEALs undergo to prepare for operational deployment. The corporate knowledge and experience of our leadership were tested at the operational level as well as the strategic level. All this, four hundred miles inland. I was immensely proud of my SEALs, indeed, all of the SOF forces under my command.

BUD/S, SEAL Qualification Training (SQT), and SEAL Platoon Training are the building blocks of the SEAL operator. Pushing yourself beyond your preconceived physical and mental limits, enduring and overcoming ambiguous situations, staying focused on the mission: these are the qualities required of a Navy SEAL. This mind-set is developed in BUD/S and crystallized during Hell Week. It is reinforced during SQT and refined in Platoon Training.

These core traits are essential to the strategic employment of Navy SEAL platoons as they deploy forward to meet SOF requirements in support of our national interests worldwide. Afghanistan was no exception. From the experienced frogman to the newest member of the platoon, fresh from SQT and his first platoon workup, these SEALs got the job done. Regardless of the terrain, the hardships, the ambiguity of the enemy and environment, or the personal risk; these SEALs adapted and they prevailed. In overcoming the enemy on his home ground, they completed another chapter in battle history of the teams. More than that, they set new standards that will serve as benchmarks for the new BUD/S graduates and the next wave of platoons that deploy forward in harm's way.

And the cycle continues. Young men join the Navy with the goal of becoming a Navy SEAL, and submit themselves to the terrible and challenging ordeal of Basic Underwater Demolition/SEAL Training. Those one in five who survive BUD/S move on to SEAL Qualification Training and other military schools en route to earning their SEAL Trident. As qualified warriors, they begin the dangerous and demanding profession of a maritime special operator—the life of a Navy SEAL. America is indeed fortunate to have had such warriors on call, in theater, at the time of the attack on our nation. It will need these warriors as we pursue this long and difficult War on Terrorism.

Appendix

Basic Underwater Demolition/SEAL Class 228

LTJG William Gallagher, Springfield, Virginia	SEAL Team Two
ENS Jason Birch, Crofton, Maryland	SEAL Team Four
ENS Clint Burke, Pittsburgh, Pennsylvania	SEAL Team Three
ENS John Green, Los Angeles, California	SEAL Team Three
ENS Eric Oehlerich, Whitefish, Montana	SEAL Team Five
MN2 Zacharia Armstrong, Thornton, Colorado	SEAL Team Three

CMSN Tyler Black, Dayton, Ohio	SEAL Team Five
ABE3 Chad Cleaver, Costa Mesa, California	SEAL Team Three
GM3 John Collins II, Portland, Oregon	SEAL Team One
GM3 Warren Conner Jr., Tulsa, Oklahoma	SEAL Team One
AO3 Brendan Dougherty, Ormond Beach, Florida	SEAL Team Four
EN3 Matthew Jenkins, Durham, New Hampshire	SEAL Team Four
BM2 Adam Karaoguz, Canandaigua, New York	SEAL Team Four
STG3 Casey Lewis, Noble, Oklahoma	SEAL Team Five
GM3 Sergio Lopez, Brooklyn, New York	SEAL Team Four
QMSN Daniel Luna, Santa Clarita, California	SEAL Team One
HMSN Marc Luttrell, Willis, Texas	Eighteen-Delta School
IT2 John Owens, Fort Lauderdale, Florida	SEAL Team Three
ET3 Larry Romero Jr., San Diego, California	SEAL Team Five
PR3 Zachary Shaffer, Pacifica, California	SEAL Team Three

The following members of the original Class 228 were medically rolled back or were able to stay in BUD/S and graduate:

ENS Chad Steinbrecher	Class 229
HT2 Pat Yost	Class 229
PR3 Christopher Robinson	Class 229
IS3 Chris Baldwin	Class 230
PR3 Grant Terpstra	Class 230
IT3 Miguel Yanez	Class 230

HT3 Lawrence "Otter" Obst was never able to regain diving status due to persistent problems with his sinuses. PR3 Sean Morrison graduated with Class 230, Ensign Matt McGraw with Class 231.

Note: Enlisted ratings may vary from the text as several members of Class 228 were advanced on graduation.

PHOTOGRAPH CAPTIONS

Page vi: Stroke! . . . stroke! A boat crew pulls for the beach. Surf passage training begins early and continues throughout BUD/S.

Page xii: During Indoc, trainees are introduced to the obstacle course. Here, trainees scale the 60-foot cargo net.

Page 14: It pays to be a winner. This BUD/S IBS boat crew, led by Ensign Clint Burke, races across the soft sand at the head carry.

Page 50: Petty Officer Zack Armstrong leads Class 228 across the Burma rope bridge.

Page 100: Ensign Chad Steinbrecher in the mud flats of San Diego Bay during Class 228's Hell Week.

Page 160: Moderate surf. Several times a week in First Phase, Class 228 takes to the Pacific for surf passage drills. Sometimes the surf wins.

Page 178: Seaman Larry Romero helps Petty Officer Pat Yost don his scuba.

Page 226: Ensign John Green prepares for Class 228's final battle problem on San Clemente Island.

Page 278: A BUD/S graduate in SEAL Tactical Training sends rounds downrange with his Mk-43 machine gun.

Page 318: BUD/S Class 228 immediately following their graduation.

About the Author

Dick Couch is a 1967 graduate of the U.S. Naval Academy. He graduated from BUD/S Class 45 in 1969, and was the class Honorman. He was also the first in his class at the Navy Underwater Swimmers School and the Army Military Free-Fall (Halo) School. As Whiskey Platoon Commander with SEAL Team One in Vietnam, he led one of the only successful POW rescue operations of that conflict. Following his release from active duty in the Navy, he served as a maritime and paramilitary case officer with the Central Intelligence Agency. In 1997, he retired from the Naval Reserve with the rank of Captain. At that time, he held the senior command billet in the SEAL reserve community. Dick Couch is also the author of four novels—*Seal Team One, Pressure Point, Silent Descent,* and *Rising Wind.* Dick and his wife, Julia, live in Ketchum, Idaho.

About the Photographer

Cliff Hollenbeck is a leading international photographer and film producer. He is the author of more than a dozen books on photography, travel, and business, including the novel *Acapulco Goodbye* and the pictorial book *Mexico,* with an introduction by James A. Michener. Cliff has twice been named Travel Photographer of the Year by the Society of American Travel Writers, and his film company has received gold medals at the New York and Chicago Film Festivals, and Tellys for travel commercials and videos. His clients include international airlines, cruise lines, advertising agencies, magazines, and book publishers. He spent six years in the Navy during the Vietnam era, three of them as a photojournalist with Special Warfare Groups. Cliff and Nancy Hollenbeck live in Washington State.

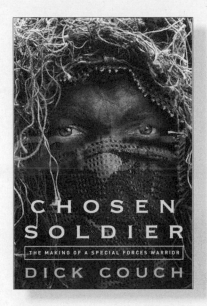

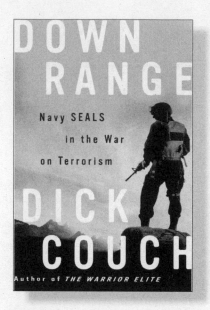